# Rare and Commonplace Flowers

# RARE AND COMMONPLACE FLOWERS

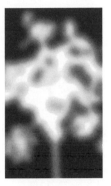

THE STORY OF

ELIZABETH BISHOP

AND LOTA DE MACEDO SOARES

## CARMEN L. OLIVEIRA

TRANSLATED BY NEIL K. BESNER

RUTGERS UNIVERSITY PRESS

NEW BRUNSWICK, NEW JERSEY, AND LONDON

*First published in Portuguese in 1995 as* Floras raras e banalíssimas: A história de Lota de Macedo Soares e Elizabeth Bishop *by Editora Rocco Ltda., Rio de Janeiro, Brazil.*
*First published in English in 2002 by Rutgers University Press, New Brunswick, New Jersey.*

Library of Congress Cataloging-in-Publication Data

Oliveira, Carmen L.
   [Flores raras e banalíssimas. English]
   Rare and commonplace flowers : the story of Elizabeth Bishop and Lota de Macedo
Soares / Carmen L. Oliveira ; translated by Neil K. Besner.
     p. cm.
   Includes bibliographical references (p.   )
   ISBN 0-8135-3033-4 (alk. paper)
   1. Soares, Lota de Macedo, 1910–1967.   2. Bishop, Elizabeth, 1911–1979.

   PQ9698.25L4816 F513 2002
   863.3'42—dc21

                                      2001019838

British Cataloging-in-Publication information is available from the British Library.

Manufactured in the United States of America

*For Mário and Rico*
*and in memory of Magu*

# CONTENTS

# FOREWORD

IN LATE 1951, the much-traveled Elizabeth Bishop, having completed her term as Consultant in Poetry to the Library of Congress (the position now known as Poet Laureate), was at loose ends. Where could she go next? She decided to travel around the world. She booked passage on a Norwegian freighter, the SS *Bowplate*, and headed for Tierra del Fuego and Cape Horn. While the ship was docked at the Brazilian port of Santos, she went to visit her friend Pearl Kazin, recently married, and some friends she had met in New York: Mary Morse, a former dancer, and Maria Carlota Costallat de Macedo Soares, the aristocratic Brazilian friend Morse was living with. Eating a cashew fruit (the fruit the nut comes from), Bishop developed a severe allergic reaction, and ended up falling in love and living with "Lota" in Rio and Petrópolis, where Lota, deeply interested in architecture, was supervising the building of a very modern house up in the mountains. Later, Bishop bought an old house of her own in the eighteenth-century mountain town of Ouro Preto. She spent nearly twenty years in Brazil.

For ten of those years she was happier than she had ever been. Orphaned by the death of her father and the mental collapse of her mother, Bishop had never had a real home until Lota offered her hers. She wrote eloquently about her new country, both its extraordinary beauties (including the loving new surroundings) and its excruciating poverty. Brazil also freed her to write about her traumatic childhood in Great Village, Nova Scotia, and Worcester, Massachusetts. When she was not writing her own poems and stories, she translated major Brazilian authors, and the remarkable diary of a young girl growing up in a small diamond-mining town in the 1890s (published in the United States as *The Diary of Helena Morley*). While she was living in Brazil, she won the Pulitzer Prize for her second book, *Poems: North & South—A Cold Spring*, which closed with her moving love poem to Lota, "The Shampoo."

In a later love poem, "Song for the Rainy Season," she and Lota, in their "open house," with its glass walls (in an area called Samambaia, after the name of a fern), are wrapped in a "private cloud." But she also predicts, almost against her will, that the richness of the rainy season, teeming with life, must come to an end, and inevitably, everything will "shrivel/in the steady sun."

Was this a self-fulfilling prophecy?

The painful distance and desiccation that eventually grow in the blissfully "unlikely" relationship between Dona Elizabetchy and Dona Lota are triggered by a political appointment. A friend of Lota's, Carlos Lacerda, had become governor of Guanabara (which, between 1960 and 1975, was the new name for the state of Rio de Janeiro, after Brasília replaced Rio as the Brazilian capital). He invites Lota to supervise the conversion of a huge area of landfill into Rio's most extensive waterfront park, Parque do Flamengo. As Lota becomes increasingly obsessed with this massive project, as the petty jealousies of the urban bureaucrats and the fallings-out among Lota's team of visionaries keep undermining Lota's genius and generosity, Bishop feels increasingly abandoned, increasingly isolated, in an exotic New World that speaks a language she finds hard to master. She goes on drinking binges. She buys a house in another city. She accepts a six-month-long teaching appointment in Seattle. She has an affair with a younger woman. And although she and Lota never stop loving one another, the breaches become increasingly irreparable.

This is the heart of the story that Carmen Oliveira tells in this compelling double biography, already a best-seller in Brazil. Not judging, never taking the side of one of her two protagonists, she performs here an act of compassionate imagination. On the basis of thorough research that includes interviews, letters, newspaper articles, and other significant documents, much of it new to print, Oliveira uses the techniques of the novelist, re-creating private events through the freedom to invent conversations, to fill in the personal blanks. As a Brazilian, Oliveira has a powerful (and passionate) understanding of Brazilian history and the Brazilian government. She brings to dramatic life the endless sequence of memos and meetings and makes them both gripping and thoroughly convincing. The passages in which she filters events through four of Lota's gossipy friends (with made-up names) are especially canny—and delicious.

Most of the letters between Lota and Elizabeth were destroyed. But Oliveira succeeds in creating a touchingly detailed image of their relationship, with a particularly vivid portrait of the witty, loving, impulsive, and compulsive Lota de Macedo Soares that will give North American admirers of Bishop's poetry a greater understanding of her remarkable friend than we have yet had—and will therefore deepen our understanding of one of our greatest poets. Literary history aside, this is a poignant love story that is as well a sad human story about the helplessness of two intelligent, strong-willed people to overcome their tragic capacity for self-destruction.

*Lloyd Schwartz*

# TRANSLATOR'S PREFACE

IN PORTUGUESE, *Flores raras e banalíssimas* tells a very Brazilian story—the first time that the Brazilian ethos so important to Bishop's life and art has been seen from a Brazilian point of view, with a rich evocation of Brazilian politics, popular culture, and society in the fifties and sixties. It is also the first time that Lota de Macedo Soares has been brought alive; the rise and decline of the relationship of these two extraordinary women are at the core of Oliveira's story. The book's form is intriguing: a biography that explicitly confesses its desire to be a novel while at the same time drawing on the kind of research one would expect of a biography.

At first I set myself the misguided goal of trying simply to conserve the climate of feeling that Oliveira's supple and many-layered Portuguese conveys so resonantly—to keep everything I could of Brazil. I thought that I could render this feeling in English. I could not. The first draft (perhaps this affliction still lingers in the last) was therefore more of a stilted report rather than a rendition. I discovered that you cannot hope to conserve, let alone render, the Brazilian world in English. My hope was produced by my nostalgia for Brazil and by my love for Portuguese; both led me astray. The structure of the language, its way of producing and conveying meaning and feeling, is not entirely portable. Portuguese as English sounds mawkish or melodramatic, the rhythms and the style, the syntax and sense of Portuguese are other. It is as if the narrator were in a hot stiff suit that could not be unbuttoned; meanwhile, arms flail in sweeping gestures, signaling in a third, unknown idiom.

Oliveira varies register and syntax according to the era, the character's class and social position, and, crucially, in keeping with the subtly shifting points of view. It is important that Bishop is referred to as Dona Elizabetchy by the women's companion and cook in the Leme apartment, Joana (or Djuana in Bishop's mouth and to Oliveira's ear), as Bishop by most of Lota's friends (as Oliveira makes painfully clear, they were alternately jealous, distrustful, and hostile toward the American poet who, they felt, seduced and destroyed their friend), and as Cookie by Lota. Portuguese and English become subjects in themselves as Lota teaches Bishop, lovingly, the sounds and rhythms of her native language. Early on, Oliveira gives us Bishop—who was reticent about speaking Portuguese in public—thinking that Portuguese "seemed a difficult and harsh language to her. Lota assured her that it wasn't, that the language was sweet and that with a little bit of botanical study, Bishop would soon become an expert in internal rhymes. . . . 'Lígula. Pétala. Plúmula,' she pronounced, very slowly and roguishly." Often, Bishop reflects on the meanings of Brazilian turns of phrase, habits of speech. Petting her cat Tobias, Bishop reflects, "You are an 'animal of esteem'. . . finding the expression amusing and already straying from her work to think of more amusing expressions."

As I worked toward an English rendition, the distinctive powers of this language began to arise. What would sound and read as more florid and Latinate in a literal rendition became what at first seemed more clipped and terse as I began to find my way toward telling the story in English. Then I realized that "clipped and terse" were qualities that inhered only in relation to the rhythms of the Portuguese that I had to let go, trusting that the essence of the story would survive this migration.

*Finally*, I hope that what remains irreducible for readers of *Rare and Commonplace Flowers* is Oliveira's passionate re-creation of some fifteen vital years in the lives of Elizabeth Bishop and Maria Carlota Costallat de Macedo Soares—"the Brazilian woman with many names and surnames"—because it is such a powerful, joyful, and sad story in any language.

I thank Carmen Oliveira for her work over the last four years, as we reflected together, during countless exchanges, in person and by e-mail, on two languages, two cultures, and two women's lives. I also thank Beatriz Marinho Strauss and Joan and Saul Gefter for various kinds of help, much appreciated, with this project. I am grateful to Barbara Schott, who read an early version of the text with a poet's eye and ear, a surgical pen, and a warm heart. Many thanks to my Brazilian family—Judith and Walter Gainsbury, Joanne Gainsbury, José Cândido Migueis Alves, Michael Gainsbury Migueis Alves, and Rochelle Taylor—for their constant moral, technical, and spiritual support over the last four years. And in loving memory of Michael Lorne Gainsbury, 1958–1983.

# ACKNOWLEDGMENTS

The author thanks the following individuals:

All those who granted her interviews or gave her statements, especially Ashley Brown and Mary Stearns Morse.

All those who provided technical assistance of various kinds, especially Nancy S. MacKechnie, former Curator of Rare Books and Manuscripts, Vassar College Libraries Special Collections, for her indispensable help with the Bishop papers, and Rosy Bleggi Peixoto, in gathering documents about the Aterro. Also: Moira Adams (botany), Suely Avelar and the Portinari Project (iconography), Ricardo Cravo Albin (Brazilian popular music), Cristina Mary Paes da Cunha (bibliographical research), Fernando Marcillac Fontes (computing), Emilia Gola (architecture), José Maria Manzo (Brazilian popular music), Regina Luz Moreira (bibliographical research), Jorge Paes (graphic arts), and Laura Viarengo (idiomatic subtleties).

To all who gave their constant support to this edition: Ana Duarte, Gary Fountain, Laura J. Menides, Alice Methfessel, Julia Michaels, Rosiska Darcy de Oliveira, Barbara Page, Paulo Rocco, Lloyd Schwartz, Carol Shields, Zuleika Torrealba, Tom Travisano, and Vivian Wyler.

# NOTE ON TEXT

This book is based on oral and written testimony. Any resemblance to persons living or dead is intentional. It should be noted, however, that Adrienne Collins, Do Carmo, Edileusa, Ismênia, Maria Amélia, Naná, Vivinha, and Zezé are pseudonyms.

# Rare and Commonplace Flowers

(Accounts of that have everything all wrong.)

Elizabeth Bishop, "Crusoe in England"

# BOSTON, 1978

A WHITE-HAIRED WOMAN WITH SAD EYES rereads the first two lines of a poem that she has been trying, interminably, to finish:

*Of course I may be remembering it all wrong*
*after, after—how many years?*

After how many years, in fact?

She looks out the window at a beautiful view of the port. There's little movement on the docks. On one of the walls of the room, the scowling face with blue eyes and horns bares its teeth. In every corner, piles of books.

It was in 1951. November, 1951. Twenty-seven years ago!

She'd been going through a bad time in her life.

She'd hated her job at the Library of Congress in Washington, D.C. Her stay at Yaddo, to write, had been a disaster. Since *North and South* had been published to good reviews in 1946, she hadn't been able to write enough poems for a second book. She was frustrated. She'd spent her life roaming the world—Paris, Casablanca, London, Mexico City, Florence, Port-au-Prince, Key West. Lately she'd been in New York, moving from hotel to hotel. She couldn't *produce*. She was drinking herself into abjectness.

Not knowing what to do with herself, she decided to take a ship and simply go to sea. Alone, since she was, in fact, alone.

She was forty.

She wanted to write. She wanted to make money. She wanted friends. She wanted to believe that love could return in her life.

The ship's first stop was at Santos. The port was a letdown: feeble pink warehouses, bags of coffee, some uncertain palms, and oppressive heat.

But Santos wasn't her destination; Rio de Janeiro was.

She knew two American women who lived there—Pearl Kazin, the sister of Bishop's friend Alfred, and Mary Morse, whom Bishop had met in New York in 1942, in the company of a Brazilian woman with many names and surnames.

Dear friend, sit down. The tale is long, and sad.

# OH, TOURIST

ON NOVEMBER 30, 1951, Mary Morse took Elizabeth Bishop to the apartment in Leme that she was sharing with Lota de Macedo Soares, on the eleventh floor, looking out onto the beach side, Avenida Atlantica.

With no sense of the eventual implications for her life of the gesture, Mary made a friendly offer: "The apartment is yours for as long as you'd like to stay in Rio."

Bishop thanked her tersely. She didn't want Morse to sense how at sea she felt.

The inevitable occurred between two shy people: neither was able to find a subject to open a conversation.

Mary opened the window so that Bishop could look out on the view. Bishop liked ocean views. She said this one was especially lovely. Then she looked around the room, admiring the exceptionally good taste. She liked the spare decor; she liked the paintings. She liked the Alexander Calder mobile. She particularly liked the two modern chairs.

Mary noticed.

"Lota designed those."

"And where is Lota?" asked Bishop.

"She's in Samambaia. She couldn't come because of the house."

Bishop took mental note of a lovely word, *samambaia*, and turned her gaze to Mary's pleasant face.

"Because of the house."

"We're building a house in the mountains, in Petrópolis."

"Ah."

Bishop wanted to know more about Lota.

Mary explained that she'd met her by chance, in 1941, shortly before meeting Bishop herself. Near the end of her dancing career, Mary had been going back to New York. On the ship she'd met Lota, who was part of Portinari's entourage; he had been selected to paint the murals in the Library of Congress in Washington, D.C. Lota loved art. In New York, she immersed herself in the Museum of Modern Art, going through it arm in arm with Florence Horn, a journalist with the magazine *Fortune* who, as Lota saw it, embraced Brazil almost too ardently. Inspired by the scope of the museum's cultural programs, Lota was determined to create the same system in Brazil. When Mary came to Brazil the following year, 1942, she was amazed to see how Lota had already formed an association of Brazilian artists and intellectuals to spread the national culture—with statutes, an advisory board, and all the rest. With the same determination, Lota invited Mary to live with her in the Leme apartment. Mary accepted. That had been ten years ago. Now Bishop must excuse her, but Mary had to leave before dark because of the road. She'd call later to schedule the day they'd bring Bishop to see Samambaia. She wished her a good stay in Rio de Janeiro.

BISHOP WAS DEFINITELY not enjoying Rio de Janeiro.

The panorama seen from the window was lovely. But the city was terribly hot and—how to put it?—slovenly.

From early on the beach would turn into a wasps' nest of people. Dark men in bathing suits played soccer all day in the middle of the street.

Instead of soothing her, the mass of people ambling along the streets of Leme produced the opposite effect. And the middle of Copacabana was another wasps' nest, adding to her sense of aimlessness. She felt paralyzed.

Sweating in only her slip, she worked at a poem in the apartment on Antônio Vieira Street:

> . . . *Oh, tourist,*
> *is this how this country is going to answer you*
> *and your immodest demands for a different world*

She was happy when the day arrived that Mary and Lota were supposed to take her to their house in the mountains.

At the time arranged, a red Jaguar with the top down pulled up to the curb. A short woman got out gracefully and smiled at Bishop. As she approached, Bishop saw that she was a good deal darker than Bishop had remembered. With her right hand, Lota shook Bishop's vigorously; with her left she caressed her shoulder. She looked into Bishop's eyes.

"Shall we go?"

Not used to this kind of contact, Bishop didn't know what to do next. Lota opened the car door, motioning Bishop to get in and sit down. Then she pulled away and they were in flight. Soon Lota had extricated herself from the buses and other cars and they were climbing a mountain, in the midst of dazzling scenery. On the left, the mountains followed each other under massed banks of clouds; to the right, the road was alive with stretches of brightly colored flowers.

"Maria-sem-vergonha—shameless Mary," Lota explained.

Bishop was delighted, wanted to stop and jump out of the car, but she was too shy to ask.

When she came to again, she saw that they were passing through an enchanting little town, its streets lined by solemn mansions, with well-kept gardens adorned with hydrangeas.

Lota explained that the emperor had chosen this town to build the holiday residence of the royal family. The last thing that would have occurred to Bishop in Rio as she dodged a soccer game in the street was that this country also had kings, princes, and princesses. She reminded herself to ask more about this subject later.

Suddenly, everything changed. They were pointed down a narrow and potholed road. While she deftly maneuvered around rocks and holes, Lota kept on talking casually:

"This stretch will get better." —Zoom— "I inherited the grounds of Samambaia from my mother ten years ago. First came the partition, after long delays; I had to divide everything with my sister into sections equal to the millimeter. Then I decided to divide it up into first-class lots. This process is also never ending; it involves a mountain of paperwork. I've only just been able to begin building the house. Later I'm going to take care of this road." — Zoom.

Bishop wasn't worried about the bouncing. The road was lovely! It had been cut through the middle of the forest, the most exuberant thing she'd seen this close up. Large trees gestured at each other, brandishing pendants. High up in the branches, the bright red of the bromeliads stood out.

As they rounded a curve, something ungainly and afflicted suddenly decided to cross the road. Bishop opened her mouth for the first time.

"A lizard!" she cried, with childlike joy.

However, they carried on as if this were nothing unusual, and Lota announced that they were almost there.

Bishop glanced casually to one side and tensed up. Oh dear: she could have sworn that she'd seen a camel. It *was* a camel beside a hedge, beyond a shadow of doubt.

The driver saw Bishop's surprise and said playfully: "Don't panic. My neighbor buys animals for the zoo. They stay here until they get sent there."

The only thing missing now was for a rabbit in a hurry to appear, checking its watch.

The Jaguar was parked.

"We've arrived," Lota proclaimed.

Bishop got out and was greeted by a capering dog.

She looked around: what an incredible place! In the distance, the bluish mountains. All around, the forest. In front, powerful, an enormous slab of granite.

"This is my house," Lota's voice came from farther ahead.

"Good morning. Did you have a good trip?"

Mary appeared from somewhere and took Bishop to the house that was being built.

Two half-naked men were perched on top of a wall.

Guided by Lota, Bishop traversed the site from top to bottom, stepping on cement that had been abundantly decorated by dog prints. This will be here, that will be there, Lota pointed out enthusiastically. A gentle touch on the arm indicated that it was time for Bishop to keep moving. Lota explained how she had planned the house, with someone whose name Bishop did not grasp. In a daze, the American woman dimly understood that a house without walls was to be erected there; or else it was a corridor, around which there was to be a house. She was arrested by the sight of Lota's lovely hands, which she used generously as she spoke.

"Here in Brazil, things are a bit—empirical. But in the end, everything turns out right," she was assured by the owner of the hands.

"LET'S HAVE a little walk," Lota said.

Bishop was about to mention that her suitcase was still in the car, but Lota was already on her way. Bishop and Mary followed.

A trail led to the waterfall. Bishop regretted not bringing her diary. She listed to herself the variety of colors: dark green, bluish green, olive, purple, rust, yellow, another yellow, blood red, white dappled with green. She heard the hidden tremor of the waterfall. Lota guided them. "Careful—thorns!" She gave her hand to Bishop, helping her around a rock or over another slippery one.

When they got to the waterfall, Bishop watched the happy meeting of the water with other living things—maidenhair, bromeliads, water plants, moss.

"The water we consume is dammed here," Lota intervened, practical. "The stream flows up ahead and runs close by the house. Come, I'll show you."

AT FIVE o'clock the men left with a wave.

"Good-bye, Dona Lota."

"Bye-bye."

"Until tomorrow, Dona Lota."

"Until tomorrow, my flower."

Bishop was taken with the affectionate form—to her mind, intimate—in which Lota spoke with the manual laborers. Actually, the same thing had happened at lunch, when Lota insisted on introducing Bishop to the maid.

"Edileusa, this is Dona Elizabeth."

"You okay?" asked Edileusa in Portuguese, and Lota translated.

Bishop said yes, and Lota translated.

Lota intrigued her. In New York, she'd been after Danish tea towels; she liked their patterns. She spoke knowledgeably of Oskar Kokoschka and Henry Moore. She spoke English with great fluency. If she made a mistake, she also made it with great fluency. Now she showed up in a sports car and was building an ultramodern house in the middle of the woods. Peculiar.

"How about a little tea?" Lota linked arms with Bishop and Mary and took them ahead.

Until at least a part of the house was finished, Lota and Mary were living in the house of their friends Walkíria and Barreto, just beneath the construction site. Bishop had already been there for lunch.

"Actually, we're not going to have a little tea, but a little maté," Lota explained. We have imported tea, but really, it's no good. You'll like the maté."

Mary watched the conversation get livelier. That is, Lota was her amusing self, and Bishop didn't hold back her laughter. Mary drank her maté in silence.

Sometime later the talk shifted to poetry. Lota wanted Bishop to read one of her poems. Bishop refused.

"Then read another poet."

This was not something to which Bishop was accustomed, but at that moment it seemed quite natural. She went to get a book.

"Do you like Marianne Moore?"

"Let's hear her!"

Bishop leafed through the pages and read several sections from "Marriage." At each stanza, Bishop lifted her light eyes to look at Lota. The brown eyes returned her questions; the room filled with silences.

"Read more," asked Lota.

Bishop read "To a Snail."

Mary yawned.

"I'm going to bed. Good night."

"Good night, dear. We're going soon," said Lota.

And they stayed.

BISHOP SLEPT unusually well and awoke unusually early. The house was quiet. Apparently, Lota and Mary weren't up yet.

She looked around the room and found American newspapers and magazines on a table in the corner. She sat down and read a back issue of the *New York Times*.

Feeling up to it, she decided to come back to her first Brazilian poem, "Arrival at Santos."

The poem described a first-world tourist who has just docked at the port of an exotic civilization, where she hopes to find a new direction for her life. While the ship anchors, she casts a disappointed eye over the "frivolous greenery" and the meager warehouses. Her first contact with the local workforce is not promising either: despite her warning cry, a careless boathook snags a fellow passenger's skirt. With the petulance of someone who thinks herself above this, the tourist makes a long list of carping complaints about the country that is to receive her.

Bishop reread what she had written. There was her traveler, astonished before a world that refused to adjust to her preconceived ideas. Now she needed to finish the poem. She had to revise some of the verses, especially some of the rhymes, and she had to shape the final stanza. She thought the poem might appeal to an American editor. With luck, she might be able to sell it to *The New Yorker*.

However, after laboring over it for two hours, she felt lost and exasperated. She hadn't been able to resolve anything; on the contrary, she'd come to disapprove of solutions she'd previously liked. She was hungry. She wanted a drink badly.

"Well, well, if it isn't our poet in action!"
Lota! How good to hear that voice.
Bishop came to herself, saved.
"I'm hungry," she said, with childlike eyes.

MARY NOTED that Bishop didn't speak anymore about going back to Leme.
She simply stayed on.

Every day, after breakfast, she'd go watch Lota at the site. Morose and irres-
olute over her writing, Bishop was amazed at the self-confidence with which
Lota took control of such a complex enterprise.

Like most of the upper-class women of her generation, Maria Carlota
Costallat de Macedo Soares had had tutors and studied in Europe, but she had
not gone to university. Yet she knew everything about architecture. Her
library on the subject was exemplary. She had closely followed the work of the
young architects in the vanguard of the construction of the Ministry of Education in Rio de Janeiro. She was a friend of the most respected Brazilian
architects.

It was to one of them, Sérgio Bernardes, that Lota turned to design her
house project. She wanted to set a shapely object in straight lines among the
ornate and sinuous forms of nature. The rigidity of iron, the fragility of glass,
the luster of the artifact, and the roughness of rocks from the river would all
coexist. Different textures, shapes, and levels would always put the observer
in front of unforeseen angles, pushing him, because it was so beautiful, to
accept what transgressed the norms. The house would express Lota's passionate ideas about modern architecture. It happened that Sérgio had his own
passionate ideas about modern architecture. The result: fireworks when the
two of them sat down to discuss the project. He held the degree in architecture, but she was Lota de Macedo Soares. Time and again Mary saw Sérgio
plead to the heavens to give him the patience to bear that woman, and then
slam the door of his sports car and take off down the road, swearing that he'd
never return.

And Lota didn't just stay at the drawing board. She had built her own first
house in Samambaia, the project of her friend Carlos Leão. Then she paid the
bills of the lawyer who had taken care of legalizing the site by building his
house. Both houses were full of the creative and unexpected solutions that
were Lota's signature.

Aristocrat, landowner, whatever you called her, Mary knew one thing
about Lota: she wasn't afraid of work. When the construction began, the two
of them took turns daily at loading and unloading rounded rocks from the

jeep. Mary could not recall a more tiring job, yet she also could not recall Lota ever being tired.

That morning, Bishop watched Lota moving from one side to another, directing the placement of trellises on the roof. To the despair of the two masons, this roof didn't have slats or clay tiles, like any usual roof. It was a mad contraption made of aluminum plates supported by steel girders.

Because the work was very expensive, Lota had decided to build the most audacious architectural elements last, after finishing a basic nucleus with a bedroom, living room, bathroom, and kitchen. The walls were already standing. Now they had to be covered, which she would accomplish as soon as she could convert her two unwilling helpers.

Bishop didn't tire of watching her. It was good for a person to dream, and then build her own house.

AT NIGHT, the friends settled in.

They'd read the back issues of *Time* or the *New York Times* that Mary was able to rescue from the mail in Petrópolis.

Afterward, Lota and Bishop each chose favorite writers.

Bishop read George Herbert aloud: "Love."

*Love bade me welcome: yet my soul drew back*
*Guilty of dust and sin.*

Lota read Mário de Andrade aloud: "Poema da amiga":

*Ontem você estava tão linda*
*Que o meu corpo chegou*
*Sei que era um riacho e duas horas de sede*
*Me debrucei, não bebi.*

The translation followed: "Poem of the Friend":

*Yesterday you were so lovely*
*That my body drew near*
*I know it was a brook and two hours of thirst,*
*I bent over, didn't drink.*

Although she rendered the poems into English, Lota insisted that Bishop pay attention to the music of the Portuguese.

In fact, the Portuguese of the poets and of the maids was what came to Bishop's foreigner's ears, since Lota and Mary spoke to her in English. It seemed a difficult and harsh language to her. Lota assured her it wasn't, that the language was very sweet and that with a little bit of botanical study, Bishop would soon become an expert in internal rhymes.

"Do you want to see? Lígula. Pétala. Plúmula," she pronounced, very slowly, roguishly.

Bishop was enchanted with Lota's humor. Talking to her was a delight; she was uncommonly cultured and articulate. As an American, Bishop especially valued Lota's European education. Miles from nowhere, it was disconcerting to find the table always set with impeccable elegance. Or, in the middle of a discussion about music, to see Lota pull Erik Satie's *Pièces froides* out of her top hat. Or talk about the scandal that attended the staging of *Parade*, with music by Satie, script by Cocteau, and scenery by Picasso.

For her part, Lota was impressed that Bishop had gone to Vassar and had celebrities such as Marianne Moore and Robert Lowell among her friends.

"I'm going to introduce you to a lot of interesting people, you'll see," promised Lota, holding Bishop's arm.

# THE INDECENT PEDUNCLE

SAMAMBAIA, PETRÓPOLIS.

With pleasure, Bishop wrote her first two words in Portuguese at the top of the page: two solid and sonorous words that situated her on the planet.

She wanted to send news to the United States of the surprisingly good moments she was living through. But when she started to date the letter, she hesitated. She began to count the days since she'd arrived in Rio on November 30 and admitted to herself that she'd lost track.

Bishop was surprised. This was a sign of how absent she felt—she, for whom locating herself was so primordial an instinct that she never went out without a compass in her purse.

She listed three possible dates, and as soon as she'd finished writing, went to have a look at the construction.

Nearing the site, she saw Lota in long pants, as always, hands on her hips, speaking vehemently to two dark men. Barefoot, their pant legs rolled up, arms crossed, the men listened. Strange apparel covered their heads. One wore a doubled over blue paper bag with a crease at the top pulled down over his ears. The other had tied on a cloth with four little knots pointed to the cardinal directions.

Lota raged. One of the men shook his head, eyes to the ground. Bishop got within earshot but didn't hear the already familiar "my dear" and "my flower."

Without a doubt, one of the reasons for the revolt was the pile of iron rods on the ground, because paper hat was pointing at them and muttering something that provoked further outbursts from the mistress of the house.

Suddenly Bishop heard a change of tone from Lota, who calmed down and, in that way of hers that startled Bishop, took hold of an arm of each of the men with a spontaneity that seemed affectionate. The three confabulated. Bishop saw the masons, apparently placated, return to their posts.

Lota came to explain.

"They were complaining that from their aesthetic point of view, the house was too way out. Mottled rocks, bricks too visible, a roof too gussied up. They argued that it's all never-ending zigzags and that they weren't going to kill themselves putting in so many decorative touches for no good reason. Then I told them that they were building a house for Carnival, and they gave in."

THAT DAY, Edileusa didn't show up for breakfast.

For Lota de Macedo Soares, the day had to begin with coffee served in bed. Understandably, Lota was quite put out. She drank a single cup of strong coffee, beans ground on the spot, and went off swearing. What the devil, what the hell.

A little later, Mary told Bishop she was worried: Edileusa still hadn't come. To Mary's surprise, milady immediately got ready to make lunch. She loved to cook.

Working with an exotic assembly of spices and chives, Bishop improvised some pancakes.

At mealtime, Lota seated herself at the table with ostentatious satisfaction, tucking in the linen napkin at her neck and rubbing her hands. As usual, she sprinkled pepper liberally on her plate, but before taking the first mouthful she stopped.

"Hmm. Really? Mary, let's wait until she tries it. Who knows?"

Finally, with the air of one who might be making a fatal mistake, she ate. Bishop was close to distress.

"Mmm. Délicieux. Délicieux."

And to the end of the pancakes, it was constant praise. Lota pierced Bishop with intense glances, at once grateful and proud. Mary waited for Lota to sprinkle some pepper on Bishop and eat her.

"I didn't know about these gifts of yours. I thought a poet spent all her time listening to the stars."

Bishop thought this definition of her vocation questionable, but she knew that she was being appreciated as a cook. Boldly, she promised that for Christmas she'd make a turkey the American way.

Does that mean she's going to stay here till Christmas? Mary asked herself.

After they'd already finished, Edileusa arrived, in a deep sulk. She'd had liver trouble.

THE STORY unfolded.

For two days, Edileusa was ill. She refused to take the usual medicines, drinking tea brewed from quickweed she gathered in the woods. She moaned, my Blessed Lady of a Good Death, help me, my Sacred Heart of Jesus, save me, while Bishop cooked. She didn't even go to the traditional party cele-brating the finishing of the roof, a splendid barbeque with beer, where Bishop saw people eating raw manioc flour for the first time.

Bishop tried hard to establish some kind of verbal contact with Edileusa, but it was impossible. Even Lota had difficulty translating the tale of the sick one. She'd had a spat with a neighbor, who'd cursed Edileusa's sister, calling her an easy woman. The heated exchange brought on the jitters in Edileusa, who got so worked up she positively quivered. It was a real blowup, and it just about did her in.

Bishop felt like she already knew Edileusa. Suddenly, she remembered: strangely, Edileusa looked like Mrs. Smith in the painting by Erastus Salisbury Field, *Mrs. Smith and Her Twins*, which she'd seen in Washington. Edileusa had the same air of concealment, probably because of her almond-shaped eyes and the smile tucked away in the corner of her fleshy lip. Except that she was, as they said here, dark. And instead of nicely behaved little curls symmetri-cally distributed on either side of her head, Edileusa had a massive head of hair, the legacy of her Indian grandmother, she declared.

AT THE END of the day, when each had done her duty—that is, after Lota had reached the limits of exasperation in getting to the next stage of building the Carnival shed and Bishop had reached the heights of desperation in trying to write one more line of her poem about the complaining tourist, the two would go for a walk. Mary would go sometimes, and sometimes say she pre-ferred to stay behind.

They would take a turn around the site, and Bishop would be introduced to the inhabitants. The giant snail moved with mysterious confidence along a trail strewn with impediments. The freshwater crab, with its ceramic lid, scuttled about in quick scurries. Lota knew everything about the forest and walked along making the introductions. *Imbaúba, begônia, samambaiaçu.* Lovely plants. Lovely sounds. From the labyrinth of branches, lianas and trail-ing vines emerged, and from the dead tree trunks, coral-red fungi. The women made expeditions to gather orchids. Bishop registered everything, touching the satin-smooth and the rough sides of the leaves, admiring the intricate patterns that looked as if they'd been embroidered by hand.

The area was rocky, and both Bishop and Lota liked to spend time admiring the lichens adorning the dark stones. For Bishop, they were like lunar explosions.

On their return, they'd sit on the ground and talk.

That evening, Lota said: "When I was a child, I loved to stay here at the farm."

A silence fell—enough time for memories to reach the eyes.

Lota said that her father had bought Fazenda Samambaia when she was about eight. Her mother was a fervent Catholic and had hired Dona Hermínia, a very strict friend, as a tutor for her daughters. Nothing they wore could be even faintly see-through; everything was very proper. Lota and her sister Marieta had to be yielding and obedient. Reason enough for Lota to break out whenever possible. She teamed up with Zette, a neighbor of the same age, and the two of them goofed around. An old ex-slave who lived nearby smoked cigarettes rolled in cornhusks. Lota and Zette would torment the old black woman into rolling cigarettes for them. Then it was smoke and puke, smoke and puke. Street kids' fun. And the bishop? There was a bishop who visited Lota's mother all the time. Dona Adélia feted the bishop with lavish excess—port, crème de menthe, cigars. One day Lota stole one of the bishop's cigars and snuck off to smoke it with her friend. They vomited their souls out. Then, the desperate attempt to hide the nausea from the implacable eyes of Dona Hermínia, or she'd force Lota to confess herself to the bishop.

Lota smiled with satisfaction at her childhood mischief.

Bishop felt uncomfortable. She didn't have tales like these to tell. She had spent her childhood living with relatives, now one, now another, always feeling like a guest, so grateful for shelter that she never argued, never disobeyed. But she was so unhappy that she developed bronchitis, asthma, eczema, even symptoms of Saint Vitus's dance. Bishop attributed her passivity, her inability to say what it was that she wanted, to the lack of an antagonist in childhood.

And in Belgium? Lota went on in the face of Bishop's silence. Lota's father had become a political exile when she was twelve. She and Marieta had gone to a religious boarding school. The poor nuns—the girls had raised hell. Lota had a pellet rifle. From outside the building, she'd aim at the eggs in the kitchen and fire. Bang, splat. The kitchen turned into a hatchery. Afterward, it was rosary upon rosary of penitence. The school was packed with chic little girls from all over Europe who thought the Brazilians were barbarians. It was very annoying. One day, the nuns arranged a big commemorative ceremony with the consuls from the various countries in attendance. They asked that a girl from each country sing its national anthem. Lota was flabbergasted. She'd always studied in French schools, as was fitting for a girl from a good family, and no one had bothered to teach her the Brazilian anthem. But put on the spot, she had no doubts. She sang, with patriotic fervor,

Ai seu Mé
Ai seu Mé
Lá no Palácio das Águias
Olé
Não hás de pôr o pé

It was a little Carnival tune from 1922, censored because of its uncouth allusions to the frequent drinking bouts of the candidate Arthur Bernardes. But Lota was lavished with praise for the beauty of the anthem. It was too bad that the Brazilian consul hadn't been able to come.

"And you?"

"I also spent the best times of my childhood on a farm."

"Imagine. Was your father a farmer?"

"No. The farm was my grandparents'. I lost my parents very early."

Bishop didn't know if she was ready to talk of her childhood. But she felt such respect for Lota that, without intending to, she gave herself over to her memories too. She had lived with her mother's parents in Great Village, a small town of a half-dozen streets in Nova Scotia. Her grandparents were people with a simple dignity. They sang hymns. Above all, they were loving. But one day her paternal grandparents came to get her. They were rich and lived in isolated opulence, had nothing to do with relatives or with neighbors, as in Great Village. Bishop was devil-may-care, didn't like dresses or dolls, but her grandmother made as if she didn't notice. The grandfather was neglectful; her grandmother taught her restraint. Bishop learned guilt. She became ill. She was rescued by her mother's eldest sister, who took her to the modest apartment where she lived with her husband. The Bishop family began to pay Aunt Maud to take care of her. Aunt Maud introduced her to poetry and let her spend her holidays with her beloved grandparents in Nova Scotia. Then Bishop went to boarding school. Her father's family continued to pay. Bishop remembered the loneliness of holidays: her schoolmates went home to their parents; she stayed at the school. In 1929, Bishop started at Vassar. She was good at writing essays.

Lota hugged Bishop, comforting her.

"How did your parents die?"

"My father died when I was eight months old."

And then, suddenly:

"My mother was put away in an asylum when I was five. I never saw her again."

They stayed there a long time, Lota hugging Bishop in silence.

THAT NIGHT, they couldn't sleep.

They read far into the night.

The wide silence was only broken by the noisy fluttering of a moth. And by the desultory flips of turning pages.

It was already almost dawning when Lota got the lantern and proposed an impromptu walk.

They went out, intent on the circle of light that guided them. Suddenly, lightning appeared and a strong wind rose.

"Run, it's going to rain!"

The two of them ran headlong, holding hands, laughing in little afflicted yelps and giggles, and got home all askew.

Flashes of lightning lit up the room. Their eyes met.

Lota took Bishop's hand softly.

"Don't go away. Stay here with me."

Bishop felt a cage shatter itself in the air, freeing thousands of birds.

A radiant rain broke loose.

Bishop looked at the face that waited for an answer and that anticipated her with a sudden kiss.

IN THE MORNING, Bishop was uneasy, and became more uneasy when Lota told her at the site that she was going to rush to finish the part of the house that was being built so that the two of them could move in quickly. She said that Mary had decided to build her own house close by.

Lota was counting on Bishop giving up everything and staying there with her.

It was typical of Lota. Always pragmatic, she didn't seem to need time to reflect on events. It was enough to trust that she could dominate them. Bishop, however, had an instinctive need to hold back.

Bishop admitted that the exuberance of Samambaia fascinated her. Lota's exuberance fascinated her. But the place was at the end of the earth. The house that Lota was offering as a dwelling didn't even have electric light. When it rained, the road became impassable, sealing them off from the rest of the world. All around their ladyships, scantily dressed mestizos spoke an incomprehensible language.

It was true that Lota was special. It pleased Bishop that Lota had a lineage; Lota's aristocratic manners pleased her. For Bishop, inexplicably, Lota's brusqueness did not seem incompatible with her sophistication. Lota's firmness almost intimidated her. But while Lota went on pointing an emphatic finger at the rest of the world, with Bishop she lowered her voice. Generally, with Lota Bishop felt herself at once attracted and frightened, as if she were in front of a masked outlaw.

Lota, so cultivated and refined, should have felt out of place in that backward country. But she seemed to want to resolve the conflict between civilization and the primitive by bringing the ultramodern into the woods. There she would be saved from the mediocrity of the world, in an ambience of her own design. When she felt the need for a Danish napkin or wanted to see her favorite expressionists again, she simply would get on a plane to New York.

But how to survive financially in that backwoods? Bishop's profession, if it was a profession at all, was to be a poet. The majority of American poets taught at a university to make ends meet. Bishop had been struggling with her poetry since her time at Vassar, where she'd revealed her literary talent and her vocation to other women. But it had been five years since she'd published her only book. As for Lota, her profession, apparently, was to be from an illustrious family. She walked around her vast property, inventing the beautiful things there would be in Samambaia one day, and the beautiful people who would buy lots to build their magnificent houses there.

However, the more impediments that surfaced in her mind, the more the tumult in her heart resisted them. Bishop admitted to herself that her wish was to stay. From the beginning it had been clear that an implacable attraction was establishing itself between the two of them. Their eyes gazed on each other's; their hands sought pretexts to touch. They never escaped Bishop's alert feelings, these moments the two of them were creating. But because of her enormous difficulty in expressing her feelings, what ended up growing between them was the silence that precedes a storm.

Now she saw herself about to give in. To doubt and at the same time to promise.

But what was this insistent fright raising premonitions in her soul, while trust, which should have been filling her heart, vanished, giving way to somber thoughts?

THAT LUNCH, Lota gave her a caju.

It was a red caju, pulpy and fragrant.

Bishop smelled it and quipped that it should not be allowed that a fruit and a cashew nut be joined in so indecent a manner.

"Try it," said Lota.

Bishop took two small bites. She found it too bitter and acid.

THAT AFTERNOON, while she was searching for an adjective to describe the color of soap in her poem about the tourist, Bishop noticed that she was having trouble keeping her eyes open; they winked, as if they were being squeezed shut.

She went to the bathroom and looked in the mirror.

"Ohh," groaned a swollen mouth in an entirely deformed face.

Her head had turned into an incandescent, rose-colored sphere. Her eyes were two mere slits. Her hands were also beginning to swell. The familiar, agonizing feeling of suffocating came over her—she lacked for air.

She felt her way along the wall in a panic, wanting to call out—Lota!—but her voice came out in a squeak.

She thought she was going to die then and there.

LOTA ARRANGED for the doctor to come up from Rio to Samambaia immediately to examine Bishop.

The doctor stuffed Bishop with medication with instructions in Portuguese and prescribed injections of antiallergens and calcium. Bishop was terrified of injections. Beyond that, she'd have to go to the hospital every other day to submit to a procedure that, as far as Bishop could see, consisted of taking blood from one side and putting it in the other. Feeling terribly insecure, Bishop decided on her own to also take the medications she was used to—adrenalin for her asthma and pyribenzamine for her allergies.

So that Bishop could have better attention, Lota moved her into the apartment in Leme and began to take care of her.

After a week, Bishop's swelling had still not subsided. Suddenly, she began to feel an intolerable itching all over her body. Rashes broke out on her skin. Her hands were covered in sores, and her ears swelled up like enormous red mushrooms. Bishop felt torn to pieces. And repulsive. Under Lota's worried gaze, she hung her head, full of guilt and shame.

But Lota quickly rallied her, joking that this was nothing more than a caju-itis, a common ailment in the Tropics. She explained that the caju lives in a terrible identity crisis, because in truth the caju is not a fruit, but a peduncle, that the fruit of the caju tree is called, in the vernacular, a cashew nut, which really turns out to be a nut with an almond within. Can you imagine such a muddle? In this way, following the law of similarity, caju illness tends to afflict people going through an identity crisis.

From then on, despite all her ailments, the itching, the anguish of the sud-den asthma attacks and the violence of their treatment, Bishop's exasperation always yielded before Lota's garrulous enthusiasm.

At one point Lota began to ponder whether the mushrooms that Bishop's ears had become were poisonous or edible. She drew on her botanical lore to make the appraisal. Let's see: from the size and the pinkish color they are probably *Pleurotus ostreatoroseus*. They're big and meaty. They developed rapidly. Yes, they could only be those tasty mushrooms.

At other times, to Bishop's horror, Lota would call her friends in Rio to come for a little visit. They would come and chatter happily. From what Lota told her, Bishop gathered that they suggested cures they'd successfully tried themselves, although none of them had ever had mushrooms like those. From the reigning atmosphere, it seemed to Bishop that these Brazilians loved to talk about illness.

They helped Lota to pamper her. When it came time for her injections, they cried in a chorus of consternation:

"Poor thing!"

Oh yes, carry me on your shoulder, sit me on your knee, console me as a mother consoles a child.

FOR THE REST of December, Bishop underwent treatment, taking daily injec-tions. Lota would bring a chair close to the bed and tell her how things would be at Samambaia. She was going to make a transparent house, where nature could come in at her will. On moonlit nights, they would sit outside, in silence, watching the valleys light up. For cold nights—because in the win-ter it got very cold up there—she was going to build a fireplace and the two of them were going to read beneath the covers. Bishop listened with her eyes closed.

One day, after three weeks had gone by and Bishop could already see prop-erly, even though her body was still covered with eczema, Lota sat on the edge of the bed and announced that she was going to build a studio for Bishop. It was going to be a little retreat only for her, to write poetry. She had already even chosen the place: it was going to be facing the creek, so that you could hear the running water. But with its back to the house, so that Bishop wouldn't be distracted with what was going on down there.

Astonished, Bishop watched Lota's magic hands designing the layout of the studio. The room with a wide window along it, the bathroom, the stove, the kitchen, a comfortable armchair. Bishop would be totally independent. Hm? The floor would be of clay tiles, it would be perfect. The walls, low. When you look out the window, you'll see the creek going by and all those trees. What do you think? You'll have the serenity to write.

Bishop listened quietly. Her swollen eyes burned. Lota's hands holding hers comforted her; everything about Lota comforted her.

Lota asked her to decide, once and for all, not to carry on with her travels.

Her hot tears finally came down, and with them everything else that was held in. She'd stay, yes. She wanted to stay. In Brazil, with Lota.

# THERE WAS ONCE A
# CHINESE KING

LOTA AND BISHOP RETURNED TO SAMAMBAIA, and when the swelling in her hands began to abate, Bishop did two things. She refused to continue taking the masses of injections, and she wrote to her therapist about the suffering she had been through.

In a torrent, she recounted all of the symptoms and treatments. Then she looked at her scabs and sores and at the world outside, and said that she hadn't been this happy for a long time.

But she didn't have the nerve to tell Dr. Baumann that she'd promised Lota she would stay in Brazil. She simply said that she'd resume traveling on the 26th of January, keeping to her schedule, if she'd recovered from all of her health problems.

THE 8TH OF February was Bishop's birthday and Lota decided to throw her a party. Bishop had finally stayed.

Lota sent for her friends from Rio, who drove up that infernal road balancing an enormous cake, which, miraculously, arrived intact. Lota's friends were in their forties, like her and Bishop; out of love for Lota, they tried to take in the sickly and insipid American. Behind the show of concern for her health, however, Bishop thought she detected flashes of hostility. Regardless, she tried to respond to the polite expressions by trying to find equivalents for some of their diminutive forms, a Brazilian habit she found adorable: "You doing fine, little sweetheart?" "Bye-bye from the bottom of my heart."

Lota had plotted with her neighbor from the zoo, and he brought Bishop a toucan with lustrous colors and electric eyes. Bishop loved the present and baptized him Uncle Sam.

The party lasted the whole day. At the end, they sang "Happy Birthday" in Portuguese and Lota opened some champagne. Bishop gave the cork to Sam.

After everyone had left, Lota gave a ring to Bishop. On it was engraved: Lota—20.12.51. That was the day Lota had proposed that Bishop stay, changing both their destinies.

LOTA AND Bishop camped out in the third of the house that was erect. Mary stayed at the apartment in Leme.

Living at Samambaia was rudimentary, but Lota as much as Bishop found reasons to see their lives as luxurious.

It didn't seem to bother them that they were living under the duress of a house in construction. After the royal morning breakfast in bed, Lota assembled her tiny crew and got to work. Everything in Lota was manorial, powerful, quick, Bishop noted, while in herself, everything was hesitant, full of vagaries. But in those first months living together, Bishop was also productive. She sent word to her friends that her work was yielding results; it had been a long time since she'd written so much!

Bishop practiced her Portuguese with Edileusa, who had the habit of speaking to the things she drudged with. House, you shouldn't gather this much dirt. Broom, please do me the favor of sweeping. Madam meat, why does your lady not wish to cook? Edileusa also had a lovely voice and liked to croon. This was a source of great pleasure for Bishop, because the only thing that made her miss electricity in the house was that she couldn't listen to music. Edileusa's repertoire included popular songs and sad ballads she said she'd learned from an aunt who was a nightingale. One of her favorites was "Vovozinha" (or "Little Grandma"):

*Tell me a little story,*
*Little grandma, little grandma!*
*Giants, a king, a queen,*
*Little grandma, little grandma!*

*There was once*
*A Chinese king*

*And a princess whose beauty*
*Made this king a slave*
*This king who was so strong and brave.*

*Ah, how sad a life is mine*
*Little grandma, little grandma!*
*I miss the time when I still had*
*My little grandma, little grandma.*

These lyrics touched Bishop, but she also liked it when Edileusa sang the story of Terezinha, lemons scattered on the ground, blood spilling from her heart—beautiful images.

The mornings and afternoons went like this: Lota conducted an allegro con brio on the construction and Bishop proceeded with her adagio cantabile, reading, writing, listening to Edileusa, and noting details of the flora, fauna, and geography to use in her poems.

At dusk, they fulfilled the ritual of lighting the kerosene lamps. The transition between day and night was an event that they shared solemnly and attentively. The crickets, bats, and owls came out from hiding. The bullfrog beat on his anvil. Giant moths with eyes on the backs of their wings drew close to the flame of the lamps. Listening to the little jumps that the owl took on the roof before lifting off in search of prey, Lota and Bishop concluded that the owl knew how to count up to five, because that was how many little steps there always were—he would always stamp to five.

Night also brought on asthma attacks, which disappeared during the day. Nevertheless, Bishop felt well. The flickering light exposed the bareness of the room, where the central figure of Lota shone. Perhaps it was Lota's love that saved Bishop from seeing desolation and precariousness there. She saw herself in a richly peopled world and willingly shared with the innumerable insects the safe space of the house.

MARCH PAINTED the woods purple. The lent trees, previously hidden among taller trees, came into bloom, turning themselves into the most remarkable presences in the forest.

There were days of downpour. When it rained torrentially, there was no way to leave the house. Construction was interrupted. With the road muddied, no one risked coming up. They took the time to be together. Lota and Bishop exchanged confidences. Bishop confessed that she'd drunk compulsively since she was twenty-one; Lota revealed details about her troubled family. Since both were spirited, they also had a lot of fun. Lota did unforgettable imitations, like the one of Alice B. Toklas just arrived at Samambaia with her book of recipes. Edileusa, of course, didn't appear. Lota filled the place with smoke trying to get the woodstove to work, and Bishop struggled not to burn up her tasty dishes. Gradually, Bishop felt her defenses yielding before Lota's tenderness. Nothing she could imagine was as good as being in her embrace, while the rain fell outside. In the autumn of their lives, it was the sudden pleasure of lent trees in bloom.

FIVE FIFTY in the morning. At Baron of Mauá Station, between the squares of Bandeira and São Cristovão, Arnaldo de Oliveira waited for the whistle of the train. Monday was the day to visit his clients in Petrópolis and that was the train that took Arnaldo and other travelers, representatives of wholesalers in Rio, to the city of hydrangeas. The train, four cars and a mail wagon, was pulled by a coal-powered locomotive. It crossed the suburbs of Leopoldina and stopped at the foot of the mountain. There, the train was taken apart and each car was pulled by a small locomotive to the station at the top of the mountain, where the train was reassembled. After a trip of two and a half hours, it stopped in the middle of Petrópolis, on Dr. Porciúncula Street. Arnaldo went straight to the Commerce Hotel, near the station. After getting the key to his room, he went out to call on his customers.

Arnaldo liked to have responsibility for the business in Petrópolis. Because he walked a lot, he knew the city well. He liked to see the banks of the Piabinha and Platinado Rivers covered with hydrangeas. He liked to see the beautiful mansions, and he knew the house of Santos Dumont, honored by Brazilians as the inventor of the airplane, and the house in which Stefan Zweig and his wife committed suicide. He liked the Imperial Residence, which sheltered the descendants of the Brazilian monarchy. He liked the climate, the flowering acacias, the people. It wasn't for nothing that the big-shot politicians had chosen Petrópolis as the place to spend their holidays—the president of the republic in the Rio Negro Palace and the governor of the state in Itaboraí Palace.

Petrópolis was very prosperous. The textile industry was healthy; the factories were famous for their cashmere and fine silk. Business was also healthy. Arnaldo had to visit innumerable warehouses, almost all of them owned by the Portuguese, and by the end of the day his feet were worn out.

He'd eat with a colleague at Falconi's or at Primavera's, on 15th Avenue. At nightfall, as he made clean copies of his orders and retraced the route of his calls, Arnaldo reflected that, being a professional traveler, he never would have the time to wax the floor of the Imperial Museum with those fuzzy slippers, as the tourists did.

Before catching his train back, Arnaldo invariably went by the D'Angelo Brothers bakery, to buy caramels, a Petrópolis specialty, for his daughter. On that day, three strange women were buying buttered biscuits. One was quite short, with long pants and a man's shirt. The others were tall and fair. They spoke a foreign language.

Pereira, a veteran salesman who had worked in the Petrópolis area for a long time and who prided himself on knowing everything about the city, whispered to Arnaldo:

"Those three over there are some American women who live way out on the edge of Samambaia."

THE SUN BURNED. A lizard lay still next to a rock, its head up, mouth open, its antediluvian eyes closed, as if it were drinking the light in peace.

Edileusa began to sing the praises of how delicious a little lizard's tail was served with black beans. Bishop had already been presented with some exotic combinations, such as black beans with pigs' ears and feet, but beans with lizard was a novelty.

Lota led her on: "What does it taste like? Is it like an armadillo?"

Edileusa didn't need to be begged. She didn't speak only about lizards but of other dainty dishes such as thrushes, flying ants, guinea pigs. Lota and Bishop felt uncomfortable. If it were left to Edileusa, there would be no more wild animals on the planet. But Edileusa was a savage, Lota noted. She was hungry; it was plausible. And what about the well-educated people who were exterminating species for nothing? Did Bishop know that the cape of Dom Pedro on display at the Emperor's Museum was made entirely of feathers of the yellow-breasted woodpecker?

Bishop thought of Sam, her beloved toucan. He certainly lived the good life. Six bananas a day, baths with the garden hose, even a pair of earrings to play with, which Vivinha had brought from a department store. The next day, however, there was a bad storm and Bishop forgot to cover the cage. When she remembered, she raced outside, without thinking of her asthma, pneumonia, or anything else she was vulnerable to, and found Sam erect, turned into a statue, soggy, immobile, his eyes shut, his beak up—a sculpture by Brancusi.

BECAUSE HER asthma was punishing Bishop, forcing her to get up several times a night, Lota put her in the car and took her to the doctor in Rio. Bishop let herself be convinced to begin treatment with cortisone, even though the effects of the drug were not yet fully known.

The first dose of cortisone gave her a feeling of euphoria that Bishop, a chronic depressive, found delightful. On a night when she added a gin and tonic to the dose of cortisone, she put a piece of paper in the typewriter and wrote without hesitation:

*A scream, the echo of a scream, hangs over that Nova Scotia village.*

In prose, Bishop narrated the instant in which a girl sees her mother cry out, a terrible scream. Afterward the mother is taken to an asylum, and the girl is left walking among the townspeople, paying attention to other sounds, trying to forget the sound of the scream.

Bishop wrote day and night without stopping until she came to the end. Lota didn't interfere. She understood that Bishop was trying to conjure with the atrocity of that moment.

FINALLY BISHOP was satisfied with "Arrival at Santos" and sent the poem to *The New Yorker.*

Inspired, she wrote her first lines for Lota.

Observing that the lichens grew on rocks without any turbulence, taking their time, she admonished Lota for her impatience:

*. . . you've been, dear friend,*
*precipitate and pragmatical;*
*and look what happens.*

Bishop juxtaposed the growth of the lichens with the appearance of the first streaks of white in Lota's hair. And confessing her love in middle age, she evoked a moment of sensual intimacy between the two women:

*The shooting stars in your black hair*
*in bright formation*
*are flocking where,*
*so straight, so soon?*
*—Come, let me wash it in this big tin basin,*
*battered and shiny like the moon.*

Cautiously, in her oblique way, Bishop had told her friends that she had to delay her trip because of illness. Now, she openly admitted that the old problems had disappeared at Samambaia. I am happy, I am happy, she boasted. Thanks to Lota de Macedo Soares, with whom she was going to the United States in April, to get her records and her books. After forty years, she had a home.

# RIO DE JANEIRO, 1994

NANÁ OPENED up the Saturday, July 2, 1994, issue of O *Globo* and, in the section titled "She," saw the call for information about Lota. "Lota changed the landscape of Rio and now is the subject of a book that rescues her from obscurity." What a surprise! After so many years.

The article took up the whole page. She recognized the photo of Lota: she was probably in her early thirties, her hair quite short, a cigarette in her hand, a faintly mischievous eye. Beside her, of course, they'd put a picture of Elizabeth Bishop. The American was very much at ease, even smiling, which was unusual. The picture was probably from the beginning, the early fifties.

Naná was about to start reading when the phone rang. What a nuisance. At eighty-four, she had some difficulty understanding what was said over the phone. And even more so because most of the people who called were more or less her age, with the same little thread of a voice.

"Dolores! Dolores!" she tried to shout, but all that came out was the little thread. Besides, what good would it do? Dolores was in the kitchen, which she never left, even if the phone or the doorbell exploded from ringing so much. When she'd gotten old, Dolores had become as deaf as a doorpost.

Naná gave up and answered. It was Ismênia. What? Ah, she'd become very annoyed at the article. There are intimate things about people that are not supposed to be made public. That's so, that's so, said Naná, as was her habit. Bye-bye then, love. A little kiss.

She came back to the newspaper and read: "A caju brought Lota and Bishop together."

She remembered clearly the first time she'd seen Bishop. Lota had called, inviting her to visit the great North American writer Elizabeth Bishop, who was staying at her apartment in Leme. Naná had never heard of the great North American writer Elizabeth Bishop, but she was never able to turn Lota down on anything.

When she got there, she found Lota sparkling. After the usual hugs and affection, she took Naná to the bedroom. Other friends were already there: sweet Mary Morse, Vivinha, Vivinha's friend of those days, and, let's see, Clotilde Pena, maybe. Proudly, Lota introduced the Great Writer. A bright pink creature was lying in the bed, as ugly as a bogey woman. The discomfort of the illustrious sick person was obvious. Naná, who was shy, got ready to be uncomfortable too. But Lota wouldn't allow it. She said very funny things and translated them for the bogey woman, who laughed, poor thing; what else could she do?

Lota, Lota, how she missed her. Naná leaned back in her chair to remember better.

The two of them were born the same year, 1910. Except that Lota, with that father of hers who was in exile every now and then, was born in Paris.

When Naná met her, Lota was living in an apartment on the Lagoa. Ahead of her time in everything, she was into the communal living that only became more accepted in the sixties. It was a three-floor apartment, each floor with a bedroom and bathroom, with the other rooms used by everyone. Ruth Berensdorf, who gave swimming lessons at the Copacabana Palace Hotel, lived on the first floor; she became a nun, then quit. A sensational person. What happened to her? The Lage brothers lived on the second floor— Alfredo, who was the right-hand man of conservative Catholic writer Gustavo Corção, and Carlos, who married Bibi. Lota lived on the third floor. Marieta used to say that Lota was Brazil's first hippie.

From the first time she saw her, Naná was fascinated. Lota was a marvel and a terror. If she met a bright person, she turned into a magnificent conversationalist. Naná, who did not consider herself particularly brilliant, maintained a reverential silence while luminous Lota imposed her presence. Surrounded by men—for whom, supposedly, the realm of intellectual activity was reserved—she forced them to overcome their prejudices and accept that a woman could be intelligent; they admired and loved her. During her life, Lota numbered among her friends Mário de Andrade, Rodrigo Melo Franco de Andrade, Prudente de Morais Neto, José Olympio, Pedro Nava, Gustavo Corção.

Besides which, Lota was mischievous. Naná smiled to herself, remembering. That party at Lage Park, for example. Lota said that it was a costume party and convinced her friends to go dressed up as contemporaries of Christ.

It was crazy, with all the costumes improvised with sheets—some were slaves, some Romans, and so on. When Antonio Lage came in a tuxedo to pick them up, confusion reigned. But in a minute Lota had persuaded him to trade in his black tie for a toga. When they got to the mansion, it was bedlam. All the Lages dressed to kill. Dona Baby in a long dress. And Lota swathed as Lazarus and covered in mercurochrome blood. Rosinha as Magdalene Before Repenting. Everybody in sheets. At the end of the party, everyone into the swimming pool. It came out in the newspapers: "Orgy in the Park."

Lota never stopped surprising her—never. One night, just after the Second World War, Naná was listening to a short-wave broadcast on CBS, aimed at a Brazilian audience. It was called "Women's Page." Suddenly, who comes on the air? Guess who. Saying, "The Americans want to help us? All the better. Let's take what's useful and leave the rest aside." Broadcast live, from a studio in New York. At that time everything was live. On that occasion the Americans were touting the politics of good neighbors. Walt Disney had even created Joe Carioca, a total fake and a bore, in Naná's opinion. Lota praised a publication of the Museum of Modern Art in New York, *Brazil Builds*, discussing Brazilian architecture. And she seized every opportunity to promote Brazilian artists, noting that Nelson Rockefeller had donated *Christ* by Maria Martins to the museum.

One thing that made Naná livid was the fiction that Lota was an Americanophile. It was true that Lota admired a number of things in American culture. The conscientious practice of solid citizenship, for example. The sense of organization. Because she was an aesthete, what charmed her above all was the fact that Americans funded the arts: how many rich people in the United States were there who left their fortunes to organizations founded for cultural ends? The museums weren't simply depositories for artwork but active promoters of art.

Naná remembered that when Lota came back from one of her New York trips, all she could talk about were the circulating expositions. Now, Lota enthused, you didn't have to move artworks from one place to another: they were photographed and reproduced by a slide projector during an explanatory lecture. These days this was commonplace, like television or antibiotics, but in 1945 it was a novelty.

Lota wanted to bring these things to Brazil. She had good connections with Americans in the plastic arts. Aside from being a close friend of artists of the caliber of an Alexander Calder, she had easy access to the cultural promoters of the time, like that director of the Museum of Modern Art in New York, what was his name? He even came to Samambaia to visit Lota. Oh, leaky head. Ismênia would know, she remembered all these names.

Here in Brazil too, Lota moved among artists. She was a great friend of Rosinha Leão, who introduced her to Cândido Portinari before he had become Brazil's best-known artist—before his marvelous painting *War and Peace* had been hung in the hallway at the entrance to the United Nations building in New York. Lota often went to Portinari's atelier, scribbling a bit, as she put it. Aside from Portinari himself, she became friends with Enrico Bianco, Carlos Leão, Roberto Burle Marx, all of them prodigies.

She was connected to everyone. She arranged for Mário de Andrade—as well known in literary circles as Portinari was for his painting—to teach a course on art at Portinari's house, while Portinari was in New York. Lota organized a series of lectures and gathered her women friends. Naná went, and was left with the impression that the modernist had misjudged his audience. Perhaps he'd expected a roomful of Lotas.

Now the family, put off by the, shall we say, independence of Lota, started proclaiming that Lota was under the influence of the Americans—the same accusation leveled at the Brazilian bombshell Carmen Miranda after her success in Hollywood. This was nonsense, because what stood out most in Lota was her European experience. But because of her connection with Mary Morse and Elizabeth Bishop, the Macedo Soares, who held a grudge against Lota—which she returned in spades—always referred to the "Americans" at Samambaia. But the peasant lady of Samambaia, as Rachel de Queiroz dubbed her, was in fact very Brazilian.

Naná was lost in her memories. She'd forgotten to read the newspaper. She'd been like this for some time: she would forget what she was doing in the middle of something. Or she'd fall asleep. Well, let's go see what upset Ismênia so much, she decided, already guessing what it would have been.

AT NEXT Wednesday's tea, everyone arrived stirred up.

Ismênia brought her scrapbook to find the name of the man from the museum. Maria Amélia brought Saturday's newspaper, in case Naná forgot where she'd put hers. Good idea, admitted Naná. Vivinha brought butter cookies, without respect for anyone's cholesterol level.

Ismênia, wishing to fulfill her mission right away, wanted to start with the scrapbook. Naná became uneasy. She had little use for photographs, which brought back so many of the dead, and they themselves unrecognizable, with other faces, other bodies. She looked at the faces of her friends surrounding the album. Time had brought its devastation among them. When she was young, Vivinha had been very pretty. Maria Amélia had that distinct, classic beauty. Ismênia, poor thing, had always been homely; she looked like a marmoset, but she had lovely hands, which she'd always tried to show off. Look at them now. They were all old bats. All in their eighties, too, except for Ismênia, or so she said. Each had her own ailment, the mandatory opening to any conversation: arthrosis, hypertension, cataracts, ankylosis. Don't even talk about teeth. Maria Amélia had turned into one of those annoying old women who complain about everything, especially about the indecency she was forced to put up with. Vivinha loved to irritate poor Maria Amélia, saying "ass" instead of rump, for example. Maria Amélia was very refined, had studied at French schools; she called her dead mother "Maman." Vivinha said that the only good thing that old age had brought her was the freedom to do and say whatever she wanted—to misbehave. The truth, thought Naná, was that no one changed with age. Age simply accentuated each one's idiosyncrasies. Maria Amélia had always been annoying. And Vivinha had always had a quick trigger. Her specialty was telling stories; you could die laughing. Nobody told the story of the Pekingese like her. Henrique Lage, heir of the National Coastal Navigation Company, an empire, fell in love with the Italian opera singer Gabriela Bezanzoni and brought her to Brazil. He built a mansion in extremely bad taste for her in the middle of a luxurious park. Among other extravagances, this Bezanzoni had nineteen Pekingese—hysterical little dogs. When she sang, they all yelped together. A butler with white gloves would clap his hands for them to stop. When Vivinha told it, it was even funnier because she imitated them all at the same time—the warbling of the contralto, the nineteen vocalists, the poor butler. It was wild.

"Naná! Come down to earth, Naná!"

Ismênia had found the blessed name: Monroe Wheeler. It was in a well-crumpled clipping from the magazine *Diretrizes*, April 1942. Naná looked at the advertisements; she loved the ads. Mappin & Webb, Ouvidor Street 100—Rio de Janeiro—London—Buenos Aires—Johannesburg—Bombay. The London Assurance: México Street 90 (The Esplanade Building), founded in 1726. Nunes House—Furniture, Curtains, Carpets, Decorations: Carioca Street 65–67. They were all gone. The Louvre, the Eiffel Tower, all the height of chic, they were gone too.

Naná read the headline: "Brazilian Artists to Gather." Below, a cartoon of Lota, sitting with her legs spread, drawn by Augusto Rodrigues.

"What bad taste to portray Lota that way."

"Maria Amélia, she was that way."

"Come on, Vivinha, she was very elegant. Very refined."

"That she was," agreed Naná. "Lota wasn't elegant in the sense of dressing in style, but she was always careful to present herself well. Her clothes, of the best quality. English tweed coat. Footwear by Moreira. Her seamstress, Esmeralda, worked with all the upper crust. Her shirts were ironed to perfection."

"That was one side of her," Vivinha cut in. "The other was this messed-up side. Swearing, son of a this, son of a that. In jeans, with her shirtsleeves rolled up. I even think it was Lota who came up with this fashion of rolled-up hems. Really, she did have this bold side."

"Well, at any rate, I was quite shocked at the way the newspaper referred to Lota and Bishop."

Maria Amélia had come to the point. Naná sighed.

"You were shocked, Maria Amélia? What did you want?"

"Come on, Vivinha. There was a love between two souls there."

"My Saintly Parakeet of the Flat Tires!"

"Lota was an austere person."

"And is an austere person spayed?"

Vivinha could be so disagreeable.

"Vivinha!"

"Maria Amélia, you want so badly to frame Lota as a frustrated spinster, because she didn't marry and have a herd of children like you did. Put this in your noodle: she was the most charming, most fascinating person in the world. She knew how to take whomever she wished to bed with her."

"Vivinha!"

Dangerous territory. Vivinha was also unmarried and had her own life. Naná would like it if the discussion stopped right there.

"Naná, what do you think?"

Oh, Lord.

"I don't know, I don't know. They were very discreet. When I went to Samambaia I slept in the guest wing. They went to their part of the house and closed the door. What went on behind the door I don't know."

"That's right. It was private."

"Come off it. We're not talking about what went on behind closed doors but what went on in plain sight. If Lota was very discreet, she was also very genuine. She always showed herself as she really was and always demanded respect for it. Didn't she?"

Lota's commanding presence filled the room. Yes, thought four old women unanimously as they remembered.

AFTER THEY'D GONE, Naná went back to her memories. She'd followed Lota's trajectory from close by, from the times they split a cheese sandwich at the German Bar to when she became Dona Lota.

She'd had a difficult childhood. Her father, José Eduardo de Macedo Soares, left the navy for journalism and politics. His life, and therefore that of his wife and two daughters, was shaken up by virulent disputes and persecutions. He was exiled by one president, Bernardes, and arrested by another, Vargas—always claiming that he was fighting for freedom. In 1932, his newspaper, the *Diário Carioca*, was raided. He had many enemies and detractors. But what most disturbed Lota's youth was the argument with Geraldo Rocha, from the newspaper *A Noite*. He wrote about José Eduardo leaving his wife, Dona Adélia, to live with Horacinho de Carvalho. Horacinho was a handsome young man. Geraldo Rocha wrote sordid stuff about their relationship. It was execrable. Lota suffered; she was extremely sensitive, and she had her own identity problems to deal with. Marieta said that Lota had even tried suicide once. Lota had never told her such a thing, and so Naná took this information with a grain of salt. The two sisters never got along.

The fact is that Lota decided to go her own way and to live alone. In those times, it wasn't at all common for a young woman to live alone. After the apartment on the Lagoa, she lived in Buarque de Macedo Street, in Flamengo. Later, she lived on Xavier da Silveira Steet, at the corner of Copacabana Avenue, where the store Elle & Lui was. Today the building was gone. Then she decided to build a little house at Samambaia. Carlos Leão designed it for her. At that point she had already become the strong person who seduced everyone. Or almost everyone. There were those who saw her strength as domineering and arrogant. Naná never saw it this way. For her, Lota was so full of light that no one could see that she was not pretty.

In the little house, Lota dedicated herself to an activity that ended up being one of her trademarks: entertaining. She was an impeccable hostess, and she provided moments of great pleasure to her select group of friends. Carlos Leão, or Caloca to his close friends, commemorated these meetings, drawing "Tiny Quotidian Flora," the "rare and commonplace flowers," playing on the fact that Lota loved botany. Each frequent guest got a Latin name, in keeping with his or her "family." Lota, for example, was an Impudent Carlota, from the Dubious family. Caloca was a panic.

Meanwhile, Lota resented not having a specific occupation. She complained to Naná that she wasn't doing anything. She couldn't find a place in which to apply not only the vast erudition she'd accumulated from her reading and her travels but also her desire to change the world and make it more beautiful. So she spent her time putting what was around her into good shape—the house, the vegetable garden.

Lota was impetuous, but once she decided to take something on, she was indefatigable. Kylso, for example. Lota had taken her car to be fixed in one of those backyard garages, the kind there used to be. While she was talking to the mechanic, she saw a little boy sitting in a wooden box, clutching a dog. Coming closer, she saw that his legs were two little twisted sticks. He'd had polio and couldn't walk; he could only drag himself along the ground. Lota was very upset. The mechanic said he didn't have the money to do anything for his son. Impulsively, Lota said that she would take him and care for him. The father agreed right away, on the condition that the little mutt go with him. So off went Lota in her Jaguar, with Kylso and Rebecca at his side. Lota paid for two or three operations for him, and he learned to walk, limping a little and leaning on a cane. Much more than financial support, Lota gave affection to the child, helping him to endure the terrible pain of the postoperative treatments. Everyone was impressed by Lota's devotion. She put him in school, and when he was still a young man, seeing that he had a talent for drawing, she got him an apprenticeship in the architect's office of Henrique Mindlin and then placed him with Sérgio Bernardes. Kylso became an excellent project designer and earned good wages. Then things began unraveling as, against Lota's advice, Kylso married early and began having one child after another. Lota built a little house for him in Samambaia, and every now and then she'd have all the children over. But nothing seemed to be enough for Kylso. It ended up with him and Lota having unpleasant discussions about money, and just at the time when Lota wasn't very well. Lota became disenchanted and didn't want to see him anymore. It was a pity that things ended this way, because Lota saved that boy. That is, she thought she had saved the boy. Who knows if Maria Amélia wasn't right? Maybe Lota saw in Bishop a wounded little girl whom she wanted to save. The truth is that everyone was appalled when Lota announced that Bishop was moving lock stock and barrel to Samambaia. At that point no one could guess what Lota saw in the sickly American. As Vivinha put it, a bit resentfully, perhaps, gracelessness sent its regards with that one.

# EVERYDAY LIFE

IN THE FIRST WEEK OF JUNE 1952, Lota and Bishop were back in Brazil.

No sooner had they arrived in Samambaia than Lota took over the work on the house again. For Bishop, it was amazing that in merely one month she and Lota would be moving to the new wing, with two bedrooms, bathroom, and a small living room with an iron stove, designed by Lota and made under protest by a local ironmonger, who swore it would never work.

Speedy Lota, besides beginning work on building the studio, decided to dam the water that went by in front of it from the waterfall, so that Bishop had somewhere to swim. She started to replant the vegetable garden. And she decided to build a new access road to Samambaia that, as Bishop understood it, would reduce the fame of the spiraled Amalfi road to dust.

Lota began early. Bishop hadn't finished her breakfast when Lota weighed anchor in her bathrobe to supervise the building of the swimming pool. The roar of explosives and the jarring thud of the sledgehammer were out of place in Samambaia. Lota wanted to speed up this phase so as to restore the silence so dear to Bishop. Although she was dizzied by the commotion, Bishop was moved by Lota's concern with her well-being and made frequent visits to the work site, bringing coffee.

On that morning, Lota was at the hydraulics section.

"Mr. Zé, that bend you're making in the drainpipe will be wide enough for peepee but not for caca." Lota's frankness scandalized Bishop. "Everything okay, my love?"

Lota smiled sweetly. Bishop felt absurdly happy.

"Look, sweetheart, it'd be better for you to go in now. Our dynamite specialist is warning that there's going to be another explosion."

Bishop had barely got inside when she heard a colossal kaboom! followed by hysterical barking. Lota raced in, furious, yanking the belt of her robe around her waist. The son of a bitch specialist had botched his calculations and nearly destroyed the toolshed. And he'd only missed blowing up the new gardener, the imbecile, by a bit; evidently he had no better place to rake than precisely in the detonation area.

The days went by this way, with Lota busy with her workers, and Bishop busy with Lota. In the middle of so much tumult, Bishop couldn't find the seclusion necessary to write poetry. Her world was Lota's world. So she started writing to her friends, recounting in detail the events of her day-to-day life, and to show how competent and admirable Lota was. Lota kept an organic garden, used nontoxic fertilizers, corresponded with a British specialist on the sensitivity of plants to electromagnetic waves. Lota was a specialist in silviculture. Lota could plan and carry out complex projects such as dams and roads. She and Lota read poetry daily, alternating in the role of authority, depending on whether the poem was in Portuguese or English. Bishop was getting used to being content. She was sleeping well. She and Lota shared a healthy happiness, almost never coming down; they stayed in their house under construction in the middle of the clouds.

Lota also wanted to convince her friends of how competent and admirable Bishop was. She was a genius, a great poet. When "Arrival at Santos" was published in *The New Yorker* in June, Lota circulated the poem. Ismênia translated it for Vivinha, who hated it.

"I DIDN'T HAVE children, I didn't transmit the legacy of our misery to any other creature."

Bishop finished reading *The Posthumous Memories of Brás Cubas* by Machado de Assis. It was a very difficult book for her. She noted dozens of words to ask Lota about. Surprisingly erudite, the Brazilian writer cited sources at each instance, and Bishop queried, to look up later, what Balaam's Ass and Sintra's magpies could be. She underlined a Schopenhauerian aphorism: pleasure is a bastard pain.

But Bishop would have liked some lighter reading. Before, she had read *Childhood* and *Anguish* by Graciliano Ramos, both dense, and both with affectionate dedications to Lota. Lota therefore suggested *Minha vida de menina*, or *My Life as a Girl*, by Helena Morley.

More than a delight, the book was a revelation to Bishop. The comments of an adolescent on daily life in Diamantina at the end of the nineteenth century were at once funny and moving, and full of delicious information. For example, that only men were permitted to use watches. Women would tell time by the church clock or the trumpet from the barracks. This was during the day, for at night the women's clock was the rooster. Alongside the facts, the diarist added her youngster's observations. In the case of the rooster-clocks, she asserted that "the rooster's crow is never right and no one is convinced. When the rooster crows nine o'clock, they say that the girl is running away from home to get married. I always hear the rooster crow nine o'clock, and it's rare for girls to run away from home."

Above all else Bishop liked the detailed descriptions of the relationships between the girl and her parents, brothers and sisters, grandparents, cousins and uncle—the preferences, the taunts, the squabbles and devotions that characterized the world of the kind of stable and extended family that Bishop had never known.

One day she told Lota that she was going to translate the book into English, not for entertainment or to practice her Portuguese, but aiming toward its publication abroad. Lota was exultant.

THAT NIGHT, with friends gathered, Lota was having one of her usual free-for-alls with the newly converted Alfredo Lage. On this occasion it was about *The Drama of Jean Barois* by Roger Martin du Gard. Alfred had been moved by the affliction of a man divided between mysticism and reason. Well, Lota refused to take seriously a man who said that women were irremediably inferior beings. This small detail had escaped the notice of the theologian, and Lota went to get the book to prove her point. Look here. Right away the inattentive reader was surrounded by other indignant women. Bishop was still unaccustomed to the vehemence of Cariocans; it seemed to her that a lynching was imminent. Then, without Bishop having noticed any transition, suddenly they were talking animatedly about something else. Someone was declaring that in Brazil, nothing was well finished or trustworthy. Lota took the opportunity to say that that very morning, Bishop had drawn her attention to a mistaken report about the United States published in a Rio newspaper.

Heads turned solemnly toward the foreigner. So this meant that, aside from always wearing that expression of someone who made her bed on the porch and forgot the blanket, the insufferable one was also a xenophobic troublemaker. Vivinha felt her hostility gathering force.

Bishop could see that each day, her relationship with Lota's group was getting spikier. Aside from the language barrier and the fetter of shyness, she had to contend with the jealousy of some of Lota's friends. In truth, almost all of Lota's friends, men and women, seemed tedious and futile to her with their forced air of festivity. The great exception was a journalist, uncommonly cultivated and a charming conversationalist, who had a summerhouse at Samambaia. After the noisy evening gatherings with Vivinha and company, it was a great relief to have Carlos Lacerda to lunch on a Saturday afternoon.

LOTA AND BISHOP already knew about Edileusa's artistic inclinations. She liked to decorate plates, for example. She'd serve the rice in the middle of a whimsical flowerbed of carrots, radishes, and cucumbers. She didn't like it if they ate the flowerbed; it was only for decoration.

Even so, it was a surprise to learn that she was an adept at art nouveau. When they got back from their trip, they came upon an enormous white bird painted on a dark rock near the house, with its wings spread and its beak open, like an irritated goose. Edileusa had used the arabesque of a lichen to serve as the body of the bird.

With her incorrigible vocation as a patron of the arts, Lota complimented Edileusa effusively. But Edileusa limited herself to a "ho-hum." Ever since her bosses' return, she'd been acting very strangely. She didn't sing anymore. She brooded. She made mistakes with the salt.

Bishop, who was always ready to assume the blame when things went wrong, tried to determine her responsibility for the change in Edileusa. Was it because of her incursions into the kitchen? But soon Bishop discovered the real reason. Zezé, the hundredth new gardener, was always under foot. It was water, it was coffee, it was a borrowed broom; it was coffee, it was water. Edileusa put her hands on her hips, teasing: "Again!!" While the young man drank his water or coffee right there, aiming his blue spurs at his goddess, the culinary activities were interrupted. And once resumed, they left much to be desired. One day Lota complained that the chicken was raw. Less well cooked it tastes better, Edileusa shot back, more interested in spotting her sweetheart through the window.

Notwithstanding her intuitions about seasoning, Edileusa was never particularly accomplished when it came to cleanliness. This got a lot worse after the arrival of her little German guy. She said that she was really ruffled. One day, Lota pleaded with her to please clean out the garbage can. When she came back for lunch, she found the can painted with black and red lilies. To needle Lota, Bishop remarked that the result was even better than the vase of Portinari's at Samambaia.

Lota got into the jeep and went down to Petrópolis. She came back with two enormous drawing pads, brushes, watercolors, and gouache.

"Take this, Edileusa. Paint."

"IT'S GOING BADLY, it's going badly."

Lota would come back from the work site, tired out, to find the house chores abandoned. One day lunch wasn't ready because Edileusa was unhappy. She'd discovered that Zezé was a big womanizer. Another day, she was late because they quarreled fiercely on the way; he had nothing but dirty things on his mind.

Lota decided to talk to Zezé. Twisting his hat in his hands, very embarrassed, Zezé finally explained that the problem was that Edileusa, who was still chaste at the age of thirty, would only give herself to him after getting properly married, complete with veil and bridal wreath. Mischievous, Lota urged him not to give up.

"What kind of weasel talk is that? Insist on your rights, my man!"

But to Bishop she revealed that she was going to arrange their wedding on Edileusa's terms.

And as always with Lota, if she said she would do it, it was as good as done. Edileusa wanted to choose the style of dress, wanted the cake to be made at a bakery, wanted a honeymoon. Lota looked after everything. On the day of the wedding, she and Bishop went to the apartment in Rio so that the betrothed pair and their guests could feel at ease.

But the results were not what was hoped for. First, perhaps because she was older than Zezé, Edileusa was extremely jealous. She spent her time going from Peter to Paul, trying to find out where her untrustworthy husband could be. Second, she found her vocation in painting, revealing herself to be, as Lota's appraisal had it, an excellent primitivist. After the goose on the rock and the flowered garbage can, Lota's intentions in providing art supplies to Edileusa had been to avoid having her share in the work of decorating the house. As she continued to show her works of art, however, Edileusa continued to confirm her talents. Lota bought canvasses and tubes of paint and encouraged her to move into oils. Children playing in a circle, young women dancing around the pole, blacks in Panama hats watching time go by populated Edileusa's canvasses. When she caught Edileusa about to smash a canvas on Zezé's head, Lota decided that it was time for her to go. With an affectionate hug, she told Edileusa that she belonged in an art gallery, not a kitchen.

That was how Lota and Bishop lost a cook and a gardener on the same day. A bit disconsolately, Bishop went back to the kitchen. Lota sent messages on the four winds that she needed a maid and a gardener with a lot of experience, who understood gardens, orchards, and vegetables. It was in this way that the four Marias came, four sisters for whom Lota designed a system of rotation that guaranteed there would always be a Maria in the house. And this is how Manuelzinho came.

IN THIS WAY, Lota and Bishop practiced the art of finding grace in the small rituals of daily life.

They established routines that were rites of conviviality. Awakening side by side. Morning greetings. Breakfast in bed. The "inspection visits" to the work site. The grocery list, the lunch menu. Reading and conversation at night. The arrival of the mail. The moment when the mail was opened was special—the moment when Bishop's friends came in to Samambaia. At first, Bishop would read and report to Lota. With time, Lota began to open Bishop's letters herself. She disapproved of depressed friends—they weren't good for Bishop. She wrote postscripts in letters to Gold and Fizdale, American pianists that Bishop had met through Lota. She sent her regards to Marianne Moore.

Rarely did Lota and Bishop part. If Lota had to go to Rio, they went together. Crossing the mountain range was always an adventure for Bishop, who didn't know how to drive. If the day was bright, the little Jaguar was a meteor. Lost to the attractions of the landscape, Bishop would stare fixedly at Lota's polyvalent hands, taken up at once with gesticulating, holding a cigarette, and finding the perfect angle through the curves. Often, the crossing was made through the middle of dense fog. Lota carried on dauntlessly. Bishop, aware of the sheer cliffs hidden in the mist, would distract herself by making up letters to her friends, recounting the spectacular alteration of course in her life. She had a home, with a stove and all. She was incorporating spicy flavors into her cooking. She was making poetry in her food; she was inventing extravagances like jaboticaba jam. How to explain to Kit and Ilse Barker the voluptuousness of the jaboticaba?

Lota and Bishop made plans, and in this way the relationship grew more solid. They would raise cows and make butter at home. They would travel to Italy. The difficulty with international travel was that while Bishop was used to traveling third class and staying in pensions, Lota would go nothing but first class. To travel like that, they needed to save some money. And how to save money, if the costs of construction were astronomical and Bishop wasn't able to write poems for her second book?

"THERE'S NO shortage of animals here," Lota remarked when Bishop revealed that zoology was one of her preferred subjects.

They'd go out on nocturnal explorations. Lantern in hand, they'd surprise the frogs which, disjointedly, mounted each other for the "reproductive embrace." They focused on the red eyes of the owls that watched for prey on the ground and moved off in Parnassian flight. At home, they heard the excited squeaks of the bats. Lota defended them, explaining that they helped maintain the forest by defecating the seeds, ready to germinate, of the plant species they fed on.

Bishop never tired of admiring Lota's cache of cultural lore. At each moment she'd make opportune and well-informed comments on whatever was on the agenda.

Captivated, Bishop wrote a poem about Lota: "The Wit."

*"Wait. Let me think a minute," you said.*
*And in the minute we saw:*
*Eve and Newton with an apple apiece,*
*and Moses with the Law,*
*Socrates, who scratched his curly head,*
*and many more from Greece,*
*all coming hurrying up to now,*
*bid by your crinkled brow.*

*But then you made a brilliant pun.*
*We gave you a thunderclap of laughter.*
*Flustered, your helpers vanished one by one;*
*and through the conversational spaces, after,*
*we caught,—back, back, far, far,—*
*the glinting birthday of a fractious star.*

Setting stone upon stone, Lota built Bishop's promised studio out of nothing. In December, Bishop sat down in *her* chair, in *her* space, feeling so happy she thought she'd weep for a week on end. As Whitman put it, "Immense have been the preparations for me/Faithful and friendly the arms that have help'd me."

Now what she owed in return was that, installed in her atelier, she should draw inspiration from the bamboo grove in front of her and write the most beautiful poems of the century. Or at least some that someone would buy.

Bishop struggled. She spent the afternoons working with the rich material that Samambaia provided her. But the next day, when she read what she'd produced, she'd ask herself how she could have written something so idiotic.

MANUELZINHO, "the world's worst gardener since Cain," introduced Bishop to the Brazilian institution of the tenant. Fascinated, Bishop watched the little man, in pants covered in patches and a straw hat painted green, bring Lota to the edge of madness.

Lota would buy kilos of the best seed, imported and guaranteed, and the whole result would consist of a three-legged carrot. Manuelzinho planted collards and red carnations in the same bed. He'd spend hours standing beside the donkey, looking out at nothing, or at what looked like nothing to Bishop. His children, with their heads stuck into Pérola sugar sacks, ran off in terror when Lota approached. Once a month Manuelzinho would take his notebook with the camel on its cover and come to "do his accounts." By his calculations, in which the decimal points were always forgotten, Lota owed him millions.

Faced with the creative vitality of her tenant, Lota swung schizophrenically between fury and condescension, exasperation and tenderness. Discerning in Manuelzinho someone who resisted the oppression of order and maintained his freedom through his imagination, Bishop dedicated a long poem to him. She installed Lota as an ambivalent narrator and made Manuelzinho into an irresistible infringer:

> And once I yelled at you
> so loud to hurry up
> and fetch me those potatoes
> your holey hat flew off,
> you jumped out of your clogs,
> leaving three objects arranged
> in a triangle at my feet,
> as if you'd been a gardener
> in a fairy tale all this time
> and at the word "potatoes"
> had vanished to take up your work
> of fairy prince somewhere.

The Marias began to get accustomed to having that gringa in the kitchen who mangled her Portuguese and mixed mangoes with curry. Many people appreciated Bishop's cooking, from Maneco, Rosinha, and Magu's nephew to the poet Manuel Bandeira, who sang the praises of her jams and jellies. Lota felt cherished when, the work routine finished, Bishop would put a batch of fresh cookies on the tea table. Cookie, she took to calling her. My dear head cook.

BEFORE BISHOP could say Worcestershire, a year had gone by. The ring with Lota's name engraved on it was dated 20.12.51. Now it was Christmas again and Bishop wanted to keep her promise to make a turkey for the dinner in the best New England tradition.

That morning the maid on duty, Maria of the Pains or Maria of the Cliff, Bishop didn't know which, came to inform her that the turkey had arrived. Bishop came down from the studio planning what she could use to substitute for cornbread mix to make the stuffing. For seasoning she would need savory and thyme—how, precisely, did you say that in Portuguese? As well, speaking of turkey, Lota had already explained that Thanksgiving Day was not translated as Dia de Dar Obrigados, as Bishop had elucidated for one of her correspondents. Well, at least they'd brought gravy seasoning from the United States to baste the bird. Bishop figured that it would take about six hours to roast.

At the door of the kitchen, Bishop halted. The Christmas dinner was standing sadly in front of her, tied by a piece of string to a leg of the table. It maintained that solemn air that turkeys are capable of, despite the scarlet pendent.

"Oh dear." What an uncomfortable situation. She'd never dreamed that the bird would come alive.

"The lady doesn't need to worry, we'll kill him. Then we'll scald him in boiling water and pluck him."

"Oh dear."

"Today we'll give him cane liquor all day; we'll kill him tomorrow."

Bishop thought the cane liquor was an act of piety, a kind of narcotic so that the turkey would cope with the execution better, poor thing.

"Well, okay."

And in this way, in the best New England tradition, the cook and the condemned one maintained their composure.

AN ENORMOUS blue butterfly, like the ones that turn into trays, glided by. From the pool Bishop followed the flight with her eyes, which ended by flying to Lota's eyes. The two of them smiled. It was January, it was Sunday; there was no work or workers, and Manuelzinho had gone down a long time ago, with his hoe on his shoulder. The water flowing over their bodies was the most refreshing thing imaginable under that blue sky. Lota came closer, slowly. I am forty, thought Bishop, incredulous at such a singular love.

Suddenly, a racket: caw, caw. It was a flock of parrots, screeching on their passage.

Lota and Bishop followed their flight into the forest. Then they resumed their smiles, lying back in the loose hammock of the afternoon and gathering together in its hollow.

"Shall we go, Cookie?"

"Let's go."

Embracing, they went to the house; for Bishop it was as if they were skaters making slow, slow circles.

At dusk they came out of the bedroom regaled and went to the veranda to have some iced maté.

FINALLY LOTA found time to realize a dream of Bishop's: to see Ouro Preto. Suspecting what it meant to travel in Brazil, Lota, a habituée of New York, drew up a long list of equipment to ensure the trip went well, from soup to nuts. She had the Land Rover tuned up and read some maps. Talking to a friend who had just come back from there, she learned that the new road had been finished. If they went by car, the trip would be much more pleasant. They shifted the voluminous baggage from the jeep to the old Jaguar, and off they went.

After some kilometers on the new road, under the marvelously blue sky of Minas Gerais, Lota and Bishop were bewildered. Suddenly there was no more new road. It had been started, but it hadn't been finished! From that point on, they had to proceed on the old road, forcing the low-slung Jaguar to swerve between the craters. They covered fifty kilometers in six hours, punctuated by Lota's copious list of cusswords. In a triumphant entrance, they got to Ouro Preto at night, dragging the tailpipe knocked loose by a pothole.

For Bishop, Ouro Preto made up for all the hardships of the trip, which had included a flat tire and hotels totally inadequate for a Costallat de Macedo Soares. Bishop fell in love with the city, with its baroque churches and eighteenth-century colonial houses. She left resolved to return there many times.

THE POOR JAGUAR got back pretty beat up. With the twelve hundred dollars that she'd been paid for "In the Village" and a little more, Bishop decided to buy a black 1952 MG. Lota adored it, flying up the future Amalfi road like the wind, making Bishop's graying hair stand on end.

But on a dark wet night, the gallant MG got stuck in the mud, and no amount of pushing would get it out. Lota and Bishop had to climb up to Samambaia sloshing through the mud, holding hands in the pitch black. Reaching home, Bishop complained because her lovely sweater, which she hadn't even worn yet, had been left in the car. It would certainly be stolen. Lota snorted, jumped into the Land Rover, drove back down through the rain and mud, and rescued the blessed sweater. She forgot about the payment for the workers, which was sitting in the glove compartment. But no one stole it.

OFTEN, LOTA would say: "Cookie, go work."

Bishop was distracted, unable to concentrate. She spent time fighting with words, unbuttoning them. Often they resisted. At other times it was Bishop who, subduing them, lost interest and went in search of others. She could not finish her poems and sell them. She wanted to be able to write poems of three and four pages, like her friends Theodore Roethke and Robert Lowell. The publishers paid better for those, and collected, the poems would make a book right away. The poems that Bishop struggled with were short; it would take dozens of them to make up the new book, which the publisher asked for constantly. Bishop wrote to them that she was near to finishing a half dozen of the long ones; wait, they were on the verge.

That week, Lota had to stay in Rio for two consecutive days. She was renting the apartment in Leme so she'd have a steady monthly income and had other paperwork to look after. When she got back to Samambaia, Maria ran to meet her in the parking lot. Dona Elizabetchy wouldn't come out of her bedroom; she hadn't eaten anything for two days.

Lota flew. Cookie!

The door to the bedroom was locked.

Lota twisted the doorknob, pounded on the door, screamed for Bishop.

Animal-like sounds came from the room.

Lota was ready to force the door when it opened. She ran in headlong.

On the floor, near the bed, empty bottles.

Bishop let herself be hugged. She began to sob.

"Help me," she begged.

THAT WAS FOLLOWED by other binges. When Bishop started drinking, she couldn't stop. She would drink herself unconscious. When she came to she would be sick, feel guilty, loathe herself. Then she'd not drink for a time.

Lota strove to prolong the periods of abstinence as much as possible. She stopped serving drinks at her gatherings of friends. If the two of them went to someone's house, she asked that Bishop not be offered anything.

Bishop was grateful for this loving protection. But she felt even more guilty, ungrateful, and irresponsible when she began drinking again. When Dylan Thomas died in November 1953, himself a hopeless alcoholic, Bishop went on a Homeric binge for all disgraced poets. At other times, Lota couldn't identify the specific event that would bring on a relapse. She was certain of one thing, however: her love alone was not sufficient to free Bishop from her addiction.

Lota spoke to Bishop and, with motherly persistence, convinced her to seek medical treatment for her dependency. Bishop agreed to take Antabuse, a medication that would make the drinker vomit her guts out at the smallest sip of alcohol.

LIFE WENT ON in this way, a small and serene life. Dewy mornings, starry nights. Antabuse.

The help constituted the major contact Bishop had with the language. Bishop tried to practice her tortured Portuguese with the Marys and Johns at hand. She wasn't always successful. One morning, while one of the young men was raking near the pool, Bishop remarked on the beauty of a crab on a rock. Without delay the young man raised his hackle and wham!, shattered the beauty.

Sometimes she missed Edileusa, now painting a lot and selling her work to Lota's friends. One day Bishop wanted to know if Edileusa was a common name. Lota explained that no, it was probably half of the mother's named combined with half of the father's, a Brazilian custom that had produced names like Rubenaldes and Cleidonires. But when Lota asked why her parents had given her that name, Edileusa said, cabbalistically, that it was in homage to Princess Isabel.

There were Sundays on which Samambaia turned into a tumult of children. Kylso, Lota's protégé, already had four children, including a Lotinha. Add to them the children of the cook and her sister and Manuelzinho's children. Put out, Bishop hid herself in her studio, read *A Naturalist in Brazil*. Lota, very practical, thought it would be opportune to translate Dr. Spock's book.

A moment of pure joy occurred when Lota told her nephew Flavio that he could bring his friends to play in the pool. From the window of her study Bishop saw ten or twelve naked children jumping from the rocks, fooling around in the water, laughing, crazy little people. Bishop, who had not had a childhood, was moved. She went to the house and helped Lota make chocolate for the crew.

Lota and Bishop's life at Samambaia was made of these modest moments.

A CERTAIN CELEBRITY arrived when, at the beginning of 1954, Lota's house won an important architectural prize. Her friends came up for a party. Some complained that they'd called Leme and found Bishop more confused than ever. No, poor Cookie, Lota laughed. The apartment had been rented to another American who was also named Elizabeth, and she didn't catch on that people were trying to speak to her homonym. It was devilishly confusing.

The glory was tarnished by their financial troubles. Like Pantagruel, the house was devouring all of Lota's resources. The enormous windowpanes were imported from Belgium at prices that Bishop thought terrifying. Inflation ruled the pay rates for labor. Bishop and Lota had to cancel their plans to travel abroad, plans carefully thought out in the comfort of their bedroom.

In the area of finances, a first difference arose. Lota thought Bishop stingy. Bishop found Lota a spendthrift. So that in the Biennial of that year, in the face of their money troubles, when Lota wanted to buy an extremely expensive bronze sculpture, Bishop resented it. The acquisition, not at all a priority, would stall the travel plans for a good while.

The mustiness of the prize house continued to afflict the bronchial tubes of the fragile American, and Bishop had prolonged asthma attacks. These delayed finishing the new book even more. After nine years of waiting, the publisher proposed an edition made up of the previous book, *North & South*, and the poems from the latest harvest, collected under the title *A Cold Spring*. Bishop resisted this strongly, but after a crisis that left her in bed for ten straight days, Lota convinced her to accept the proposal. As Vivinha put it, Bishop's luck was that she was asthmatic, but Lota was axiomatic.

NEWS ABOUT THE political situation in Brazil came to Samambaia by way of the brilliant neighbor. Since the day she'd met him, Bishop had found Lacerda caught up in furious combat with President Getúlio Vargas through Lacerda's newspaper, the *Tribuna da Imprensa*. To Lacerda, Vargas was a corrupt populist. The other versions of Vargas, as "father of the poor" and the man who modernized Brazil, did not resonate at Samambaia. On one weekend or another, Lacerda would find the time to toast them with an eloquent summary of his activities as the champion of democracy. Lota liked to needle him. Bishop wasn't quite comfortable with all the ferocity. She liked it much better when the subject was literature.

One morning Lacerda was shot at, at the door of his house. When she heard, Lota anxiously called up Letícia, Lacerda's wife. He was all right. Major Vaz, however, had been killed.

From then on, Lacerda began to plan the overthrow of Vargas, to whom he attributed responsibility for the attempt on his life. Bishop had a Yankee aversion to coups, but as far as she understood, public opinion, as well as that of the majority of politicians and the army, was with Lacerda.

Suddenly, the situation was reversed. With the suicide of Vargas, the public became indignant with Lacerda, who had to go into hiding—although this did not stop him from receiving an overwhelming vote in that year's elections.

"Oh this incredible country," wrote Bishop to her friends, since she didn't have the nerve to say it aloud.

VIVINHA TOOK her nephews to see *Carnaval Atlântida*. She loved the film, which she found the essence of kitsch. Vivinha recommended to Lota that she take Bishop to see it. She needed to learn about Brazil.

Lota wouldn't even think of going to see a film in which Oscarito the clown was Helen of Troy and didn't mention the notion to Bishop. Bishop was already getting her dose of Brazil, working arduously on her translation of *My Life as a Girl*. The decision to close off the production of poems for the new book had brought great relief to Bishop, who now was devoting herself to finishing the translation. At the end of each day, Lota copyedited Bishop's work. She thought the book was going well.

Finally, in August 1955, *Poems: North & South—A Cold Spring* was published in the United States. The book closed with "The Shampoo," a poem for Lota.

# THE GREENGROCER
# BRINGS LUCK

EARLY THAT MORNING, they were awakened by thunder and lightning. A bolt struck near the house. Crack! Tobias ran into the room, fur bristling, and jumped onto the bed. The noise of the hail on the metal roof was infernal. Lota and Bishop were startled out of their embrace. Lota had to light candles because the wiring had been damaged and the power was out. Bishop found that they had no telephone line either. When day broke, the storm let up, and Lota and Bishop went out to check the damage.

> The cat stayed in the warm sheets.
> The Lent trees had shed all their petals:
> wet, stuck, purple, among the dead-eye pearls.

Bishop drew on the episode to write "Electrical Storm" and make Tobias famous. Too much of an honor for that fussbudget, in Lota's opinion, who got irritated with Tobias's habit of strewing on the kitchen floor the pieces of rat he didn't wish to eat.

Other animals Bishop observed appeared in the new poems she created in the studio. The armadillo fleeing from flames in the forest that were caused by a fire balloon. The lizards circling, red hot, the female, her wicked tail straight up and over. The sandpiper running obsessed along the beach, looking for something, something, something. Perfectionist that she was, she worked through the verses over and again, polishing them in an agony of revision.

When Bishop finally set the poems free, A Cold Spring was published, to the highest praise from North American critics. Among Brazilians, however, Bishop continued to be solemnly ignored. Not happy with this, Lota used her influence to have an unpublished poem of Bishop's appear in the magazine Anhembi, edited by Paulo Duarte, with an introduction of the poet to its readers. "Squatter's Children" was published in English in the April 1956 issue, alongside an article by Benjamin Péret, about the most famous Brazilian hideout for runaway slaves, "What Was the Quilombo of Palmares?" and an analysis, by the publishers of the magazine, of the Twentieth Congress of the Soviet Communist Party.

The introduction explained that Bishop lived in a poetic retreat on the peak of a mountain, in the beautiful rustic house of Lota de Macedo Soares, and that the suggestions about Brazilian nature being gathered by her sensibility could already be seen in some of the poems of A Cold Spring. Meanwhile, the piece continued, the illustrious guest was not read very much even by the great public of her own country, because she was "the mistress of an art that insinuates rather than imposes itself."

Naná felt relief at the reservation expressed by the author of the article in Anhembi. She knew that Lota was waiting for her to comment about "Squatter's Children," but she felt insecure. She didn't know what Bishop's political stance was, but the poem seemed to her to be a caustic protest against social injustice in Brazil, making the ironic observation that although they were destitute of land, the children surprised by the storm had an inalienable right to mansions of rain. Bishop's art demanded a mastery of the English language that Naná definitely did not possess. It was different from reading the Times. The poem "The Shampoo," for example, which closed Bishop's book, was supposedly about Lota. It spoke of lichens, of rings in the moon, of shooting stars and patient heavens. It said that Lota was hasty and now she had to wash her hair. Really. Naná could not fathom the poem's theme. It was a pity that Ismênia was out of the country. She'd be able to decipher all of that, as she'd done with Bishop's very strange story about childhood published in The New Yorker.

Naná knew that Lota considered Bishop a genius. When one friend or another raised the issue of the, let us say, inconveniences that Bishop had brought to Lota's life, with her precarious health, her odd temperament, and above all else, her alcoholism, Lota would always say that Bishop was a genius, as if with a genius one had to tolerate everything.

Because of all the genius, the alcoholism, or whatever else, the truth was that Lota was gradually withdrawing from the happy weekend get-togethers with her friends. The spontaneity had been lost. If the conversation was in Portuguese, Bishop hardly participated at all. If it was in English, the conversation adjusted itself to the varying levels of fluency of the participants; it became a muddle, Bishop shaking her head condescendingly and Lota making asides to smooth things out. Lota would say that Bishop was terribly shy. But Mary Morse was also shy and a Bostonian, and in Mary's time things were a lot more lighthearted. Card games, evening parties; Caloca and his fooling around. Well, what could you do if after five years in Brazil Bishop still didn't speak Portuguese!

THERE ARE TOO many *coitados*. Ordinarily, Pearl Kazin's remark about the first draft of *The Diary of Helena Morley* would have sent Elizabeth into crisis. Elizabeth was just as hypersensitive to unfavorable reviews or reservations as she was to fungus or to streptococcus. However, Bishop took her friend's proviso well; Kazin was suggesting a new literary agent for her in the United States. The reaction was even more heroic because Elizabeth was in that circle of hell reserved for those who transgress the laws of art; she'd been hurled there by a negative review of *A Cold Spring* written by a certain Edwin Honig.

Lota was speaking to Vera Pacheco Jordão. Vera had prepared herself to go with Bishop to Diamantina, which Bishop wanted to see in order to write an introduction for the book. Lota was aware of Bishop's deep commitment to the book set in the state of Minas Gerais. After having spent years working on the translation—even accepting, with incredible nonchalance, the demand that the husband of the author would "revise" Bishop's English— Bishop was determined to find a publisher for the book. She even reached the point of telling her new agent that she should make submission of Bishop's manuscript for her next book of poems conditional on the publisher's agreeing to publish first *The Diary of Helena Morley*, as Bishop's English translation of *My Life as a Girl* was titled. With the introduction, the work would be finished; it had involved Lota herself, analyst of the solutions Bishop had devised to render into English some of the phrases particular to Diamantina, such as the "Jew's horse" and the big pot, the *caldeirão* of diamonds. And it had even involved Mary, who almost went crazy with the typing. Vera was a sweetheart to go with Elizabeth. The house construction was almost finished, and Lota definitely could not leave Samambaia.

THEN EVERYTHING CHANGED.
Bishop was called to the phone. It was a reporter.
"You've won the Pulitzer Prize."

"Please?"

"The Pulitzer. Your book has won the Pulitzer."

From then on, it was god help us. People from the U.S. embassy, photographers, reporters, even filmmakers made the pilgrimage to the top of the mountain. The Brazilian friends who had doubted that Bishop was really a poet were constantly on the phone.

The next day, Vivinha, who had opened the newspaper to see where the film *Guys and Dolls* was playing, because she wanted to see Marlon Brando dance, came upon Bishop looking at her, with Calder's unmistakable mobile behind her. Look at that. Vivinha began reading.

"In the company of Senhora Carlota de Macedo Soares, who is her host, Miss Bishop lives an austere life, surrounded only by books, objects of art, a dog and a cat. She doesn't even own a radio."

What a joke. The reporter, as usual, made his contribution to culture by supplying titles for Bishop's remarks: "Seduction of the countryside"; "Infinite, the Subject of Poetry." Bishop explained that it was her habit to write a poem today, put it away, and only reread it years later. She listed her favorite writers: Chaucer, Shakespeare, Homer, Aeschylus, Euripides, Aristophanes, Virgil, Dante, Cervantes, and Camões. What did she have against Sophocles, Vivinha muttered. Miss Bishop declared herself surprised at the honor and guessed that she'd receive about five thousand dollars for the prize. She'd probably use the money to take a trip. The reporter added: "Nevertheless, she would come back to Brazil, because no other country exercised a greater seduction over her spirit":

The piece ended like that, with a colon—maybe a typographical error, or maybe the journalist was paying homage to the vanguards of syntax. Vivinha sighed. She'd come back to Brazil. Seduction over her spirit. Why couldn't she bring herself to like that American?

THE GREENGROCER also recognized the picture of Bishop in the newspaper. He told Lota he was very happy. The week before, another customer had won a prize in a raffle. Now it was the American's turn. Clearly, he brought a lot of good luck to his customers.

IT WAS A prodigious night, one of those nights that perhaps we only see when we are young, dear reader. The sky was so clear and deep that, staring into it, there was no avoiding the involuntary question to oneself whether it was possible, under such a sky, for evil to be or for monstrous creatures to exist.

Lota and Bishop were sitting on the sofa with a blanket over their knees. It was cool. Only a small lamp on the wall was lit, giving off a diffuse light.

Bishop surrendered herself to the soft calm of the moment. She was happy. After four years of torment trying to write, with 1956 serenity had come: she had published a book, and she had received the most important prize for it. It was true that instead of the anticipated five thousand dollars, she'd received only five hundred. However, she'd also received an unexpected grant from the *Partisan Review*. She'd finished the translation of *My Life as a Girl*, which became *The Diary of Helena Morley*, and succeeded in having Farrar, Straus and Giroux publish it. She was already writing new poems.

Lota was proud of her Cookie. For her part, she promised: she'd import, she'd improvise, she'd go crazy, but by the end of the year the house would be finished. Then they could go to New York together and stay as long as Bishop wanted.

As she had for almost five years, Bishop listened quietly, hand in hand with Lota, whose voice fell softly through the half shadow. Bishop wanted to sing the intimacy, the sweetness of that touch—the real meaning of this seemingly small and obscure life in the middle of the forest.

A psalm began to trace itself. In the days that followed, Bishop began a poem of praise for this love, praising this house. Not as an architectural monument, but as a house permanently open to nature, where fog came in through the window and indolently crossed the room in the middle of a conversation. She called the poem "Song for the Rainy Season."

*Hidden, oh hidden*
*in the high fog*
*the house we live in,*
*beneath the magnetic rock,*
*rain, rainbow-ridden,*
*where blood-black*
*bromeliads, lichens,*
*owls, and the lint*
*of the waterfalls cling,*
*familiar, unbidden.*

*. . . vapor*
*climbs up the thick growth*
*effortlessly, turns back,*
*holding them both,*

*house and rock,*
*in a private cloud.*

. . . . . . . . . . . . . .

*House, open house*
*to the white dew*
*and the milk-white sunrise*
*kind to the eyes,*
*to membership*
*of silver fish, mouse,*
*bookworms,*
*big moths; with a wall*
*for the mildew's*
*ignorant map*

IN 1957 LOTA and Bishop spent six months in New York.

They kept busy in a whirl of social occasions and shopping, in a manner they thought they'd forgotten. All her friends noticed how Bishop had changed: she was happy, healthy, well dressed, well groomed. Everyone noticed, too, that the reason for the change was at her side. It was that brown woman, very short, sophisticated, diverting, electric, devoted.

Besides taking up again with her old friends, Bishop went to conferences and talks, at which she felt very insecure. Lota, her shield-bearer, went everywhere with her.

It was Bishop who wanted to return. She was finding well-to-do America depressing. They packed up their twenty-odd suitcases, seven trunks, all of their crated boxes and barrels, and boarded ship.

The trip was eighteen days' worth of recovery for Bishop, who loved traveling. She loved taking a long time to arrive. Whenever possible, she chose voyages by sea. The trip was eighteen days' worth of excruciating boredom for Lota, who if she could would have invented a machine that dematerialized her in New York and rematerialized her at the door of her house.

WITH THE BULK of the work done, Lota loathed the little left to do at Samambaia. The financial situation remained unstable. And the arrival of menopause aggravated her insomnia and brought new inconveniences, like an infamous case of gingivitis. Because of this, perhaps, Lota became impatient when Bishop came to ask for another toucan. Poor Sam had died, poisoned, when Bishop sprayed the cage with DDT, thinking that the insecticide—the man had guaranteed it!—was inoffensive to animals. No ma'am, no more toucans for now. But right after, to console her, Lota designed and built a splendid cabinet for the hi-fi that Bishop had brought from the United States. Bishop spent hours listening to Rosalyn Tureck playing Bach's variations, and Gold and Fizdale playing Poulenc's concerto for two pianos.

"Cookie, go write," Lota said.

They kept their habit of reading to one another. Bishop read Lota Marianne Moore's praise of *The Diary of Helena Morley*. Lota read Bishop the description of the masculine attire in which the painter Flávio de Carvalho had paraded through downtown São Paulo—an outfit extremely well-adapted to the Brazilian climate and of ultrapractical conception: a petticoat with pleats to guarantee freedom of movement, ballerina's stockings to hide varicose veins, openings under the arms for ventilation, and cloth that didn't need to be ironed. Then they would spend hours discussing the news, laughing to excess.

A very welcome guest in those times was Flávio, Lota's nephew. Flávio and Lota had one of those specially attuned relationships that can develop between aunt and nephew. Luckily he adored North American literature, and he became a cherished interlocutor for Bishop as well. Both were asthmatic, and sometimes they'd discuss poetry together, each breathing with an inhaler.

# BEAUTIFUL PALM COUNTRY

THE HIGH FEELINGS over Brazil's Soccer World Cup victory in Sweden hadn't quite subsided when Samambaia was honored with the presence of Aldous Huxley. In the beginning, even Lota felt a little intimidated. But everything went very well, and finally Huxley and his wife invited their hostesses to go with them to Brasília and from there to the Amazon. Lota declined, but Bishop accepted on the spot.

When it was confirmed that the backcountry specialist Cláudio Vilas Boas would meet them at the station of the Protection Service for Indians on the shore of the Tuatuari, Bishop was ecstatic. Lota was moved by all this joy. Feigning worry, she asked Bishop if she were ready for all the frontal nudity she'd find up there. She quoted from the letter of the scribe Caminha, who came with the fleet that "discovered" Brazil and wrote the king of Portugal in 1500: "The young women are very gracious, and their shameful parts are plump, tight and clean of fur."

Bishop laughed, "Lota, you're no good." Lota told her various things about Indians as they had been described by Caminha. That they spat out everything the Portuguese gave them to taste. That they exchanged their beautiful bows for any old cap. That the captain had decided to take two Indians by force for the scrutiny of the king. But then he decided to leave two outcasts on shore instead, ordering them to infiltrate the Indians and report on them to the next expedition, in this way inaugurating Brazil's secret service.

Bishop took to making notes, as was her habit. She decided that she would also write an account of the trip, without embellishment or disfigurement. *The New Yorker* would have to like it.

THE RESPECTED WRITER and journalist Antônio Callado covered the Huxley and Bishop trip for the *Correio da Manhã*. The piece, "A Wise Man among the Indians," was published on August 21, 1958.

The Anglo writers experienced culture shock, traveling directly from the ultramodern new capital, Brasília, to the Indian camps on the Xingu River. Warriors from the tribes of Caiapó, Uilapiti, Camauirá, and Meinaco, wearing nothing but *urucum* red paint on their hair and *jenipapo* brown paint on their chests, approached and greeted them with smiles.

While Callado snapped a shot of a lovely moment—the author of *Brave New World* surrounded by a cloud of little butterflies—Bishop was asked for her hand in marriage. At least that's what they told her when a warrior, touching her pale skin, suggested something exotic in the Txucurramãe language.

Bishop came back fascinated. She wrote a piece about her adventures with Huxley among the savages, but to her disappointment *The New Yorker* wasn't interested in publishing it.

PROFESSOR SANDRA CAVALCANTI, who had been a councilwoman in Rio and had hated the experience, came to spend the weekend at Lacerda's country place. Lacerda, who at this point was a congressman, was committed to approving a new law that would reform Brazil's educational system, and Cavalcanti pulled together a volunteer support group for him composed of eminent Brazilian educators, herself among them.

Lacerda invited Cavalcanti to visit his neighbor, a sensational woman, who had cuttings of a new type of rosebush.

Sandra Cavalcanti met a very short woman with fine features, with a straw hat tied over her head, tattered clothes, and beaten-up shoes. She conveyed the disturbing impression of being at once very strong and very weak.

Introductions over, the grower of roses struck up a conversation about gardening with Lacerda, totally ignoring the young woman who accompanied him.

Later on, Lacerda tried a second introduction.

"You know, Lota, something very interesting about Sandra is that she raises hummingbirds."

Lota turned and looked at Sandra.

"What's this about raising hummingbirds?"

"I don't raise them, I put out little bottles and they come."

She explained that there were lots of hummingbirds where she lived. Sandra had learned that Coke bottles had a certain spot where you could make a hole, because the owner of Coca-Cola liked hummingbirds. So, with a special drill bit, you made a hole in that spot and put in a little straw or a paper flower.

Lota called the gardener.

"Go get me a Coca-Cola bottle."

She's going to check this out, thought Sandra.

And she did.

The credit afforded to Sandra for her understanding of hummingbirds and soft drink bottles was not enough for her to be admitted into the conversation. On their way back, Lacerda tried to rehabilitate his friend: Sandra, Lota is one of the most competent people in Brazil in knowledge of plants. One day you'll get to know her better.

IN SEPTEMBER Callado came to Samambaia. These were very pleasant hours; Lota and Bishop made a very special couple. Lota was unrestrained, Bishop withdrawn, but both were excellent company, intelligent, and spirited. They conducted themselves with elegant discretion. But the writer's sensitive eye caught the subtleties of a constant relationship, a familiarity that announced an old, good love. Callado attested to an event that he defined for himself as follows: a couple at the high point of their union.

THE DIARY OF HELENA MORLEY, to which Bishop had devoted years, had received fine reviews, but it wasn't selling. Lota wasn't selling land. And with inflation running at 30 percent, Lota's difficulties grew. Bishop decided to consult the president of the U.S. bank that held her investments, the Agricultural National Bank of Pittsburgh, to inquire about the possibility of transferring her funds to Brazil. Laurence C. Connor replied that Bishop would be making a terrible mistake and that he was totally against the idea. Bishop conceded, but she wrote to her friends, depressed, that she and Lota were living in the luxury of bankruptcy.

Bishop went about in a foul mood. Her asthma attacks had worsened so much that her doctor had put her back on cortisone. And the news in the Brazilian papers was not encouraging. The headlines were about the ill-fated Aída Curi. After being threatened with gang rape, the young girl threw herself or was thrown off an apartment balcony. The latest political news reported that Lacerda had been stoned on his "Truck of the Masses" and that

Cacareco, a rhinoceros in the Rio zoo, had gotten the most votes for coun-
cillor. It was understandable that Bishop, forty-seven, a sensitive poet who
had published two books, got drunk so as not to feel too lucid.

The big gift of the end of the year was the completion of the library. Lota
and Bishop organized their books, which already numbered over three thousand. Bishop was impressed with the number of titles Lota had collected in
the areas of botany, art history, agriculture, psychology, and especially architecture and urban studies. Bishop helped to put them on the shelves: Roland
Martin, *L'urbanisme dans la Grèce antique*; Norbert Weiner, *The Human Use of
Human Beings*; Eric Larrabee and Rolf Meyersohn, *Mass Leisure*; William
Thomas, *Man's Role in Changing the Face of the Earth*. After seven years
together, Bishop's admiration for Lota was vast.

IT WAS A BLESSING WHEN, in February 1960, an opportunity arose for Bishop
to make a trip to the Amazon with Rosinha and her nephew Maneco. Traveling on a crowded steamboat was not anything Lota aspired to, but even if
she had wanted to she couldn't have gone. Alexander Calder was in Brazil,
and Lota had committed herself to trying to sell his pieces. She had also
decided to resolve her wrangling with Kylso once and for all; he was creating
an uncomfortable situation on the subject of his alleged rights.

Although she felt guilty about leaving Lota at a bad moment, Bishop
turned herself over passionately to the Amazon experience. She saw scenes
that she thought pungently lyrical. The arc of umbrellas opening up syn-
chronically over the canoes when the rain started. Chickens sailing on top of
a boat, untied, dauntless, their feathers ruffling in the wind. A barge that
served as a house, with the phrase "As the Lord wills it" on top.

Living with Rosinha and Maneco was very agreeable. They maintained a
stoic diet of cream crackers and bananas, broken only by local fruits such as
*cupuaçu* and *graviola*. Bishop and Rosinha caught themselves wondering what
would Lota think if she saw us in these sandals with this purse! News came
very late. Queen Elizabeth had had a child. Chateaubriand, the powerhouse
of the Brazilian press, was dying.

By chance, they met the plastic artist Anna Letycia and the playwright
Maria Clara Machado, who were on their way back. Through them, Bishop
sent a letter to Lota. Drive carefully, she wrote.

LOTA TURNED FIFTY.
After the party, her friends talked. Ismênia, who had stretched her holidays
just to stay for the birthday, thought that Lota looked a bit tired.

"You'd be tired too if you had to drag that instance of stupidity from one place to the next," said Vivinha, who else.

"You're unfair to Bishop. She seems to be this burned-out person. But her poetry shows her to be extraordinary."

"She'd have to be, otherwise Lota wouldn't like her so much," added Maria Amélia, who had struggled to understand "The Shampoo," although she prided herself on being the only person in Brazil who had read *The Innumerable Heart*, by the Countess of Noailles, in the original.

"Well, then you can only measure her geniality in English. I don't know English. In Portuguese, she's a land crab."

"It's difficult for her, with her New England puritanism, to live in a country where people are out in the street dancing and beating drums, throwing flowers to Iemanjá, the goddess of the sea, loving doing nothing." Ismênia was working in the United States.

"Nonsense. No one likes doing nothing more than Bishop. Listen, I don't believe that she was going to Patagonia, as she says, and then the ship stopped in Santos and she decided to just have a bit of a look. It's the same false rumor as the one about Cabral discovering Brazil by chance. To me, Bishop came to Brazil intentionally, after Lota. Or Mary. Just a minute, I'm coming!" Vivinha's companion was signaling from the door.

Maria Amélia and Ismênia turned to look at her. What, a new little friend?

"Well, I'm off. Bye-bye."

"Bye."

"Bye."

LOTA WAS WORN DOWN. She had nothing substantial to take on. Aside from taking care of Bishop, to be sure. She was fifty years old, had a wealth of knowledge, and didn't know what to do with it, she thought, as she finished designing a wood stove for Lilli and Ninita. The routine at Samambaia was monotonous. Lots of rain, the road impassable, the telephone not working, volatile maids, so that she was constantly obliged to train new ones. Right now Bishop was teaching another Maria how to cook.

Bishop was also bored. She wanted to travel; she needed to travel. They were always putting off their trip to Italy, which was now scheduled for the following year. At least they'd gone back to Ouro Preto, which Bishop never tired of admiring.

Bishop finished "Song for the Rainy Season," which was bought by *The New Yorker*. To the verses that celebrated daily life in the house under a private cloud, Bishop added a premonition. Time changes things. In a new era, nature once comforting and lavish becomes sterile:

*(O difference that kills,*
*or intimidates, much*
*of all our small shadowy life!) . . .*

. . . . . . . . . . . . . . . . . . .

*. . . and the several*
*waterfalls shrivel*
*in the steady sun.*

Lota was very unhappy about the direction of the country. She was encouraged when the Jan-Jan ticket won the October 3rd presidential election. Jânio Quadros was the perfect presidential candidate for her party, the National Democratic Union. Jango Goulart, although he was Vargas's creature, was only the vice presidential candidate. Lacerda was a candidate for governor of the new state of Guanabara. Who knew if better days weren't coming? There is no cold night, long as it may be, without its day.

# DONA LOTA

THE CAPITAL OF THE COUNTRY was moved to Brasília, and the government moved into the ultramodern palaces designed by Oscar Niemeyer. Juscelino Kubistchek—the smiling J.K., the president who conceived and built Brasília—wanted to show the world and Brazilians that the country was moving into a new era and seeking its own future. The city of Rio de Janeiro, the country's capital since the time of the empire, was unhappy with its loss of prestige; as a consolation prize it was elevated to statehood. In honor of the bay in which it is set, Rio was transformed into the state of Guanabara. Lacerda took office as the first governor of Guanabara on December 5, 1960. There was a big party at his apartment on Flamengo beach, to which, obviously, Lota and Bishop were invited. Sandra Cavalcanti barely recognized Lota, elegant as she was.

Lacerda was exultant. He knew he had beaten Sérgio Magalhães only because Tenório Cavalcanti had carried off votes from the lower class—votes that would have been Sérgio's. But this would be forgotten as soon as Lacerda showed his capacity as an administrator. For now he circulated among his guests, demonstrating to his friends his capacity to captivate them.

Lota was on the veranda, talking to Vera Pacheco Jordão. Lacerda came up to her affectionately. He repeated to Lota that she would have to be part of his government. He needed her. She should tell him, that instant, what position would please her. Lota argued that Lacerda could not appoint her because she didn't have a university degree. Lacerda dismissed this trifle with a wave of his hand.

"Tell me what you want."

Lota pointed to some rubble directly in front of the governor's apartment. It was the continuation of the Gloria fill.

"Give me this fill, this *aterro*. I'll make it into a Central Park."

On January 20, 1961, Lota was appointed to "advise, without obligation to the State, the Parks Department, subsection of the General Secretariat of Works and Transportation, and the Superintendency of Urbanization and Sanitation (Sursan); and, especially, to study the urbanization of the surfaces arising from the Aterro of Flamengo."

THE GOVERNOR HAD to pull strings to accommodate Lota's situation, creating an associate's position for her. It happened that Sursan was, by its nature, the special territory of engineers and architects; for Lota to be given a position assisting them in an urbanization project of such wide scope, they would have to recognize her as someone with specialized technical knowledge. Resentful, they preferred to understand the decree simply as creating a space and a supporting role for a friend of the governor who was sufficiently rich to work for free.

Lota, however, had understood clearly that the Aterro was *hers* and took advantage of the vagueness of the decree to seize the initiative. Officially, she asked Dr. Djalma Landim to inform her about what had been done on the Aterro. Landim sent her a copy of a document titled PA-7175. PA meant "Project Approved," so it became clear to Lota that the design of the Aterro had already been drawn up. The document indicated that the work of building a seawall, fill, roads, and walkways for pedestrians had already begun; it also showed the locations of the nautical clubs. Lota read it carefully and made various annotations.

Lota also contacted various friends, distinguished practitioners of architecture, urbanization, and landscape design, to engage them in the project, offering herself as warrant for the governor.

Exactly one month after her appointment, on February 20, 1961, Lota wrote her first message to Lacerda.

"My dear Governor,

"The area that has been rescued from the sea in Flamengo, along with the result of the razing of Santo Antônio Hill, are the last two large areas in the center of the city that offer possibilities to your Government to create a work, not simply of the greatest public utility, but also of great beauty.

"The area of the Aterro *pleads* for special care in *conserving* its privileged landscape and the sea breeze, and of transforming a simple corridor for automobiles into an immense treed area, which will soon become a mark of the city, as famous as Sugarloaf and the sidewalks of Copacabana."

VIOLATING THE rigid hierarchical principles of the civil service, Lota began to call formal meetings with the Sursan technocrats to discuss the progress of the construction. There was wailing and gnashing of teeth, but they went.

It became unfeasible to continue living at Samambaia. Lota spent too much time moving from one place to another. She decided to live in Leme and asked Bishop to come with her, even though she knew well her friend's distaste for the "marvelous city." They'd spend the weekends at Samambaia, Lota promised.

Bishop saw the commander in chief of the early days at Samambaia reborn. There was the old Lota, taking hold, arguing, deciding. Now she wasn't leading stonemasons or caretakers, however, but the *real guys*, all professionals with degrees. Bishop was happy to see her so enthused again. She would make dinner and wait for Lota to return and tell her, in her entertaining way, the vicissitudes of the day.

Except for Tuesdays. Tuesday was the day of the Sursan meetings. Lota would wake up already spent, and she came home mortified. Bishop would try to calm her with consolations she knew were innocuous.

"We're still at the beginning."

"Nice beginning, you can already see the even nicer end," interrupted Lota, immune to consolation.

"Carlos."

"Carlos?! As if you can speak to Carlos?"

"Didn't Carlos *say* he wanted the park?"

"Cookie, Carlos said he wanted the park. The problem is that this bunch of donkeys doesn't want any park at all. They don't give a damn about gardens or where people spend their Sundays. All they want is roads and more roads with cars zooming by. Now here's a good question: why would that be?"

After almost ten years of living together, Bishop knew this wasn't the time to argue with Lota.

"Come on. Let's take a little bath and relax."

FOUR MONTHS had already gone by with meetings on Tuesdays.

The directors of the Superintendency of Urbanization and Sanitation, Sursan, saw Lota form a commission of notables and, with great satisfaction, name herself president. Lota went everywhere with the commission, which usually participated in the discussions with the Sursanlets, a term coined by Lota to designate the stature of her interlocutors. Flabbergasted, the high functionaries of the state did what they could to neutralize the impetus of their designated adviser.

Lota was reaching saturation point. She took advantage of the May 1 holiday to write to Ismênia, who was a civil servant and would understand her.

"The first concern, naturally, was to invite collaborators. Roberto Burle Marx was the only person appropriate for the gardens. Reidy, who has thirty years' experience with city hall and urbanization, would be the urban consultant. Jorge Moreira and Sérgio Bernardes would take on the architects' roles. It was difficult to persuade Reidy and Jorge—both very skeptical—to collaborate. They only signed on to please an old friend.

"Then we had to verify whether the project was doable in four years. We arrived at the conclusion that it would be hard work, but possible.

"Perfect. Then we balked at the problem of how much of the area was usable for gardens. We thought of two roads. But Sursan defended with tooth and nail the idea that the Aterro would be crossed by four roads. It's as Mamede said, a psychosis about roads.

"In 1954 Sursan should have ordered a hydraulics study of the seafront. Why hadn't they ordered it to this day? Mystery. Sursan said: You make the whole ground plan for the Aterro, with beaches, restaurants on the seashore, etc., and then we'll order the study. Hell, this would mean making two plans, since the hydraulic study would tell us whether or not the beach that we are planning would be naturally formed by the sea, or whether it would have to be helped artificially. Every Tuesday we get different information. The timelines for the completion of the study go from six months to two years. In short, either it's not very clear reasoning, or it's ill will.

"And the students' restaurant? It goes like this:

"One Tuesday:

*The Commission:* To continue with these two roads that have already been constructed we'll have to remove the existing students' restaurant, otherwise we won't be able to finish the project, connect the gardens, etc.

*Sursan:* No, you can't remove the restaurant! The students will yell, and the government won't have the courage to go against them.

*Dona Lota:* The government will have to remove the restaurant because this one is provisional, and the students won't yell because they're going to get another one, and even better, it's more central.

*Sursan:* Ah! Ah!

"Next week:

"The commission, after going personally to the restaurant, ascertains that it's a big mess but that it serves nine thousand meals per day. The commission looks for another large shed.

"The next Tuesday:

> *Dona Lota*: What about that new shed on Chile Street?
> *Sursan*: We can't use that one. It's empty, but we're going to straighten Chile Street, which is out of alignment and off level.

"(Constructed by Sursan . . .)
"Now what? Let's think . . .

> *Sursan*: We're going to talk to the students.
> *The Commission*: No! We've already asked that you don't talk about this. Let's study the situation and see what we can come up with to resolve the issue.

"The next Tuesday:
"The issue of the hydraulics study, etc. returns, and Dr. Landim makes his great and single contribution.

> *Dr. Landim*: I have a big shed, the Hime foundry.
> *The Commission*: Very good, very good—congratulations!

"The next Tuesday:
"Here's the floor plan of the foundry, it's five thousand square meters.
"Perfect, says the commission.
"We need to talk to the students.
"No, says the commission.
"But I want this foundry for a garage for Sursan, says Dr. Raposo.
"Ah!, says the Commission, a five thousand square meter garage???
"Look, Dona Lota, says Dona Dea, we're going to spend thirty-five million to convert this into a restaurant.
"What? says the commission. The walls and the roof are perfect, we just need to pave the floor.
"These walls are a meter thick, but it's better to tear them down to put in the piping, says the architect who brought the floor plan of the foundry.
"What? Put piping in the room? You only need piping in the kitchen, and it can be external, says Jorge. There are bathrooms already.
"Back comes Dona Dea.

> *Dona Dea*: I think thirty-five million is a lot, you can see—five thousand square meters at seven thousand cruzeiros a square meter—I was stupefied

and called a friend to see if my calculations were correct: 5000 × 7000 cruzeiros. (That's the way an engineer talks.) If you think that seven thousand per square meter is expensive, what do you want to spend, a thousand cruzeiros a square meter?

*Jorge*: Dona Dea, the problem isn't seven, or one thousand; it's to see whether there's an economical way to improve the shed so that it will replace what is going to be taken out.

*Paula Soares*: My opinion is that we should ask the students.

"Dona Lota has already heard this twenty times, she smokes inside and out and doesn't say anything."

LOTA THOUGHT THAT Affonso Reidy and Jorge Moreira had entirely too much patience with the Sursan folks. One Tuesday the Sursan engineers announced that they were going to put in a viaduct on the road near the airport in case an airplane wing had to be transported. Another time they presented a fastidious profile of the traffic volume that was to serve as the basis for calculating how many roads there should be—except that they clocked the volume of traffic at the wrong place. Jorge and Reidy endured hours of free-for-all with stoic equanimity.

"I'm scandalized by the level of intelligence and efficiency of our countrymen," complained Lota.

A neophyte in the pathways of the bureaucracy, Lota had imagined that Carlos would be available at any time to hear her justified complaints and providential suggestions. This did not happen. His Excellency was never there. Lota got irritated. At a dinner at the Museum of Modern Art with the government team, seeing Lacerda surrounded by people she considered cretinous toadies, Lota sulked and spent the night with a long face. The next day, Lota drafted some comments to Lacerda, thinking that the letter route was the best way to alert him.

"My dear Carlos,

"Many thanks for your good words at the museum dinner—I'm not discouraged, but rather *infuriated* by the difficulties with the issue of the fill—this is excellent, because I will not let go of this bone in any way unless you let go of me. I'm very satisfied with my group—despite being very busy, neither Jorge nor Reidy nor Roberto ever miss any of the meetings and always work late, and they are heroically persistent and patient with Sursan.

"As far as Sursan goes, I don't believe that you can keep Landim and Raposo as president and director—although they are honest and good people, the *incompetence* of the two of them and their ill will toward your administration are patently obvious. In all the meetings the same problems are seized on again and revisited and they don't shift position. It's deadly."

Carlos had to get rid of poor assistants. She had already been sounding out other names with Berta Leitchic, an engineer from Sursan whose competence she trusted. To show that she was attentive to all the details, Lota wrote a minutely detailed formal report justifying the two roads for cars, the necessity of completing the fill with earth from a source other than Santo Antônio Hill, and the urgency of finishing the civil construction work so that the garden could be planned.

She read the report over and was dissatisfied. It wasn't enough, she decided. She'd have to show Carlos that he had to intervene in the progress of the work. She started a new page:

"The Governor of Guanabara asks for the following information from Sursan:

*"The Fill of Widow's Hill*—Ignoring what is left from the dismantling of Santo Antônio Hill—as it will depend on Urbanization projects, legal actions, the end of the concession of the Ferro Carril Carioca Company, etc. to be used—with which earth and on what timeline Sursan proposes to have the fill of Widow's Hill completed.

"Reply: 8 days

*"Roads, cloverleafs, and pedestrian walkways*—From the project already approved by Urbanism, what timeline and budget for executing the plan.

"Timeline for replying for this study: 15 days

*"Students' restaurant*—Do not notify or inform the students of anything whatsoever. Make a definitive survey of the Hime foundry and see what can be moved there from the old restaurant, with the minimum expenditure and the minimum loss of time for this move.

"Timeline: 15 days."

Lota read over the executive order from the governor which she'd just finished composing. That was it, exactly. Very well, sirs, let's see how many pieces of wood it takes to make a canoe.

LIFE GOT VERY BAD for Bishop.

The heat in Rio depressed her. The apartment wasn't air conditioned.

Lota was completely absorbed in her work. At the beginning, she would only leave for work after lunch. Now she jumped out of bed and headed for the telephone, opening the day's vociferations. Right after that she'd leave, saying, with undisguised animation, that she was going to have a terrible day.

Bishop felt very much alone. The feeling was not exactly one of solitude but of abandonment. She walked around the empty apartment, repeating that she had to write, she had to write. She wrote letters. She told her friends how happy she was that Lota had finally been recognized and had found a place to use her enormous talents.

The second time that she found herself sitting at the table set for lunch and Lota phoned, at that very moment, to say that unfortunately she wouldn't be able to eat at home, Bishop collapsed. What was she doing there, after all? She felt petty because she couldn't manage to be deliriously happy about what was happening for Lota, but the truth was that she couldn't. And her? What about her?

When Lota got home that night she found Bishop drunk.

"Elizabeth, you're not going to pull this on me *now*."

Bishop couldn't speak. But Lota could read her eyes and saw all the old shipwrecks again. She calmed down.

"Leave it to me. Tomorrow I'm going to fix this."

LOTA PUT AN announcement in the newspaper, looking for a maid to work business hours. Joana dos Santos appeared, and Lota liked her immediately. Without considering the domestic budget but thinking about Bishop's well-being and her own peace of mind, she proposed that Joana sleep at the apartment and work full time.

Hmm, Joana thought. She was already committed to a job during the afternoons. Her boss was a fine person. She'd answered the ad because, with a job in the mornings, she'd improve her income. She had a son to raise. Joana looked at the nice white-haired lady. She hadn't asked where Joana came from, whether she was single or married. Lota had decided on Joana at a glance. Now Joana decided:

"I'm for it. Dona—?"

"Dona Lota." And pointing to another lady who looked worn out, sitting in a corner: "That one there is Dona Elizabeth."

WITHIN A SHORT while Joana was totally integrated into the rhythm of life in the apartment in Leme.

Dona Elizabetchy didn't need to go out every day to work, like Dona Lota, because she was a writer. She worked at home. She stayed there, reading, writing, reading, writing. Sometimes she'd stick her head in the kitchen, a place that Joana didn't think appropriate for writer-people. But Dona Elizabetchy knew how to make some marvelous American cocktails, when friends came over, such as Rachel de Queiroz, Burle Marx, Oscar Simon, Dona Rosinha. And to tell the truth, Dona Elizabetchy cooked very well, American and Brazilian food. Sometimes the two of them crossed paths in the kitchen, and Dona Elizabetchy got nervous, spoke English.

"Hey, don't swear at me, okay?" warned Joana in Portuguese.

"Okay, Djuana, Okay."

Now, Dona Lota didn't cook anything at all. For what, if I have my Joana? Tender, more than tender. It was my flower here, my flower there. And she was very kind. She gave a little radio to Joana, because Joana liked samba a lot. And every time that Dona Lota and Dona Elizabetchy went to eat chocolate at the Kopenhagen store, they took Joana with them.

Those two were funny. Dona Lota wore men's shirts, pants. Strange. Dona Elizabetchy would sing songs from her country; she had a pretty voice. The two of them lived very well. When Dona Elizabetchy was in the office, she'd hear the key in the door and come running. Lota, you've come home? Oh, I'm so tired! The two of them would go walking and talking and pretty soon they were laughing. Joana didn't know what was so funny, because they'd laugh in English.

BISHOP WAS MAKING a heroic effort not to drink. The solid presence of Joana was good for her. Joana was intelligent and helpful, and it was as if she'd always been there. On weekends, the three of them squeezed into the Italian car, as Joana called it, and went to Samambaia.

Mary was living in Lota and Bishop's house, while construction on hers alongside was finished. There was something new: Monica, a baby that Mary had adopted. Lota adored Monica. Even Bishop, who was more reticent about children, admitted that it was a joy to see a smiling baby in bed at her side.

All alone in the studio, Bishop reflected that Lota, with her Aterro, and Mary, with her daughter, had both found new motivation in their lives. It was time for her, too, to find new motivation. She decided to accept the proposal from Time/Life that she write the volume about Brazil for the Life World Library. It was a big challenge, because it would be her first experience writing a piece of journalism, and the deadline, in light of Bishop's chelonian pace, was draconian. It was now June, and one hundred pages would have to be ready by August, and the complete manuscript by November. Whew. But, besides representing a concrete opportunity, the contract offered Bishop two fundamental things. The possibility of traveling around Brazil, with expenses paid by Time/Life. And ten thousand dollars.

# WHY?

TO LOTA'S STUPEFACTION, another month went by with all quiet on the western front. Landim and Raposo continued secure in their positions. Sursan continued hampering the work. Carlos hadn't intervened, or demanded, or decapitated, as Lota had explicitly suggested.

After drinking the instant coffee that Joana brought her, Lota grabbed the telephone and called the governor's private office.

"I want to speak to the governor."

". . ."

"IT'S LOTA DE MACEDO SOARES!"

". . ."

"Very well."

Lota hung up. Carlos had a bad cold and hadn't been able to get out of bed. Taking pen and paper, Lota got straight to the point, without bothering to write my dear this or my dear that:

"I'm taking advantage of your being stuck at home with a cold to talk to you more about the roadways on the Aterro. . . ."

And she bombarded the governor with new chapters in the romance of the four roads that had to be two, saying that Sursan continued to agitate for the four damn roads, and that the commission had asked Mamede to redo the project, changing it from four roads to two, but Mamede alleged that he was overloaded with work, and that Mamede had to be *squeezed* to finish the project in ten or fifteen days, and that a meeting had to be called with Brigadier Eduardo Gomes, of the National Democratic Union, and Mamede and the commission in front of the governor, so that things would be made clear and this show could be put back on the road again, and that Sursan should also be invited to defend its position, and that the commission was tired of going to Sursan to ask the same fruitless questions, and that the governor had to *authorize* the commission, and that its members were *fed up*.

She went to Lacerda's apartment in Flamengo and left the letter with his wife, Letícia.

FINALLY, LOTA FELT that they were making progress. With feverish eyes, Carlos ordered the combatants to reach agreement, or they would be thrown to the dogs and served up as food for the birds. Lota's enemies backed off for the time being, except for Raposo, who persisted and fell. The air was cleared, in Lota's opinion; she felt encouraged to continue assailing her friend the governor with lectures and advice.

"A LITTLE ESSAY on administration

"(I love pompous titles for a bouquet of wildflowers)

"Just as the democrats are on one side of the Berlin Wall and the communists on the other, so in administration there are those who think well and those who think poorly, and these positions are as rigid and incapable of cooperation as political positions. . . .

"Your problem therefore is the following: as long as you don't know, when you invite people into key and decisive administrative posts, how your candidate thinks, you run the risk of having one group jamming up or even making useless the work of the other. You're the one who gives the orders and decides, but not being in the position of carrying them out, you don't see to how impossible it becomes for opposing groups to help each other.

"That's why it was so easy and fast to build Brasília: a tiny group planned it, and the great mass of thieves in Brazil carried it out. There was no contradiction at all."

BISHOP WAS BEHIND SCHEDULE. It was already mid-July, and she hadn't even been able to begin the book on Brazil. The photographers from Time/Life had already been in Rio; they had been directed to take pictures suggestive of a "developing country." Bishop wanted them to take pictures of orchids and hummingbirds. She wanted to write about Brazilians' sense of humor as expressed on truck bumpers. She wanted to describe the poetry of a bamboo birdcage or of pots put out in a window in the sun. She wanted to show that this country had Parati, Cabo Frio, Ouro Preto, jewels in front of which Brasília was just a glittering gewgaw. She wanted to say that in Brazil, a delightful intimacy really existed between bosses and servants, that the building's caretaker greeted her with a hug, asking, how are you, my daughter? She wanted to speak of the insight and malice of the lyrics of Brazilian popular music:

> *I'm so amused I get curled up*
> *when people say*
> *that the weaker one is the woman*
> *for man*
> *with all his fortitude*
> *comes down from virtue*
> *and does what she wants*

Sinhô, Noel, Monsueto: great popular composers. She wanted to speak of the sculptor Aleijadinho, the little cripple, of the painter Ataíde, of the sensation of looking at the ceiling of the Church of São Francisco and seeing a mulatto Virgin gloriously showing her little mulatto Jesus. Or seeing the prophets of Congonhas, deformed, tormented, testifying to God with their sightless eyes.

She wanted to make use of her diary notes from her trip to the Amazon on the steamboat *Lauro Sodré*. At every stop, the entire population coming up to sell pigs, fried shrimp, fruits, furniture. Mothers carrying beautiful children hitched to their hips. The people on board wanting to go down; those on shore wanting to come up. The absolute silence of Santarém, wood ferns growing on rooftops. And the meeting of the waters, the confluence of two great rivers, Amazon and Tapajós, without either surrendering its identity, each maintaining its brown, its blue in a dazzling dialectic.

If she and Lota could meet in this way, without her feeling diluted in Lota, swallowed in Lota's current.

Nonsense. Lota was not to blame if Bishop couldn't even organize the facts she'd collected, never mind write something new. At that moment Lota was confronting her engineers and brigadiers, fighting to transform a garbage heap into a garden, while she didn't even know how to begin her handsomely paid-for book.

Djuana's little radio was strident, playing at untuneful heights. Bishop felt anguished. She reached a decision and got up.

BRI-GI-TTE BAR-DOT, Bar-dot! sang the radio, while Joana swept the room. After she finished the living room, she went to the office. Strange, Dona Elizabetchy wasn't there. She glanced in the bathroom. Empty. Joana had a bad feeling. Dona Elizabetchy didn't usually go out alone.

It was almost lunchtime when the phone rang. It was Dona Lota. Dona Lota, Dona Lota, Dona Elizabetchy's disappeared! Dona Lota asked Joana to look around the neighborhood, especially the bars.

Said and done. Joana found Dona Elizabetchy with a handful of dollars, hidden behind the partition in a bar. Drinking her face off.

"Yes ma'am! Is this a thing to do? Let's get right home!"

Dona Elizabetchy couldn't stand. Joana put her across her shoulders, like the giant codfish on the label of a bottle of Scott's Emulsion, and half-dragged her boss down the street.

"Why, why?" wailed the drunk one, heavy as she was.

"I don't want to hear a peep, understand? Not a peep!"

Joana got to the apartment exhausted. She laid the big American on the sofa and went to draw a bath. She poured bath salts in, imported soap. Then she carried her to the bathtub. Splash! Joana got a face full of foam.

It was then that Joana's sadness began, which was that Dona Elizabetchy drank.

IT CONTINUED TO be very difficult for Lota to speak to the governor in his palace. The differences between Lacerda and the president of the republic Jânio Quadros had become clear since the beginning of the year, and the rift between the two widened with Quadros's invitation to Che Guevara, at that point the Cuban minister of industry and commerce, to visit Brazil. Obstreperous, Lacerda preached against communism and Castro, having supported the debacle of the failed U.S. invasion of Cuba in April. Lacerda went to the Alvorada Palace to condemn Quadros, and he was inflamed when the president, learning that Lacerda intended to spend the night at the palace, ordered Lacerda's luggage returned to him.

On August 19, 1961, while Quadros decorated Guevara in Brasília, Lacerda decorated Manuel Antonio de Verona, director of the Cuban Democratic Revolutionary Front, in Rio.

It was a precarious moment. Lacerda warned that a coup was being plotted by the federal government. He had to keep an eye out for any suspicious movement in the capital, because his political future was at stake. He was the most prestigious member of the National Democratic Union, the UDN, at the moment. And although U.S. president John F. Kennedy had ordered that the funding for the Brazilian government's share of the Alliance for Progress be suspended, he had sent substantial resources directly to the government of Guanabara. It was evident that it had not even crossed Lacerda's mind that poor Burle Marx was working on the Aterro without a contract or that Paula Soares was maneuvering to retain the notorious four roads.

But Lota had only one thing on her mind. She took Rosinha by the arm and went to Carlos's house. He was in a political meeting and didn't show much enthusiasm for the after-hours visit. Lota left fuming from all vents. She allowed herself two days to cool off and then sent him one of those little notes:

"August 24, 1961

"My Dear Governor

"Congratulations on your success in São Paulo. I got a phone call from Hilda Forbes, saying that even she was thrilled to see you on TV.

"With reference to our last interview at your house, at which Rosinha and I must have fallen like a hair into the soup, as the French put it, I'd like to say the following to you: I ask you to do me the favor of *not scolding me* in public. Only I, who have worked with Sursan for five months, *know* whether or not Landim is 'a poor little thing against whom I'm making mischief.'

"Today at 4:30 our dear Brigadier is going to bring you three issues of the greatest importance—a contract with Roberto, a license to move the students, and a reply to the students' letter—Everything is 'chewed up,' discussed, etc. All you have to do is sign."

On the next day, the 25th of August, Quadros resigned, alleging that he was being pressured by "hidden forces." Lacerda had lots to do. He answered Lota with a short note on green paper, from the governor's office:

"Dona Lota de Macedo Soares

I've read your letter of August 24. Don't you understand when we're joking? I demanded from Landim the priorities you asked for. All best."

WHILE SHE GOT DRESSED, Lota tried to explain to Bishop why it was fundamental that Carlos make the commission official.

Bishop didn't understand why Carlos couldn't resolve the situation at once, sparing Lota so many annoyances.

"Cookie, the political situation is catching fire." She pulled her long hair back, tied it in a knot and put in Calder's clasp with precise and elegant movements. "Carlos is always very busy, he's even going to have to sell the *Tribuna da Imprensa*, imagine. And you don't think that João Goulart is just going to quietly swallow this business of parliamentary procedure."

Jango, as Vice President João Goulart was known, was in China when Jânio Quadros resigned. The military had identified him as a Communist and did not want to hand power over to him. Creating a parliament looked like the only way to get rid of him. Lota saw trouble ahead.

But Bishop had turned off. She hated politics. She hated to see Lota bound up in that dirty world. And as for Lota's relationship with Carlos, Lota was behaving like a woman mistreated by her husband—she spends her life complaining about her misfortune, but God help anyone who says one word against him. From the perspective of Bishop with her self-contained style, Carlos was excessive; he was always making interminable speeches, "denouncing" things. Bishop discovered that she didn't like his gaze. He had that look seagulls have, circling, cunning, and then suddenly lunging.

"It's good that you trust him," said Bishop vacantly.

Lota was going to retort, but she had to go.

LOTA THOUGHT she had the reins in her hands. She had already drawn up the memorandum for the decree of nomination. The commission would now be called the work group, constituted of seven members, all of them experts, including herself, Dona Lota, whose lack of degrees was made up for by working without pay. It would be clear that it was incumbent upon Sursan only to execute the projects that the work group had planned. Hmm, they were going to bite themselves. It was the work group that would make all the pertinent decisions about the Aterro and the seashore. Any allotments, cession of lands, or construction not in agreement with the urban plan created by the work group would be summarily vetoed. Even more, the work group would have to advise on the eventual acquisition or placement of any art work in that area. Lota wanted to prevent the Brazilian habit of erecting a bust on every street corner from turning the Aterro into a forest of statues.

Decree 607 of October 4, 1961, creating the work group, was published in the Diário Oficial of the next day. All of the prerogatives stipulated by Lota were recorded in the decree.

Imagine how shocked Lota was when, reading O Globo of October 16, she came across the declaration by Gilberto Morand Paixão, Sursan's chief engineer of the Twelfth District, about the work on the Aterro: "It is not known how the space will be used, except for the four roadways for vehicles."

Lota climbed the walls. Not content, the engineer revealed that the students' restaurant would have to be demolished. This, after Lota had spent months asking for silence on the subject!

Bishop watched her burst out of the armchair for the telephone. Where is Carlos! Carlos wasn't in. Then she'd speak to the vice governor.

"Rafa, this is so that you'll see how urgent it is that you take the measures you want to in this sector! Naturally, we're already taking action with respect to this interview!"

Lota spent the day on the telephone. Finally, at nine that night, she suc-ceeded in getting the Brigadier Gomes to agree to send a memorandum to Sursan saying that he would approve only the two roadways.

Lota, jubilant sower of tempests, celebrated.

Bishop looked at the white page. Brazil.

IN LACERDA'S ABSENCE, Lota began to pass on to Rafael de Almeida Magal-hães, the vice governor, all her admonitions and secret information. She'd annotate in the margin of the paper: confidential. And in the other margin: to read at home. The letters and notes piled up in the drawers of the admin-istrators of Guanabara.

Looking for solutions to administrative problems, Lota bet on the efficacy of commissions. Because those she appointed were not well enough known to have any political clout, she would quickly put them on a commission that she herself had devised to study a specific question. Although Carlos made a habit of turning a deaf ear, Lota didn't give up trying to open a route for those she thought deserving.

That was how it was with Luiz Emygdio de Mello Filho. Lota asked for Carlos's agreement to use him on the Aterro:

"We're going to have to find and transplant thousands of big trees. And you know that this is going to be a real fight. Heck, Burle Marx isn't in any shape to do this, or else he'd do it for an *astronomical* price. What we're going to ask Roberto for is just the plan and the supervision. This will avoid any criticism of you, and it will be much cheaper, because the administration will do the rest, with the means they have, without any other onus. Luiz Emygdio was very generous not to be upset at not being named to Parks and Gardens, and said that he'd like to help anyway. The idea is as follows: you designate a commis-sion, headed by Luiz Emygdio, a representative of the Highways Department (this because of the trucks, winches, personnel, etc.), someone from the For-est Service, and another person or two that will be needed in this case.

"All this is *confidential*, because Roberto is a man of great generosity, but the partners and brothers are dreaming about millions, and I want to present them with the issue already resolved in this way. Speak with Dona Ruth if you're in agreement.

"Goodbye, my dear governor, I miss hearing you telling stories. The devil is that I can't catch you at home. Hugs."

Hugs, hugs, my dear governor.

LOTA NOTICED THAT Bishop was nervous, smoking a lot.

"What's the matter, Cookie?"

Bishop resented Lota's not guessing the motive for her anxiety. The truth was that in recent months each had found it tiresome to listen to the other's daily account. Many times Lota came home already hooked up to a telephone call or with a pile of papers to study, and she could barely disguise her exasperation while Bishop read the scanty lines she'd managed to write.

The difference in the nature of the chores of the two of them hurt Bishop. She was working for money at something she disliked; Lota worked for free, to be able to complete a tough assignment that seduced her. Could it be that Lota didn't see that it was only weeks until Bishop had to finish the book and go to New York to work on the revisions? Could she be that distant?

"It's because of the book, isn't it? Don't worry, sweetheart, everything is going to turn out all right. Finish in whatever way is possible. We'll go to New York together and there I'll help you to fix what's needed."

Bishop was placated. She hadn't had the courage to suggest that Lota accompany her, as involved as she was in the wrangles of the Aterro. And now, spontaneously . . .

"But won't this trip get in your way? Are you going to be able to get away at this moment?"

"Elizabeth, you are the most important thing in my life. You can be sure I will never fail you."

GOING WITH BISHOP meant that Lota would have to be away until the end of the year; she wanted to leave a detailed report for the governor, evaluating the eight and a half months' work on the Aterro. She made several outlines. Finally she gave the secretary the definitive version, which took up eight typed pages.

Before signing it, Lota reread the text. First, the hydraulic studies. She let loose a sigh. Lota had shown Sursan and also the governor photographs of the tetrapods of the beaches at Cannes, which broke the waves before they reached the edge of the dock. To her exasperation, Sursan insisted on looking for less advanced solutions. If we're going to use nineteenth-century methods, I don't know why we should spend twenty-five thousand contos, she protested. Lota thought it was idiocy, under the pretense of nationalism, that the state should spend a fortune to reject international solutions.

Then she read the paragraphs on illumination, the channeling of the Carioca River, the question of the roads. They were good. Lota wanted Lacerda to be sure that when she presented him with a solution, it was the best solution: he could believe in it blindfolded.

Next came a detailed account of the "insensitivities" that surrounded the circus over the moving of the students' restaurant. The governor's plans had been baldly disrespected, to the point that Sursan had had various talks with the students. Dr. Paula Soares thought that they should give five or six million to the students and bulldoze the restaurant. For Lota, the result of this tactic would be that the money would be used for campaigns against the government, there would be lovely demonstrations of displeasure on the part of the nine thousand without meals, and Lacerda would be obliged to give another restaurant to the famished.

Lota lit another Lucky Strike. Now the most important: the work group considered it impossible to work while Dr. Paula Soares was directing Urbanization and Sursan. We lament making trouble for you, dear, but that's what administrating is—choosing and supporting. We've already had nine months of patience.

LOTA AND BISHOP spent five weeks in New York. To save money, they stayed in Loren McIver's apartment in Greenwich Village.

Every day they'd go to the publisher's, where they'd stay from seven until seven, studying the text after the revisers' editing. Bishop felt as if she'd been demolished. Without counting some ridiculous interferences, like the objection to the existence of a Mister Silva, because Silva ended with an *a*, and in Portuguese words that end in *a* are feminine, the editors of Time/Life had made her text unrecognizable. Bishop simply would not claim authorship of the book. Everything had been changed, she explained to Lota, inconsolable.

Finally, she decided that she had sold her name for ten thousand dollars. The book was printed with the register of a co-author: Elizabeth Bishop and the Editors of *Life*.

There wasn't even the compensation of a few days of holiday in New York for the companions. Bishop was advised to return to Brazil right away, to avoid paying fifteen hundred dollars in income tax.

BISHOP LOOKED around the room. How hot it was. They had come out of the New York winter directly into this furnace. It had been exactly ten years since she had sat down for the first time in this same room, feeling lost and unloved. So much had happened since then. She had met Lota and with her had found the happiness of living. Lota had held her in that crazy country, offering her the protection of the only home she'd had in her life. Against the untiring memory of pain, Lota had counterpoised her overwhelming joviality, her ferocious determination. With Lota she'd known the relief of an ordinary daily life and the simple contentment of sharing the days with another being who recognized her. Now things seemed cloudy. She didn't feel happy. Lota, meanwhile, seemed happy. Bishop had expected that as soon as they returned from New York they'd go straight to Samambaia. After *Brazil*, Bishop felt violated and, as happens with violated people, disconnected. She wanted to see the clouds again, the mountains, the water, to hear the silence of Samambaia. But Lota said that she needed to know what had happened during her absence. Later they'd go up.

Bishop felt thirsty.

"Where does ma'am think she's going?"

"Djuana . . ."

"No ma'am. Dona Lota said for ma'am to wait here. You can sit right there, because she's coming right away to take us."

# THE SHED

IN NEW YORK, Lota consulted an international recreation group to get a recommendation for a specialist. To her surprise, they recommended a Brazilian, Ethel Bauzer Medeiros. But Medeiros resisted when Lota invited her to join the team on the Aterro. She had already spent much of her professional life working without pay on public projects. Nevertheless, they arranged to meet on the 10th of January.

Lota wrote it down in the appointment book she'd brought from New York. She loved appointment books. The 10th was pretty booked up: at nine she was going with Reidy to talk to the secretary of works, Enaldo Cravo Peixoto; at ten, an interview with Ethel; at six, a meeting with Carlos at Guanabara Palace.

Ethel was persuaded when she saw the Shed, a precarious building on the Aterro in which Lota was conducting business. Lota managed to get everyone to stay from dawn to dusk in this flimsy contraption, in the middle of an abandoned fill, as if they were in the best workplace in the world. These people were a group of top professionals, moved by idealism. Ethel felt herself particularly captivated by this gesture of Lota's, a pioneer in the country—calling in an educator from the beginning of the planning of a park.

Lota revealed that this wasn't to be a conventional park, with a fountain, benches, and seesaws for children. The premise of the park was that it would help improve the quality of life and become a site for lifelong learning. Ethel agreed to plan the playgrounds for the Aterro. She'd work for a symbolic honorarium.

At the end of the day, Lota went to meet with Lacerda. She was instructed to take a boat to Brocoió Island, where the governor would meet her. Carlos got there at ten that night, and they talked until four in the morning. The next day, a Thursday, Lota returned to Rio at nine-thirty in the morning.

Ten days later, the routine was repeated. On a Sunday morning, the whole work group went to Brocoió to give Burle Marx's draft plan and a twenty-page report to the governor.

Again, on the first of February, Lota spent the night at Brocoió. Bishop would have liked to understand why this was the only way for the president of the work group to meet with the governor.

ON THE 29TH OF FEBRUARY, Ethel unveiled her plan for a living park to the group's architects as well as to the landscape designer Roberto Burle Marx.

She explained that specific areas should be reserved for babies, for children, for teenagers, and for the elderly. The design of the park should make it easy for people to relax outdoors, allowing them to forget that they were surrounded by automobiles. The idea wasn't to fill the park with recreational equipment but, on the contrary, to leave lots of open space, so that people, especially children, could feel at ease.

Because the playgrounds were to be located between roadways, Ethel asked the architects to take various safety measures—sloping banks around everything, drainage around the equipment.

As far as spaces for pickup soccer went—an idea of Lota's that Ethel loved—they shouldn't conform to official dimensions, so that they wouldn't be turned into practice fields for professional teams. The parking lots should be outside of the playgrounds, so that people would be forced to walk in the park.

After so many months of struggling with abstruse proposals, Ethel's straightforward plans were a balm for Lota. She handed out assignments to those present, establishing dates for completion. Finally, the park that she had imagined was going to emerge.

TO BISHOP'S DISTASTE, the agreement that weekends were to be sacred began to be violated. Lota's advisers started coming up to Samambaia, and Lota spent Saturdays and Sundays in turbulent discussions.

Friday March 16 was Lota's birthday. They agreed that Bishop would meet Lota at the Shed and from there they'd go straight to Petrópolis. Bishop wanted to celebrate with a special lunch on Saturday, something intimate; it had been a long time since they'd had a moment for just the two of them.

"Lunch is fine. For dinner I've already invited Rafa and his wife and a few others. Let's see if in a more relaxed atmosphere things might get resolved.

We'll take the opportunity to show people your book on Brazil, what do you say?"

That afternoon Bishop arrived at the Aterro completely drunk. She behaved badly in front of the employees. Ill at ease, Lota took her to the car. Bishop resisted, forcing Lota into a little game of catch as catch can to get her in. On Mauá Square, Bishop jumped out in the middle of the street, insisting that she wanted to go back to Rio. Again Lota had to convince her. It was a grievous trip to Samambaia. "X awful," Lota wrote in her appointment book.

On Saturday, in fact, there was a dinner with the vice governor Rafael de Almeida Magalháes (Rafa to his friends). Lota, in fact, showed the book that Bishop had renounced. And, in fact, they talked about the Aterro until one-thirty in the morning, without, unhappily, any change in the general plan. Rafa admitted that he was not considering replacing Paula Soares. Bishop remained withdrawn in her quarters.

The next day, seeing that she wouldn't be able to bridge the distance separating her from Bishop, Lota decided to go back to Rio alone. That night she went to dinner at Le Mazot with Bertha and Marc. During the week, Lota kept herself busy day and night, trying to obliterate the fact that when she came home she wouldn't find Bishop. She wrote down in her appointment book: dinner with Pedro and Verinha; chat with Oscar Simon till one in the morning; bought a vacuum cleaner; inspection of the horticultural nursery with Luiz Emygdio and Magu Leão, who had been added to the team; ordering the lamps from Dominici; talk with Alfredo Lage till three in the morning. It didn't help; she missed her Cookie. She was happy when the weekend arrived and she went to get her.

ETHEL'S INTERVENTION brought on the first tremors in the Shed. Reidy, who was responsible for the overall urban plan for the park, was put in charge of designing the pavilions and the playgrounds. Ethel worked directly with him, impressing him with her creativity. The plan for the City of Children was the responsibility of the architect Maria Hanna Siédlikowski. Carlos Werneck de Carvalho was to build the puppet theater. The problem was that Burle Marx wasn't happy that the recreationist would be in charge of the playgrounds. Hadn't it been agreed that he would be the one to do this? Jorge agreed with Roberto. Lota and Jorge argued. Lota, you does . . . you wants— Jorge got tongue-tied when he was nervous. Lota decided that she had to put a lid on the discussion. Summarily, she reaffirmed that Ethel would do the playgrounds and Roberto would do the garden. Jorge pulled a sour face for a long time.

Lota began to feel worn out. Besides being unprepared for the chicanery of professional life, she had to minister to the conniptions of a bunch of prima donnas. Jorge pulled a sour face; Roberto didn't want to defend his proposal; Luiz Emygdio, who needed the tow truck in the garden to hoist large trees, wouldn't confront Fontenelle, who was always taking the truck off somewhere—in sum, a pile of crap.

Coming home at night was no relief either. Bishop was devastated by the book on Brazil. She spent her days making corrections by hand in the copies that she sent to her friends. Electricity was being rationed; frequently they were in candlelight. In sum, another nice pile of crap.

On that Sunday, however: "Out of that bed; today we're going to go out!"

Bishop was taken aback: Dona Lota had disappeared, replaced by tender, lighthearted Lota, the animated Lota who always enchanted her.

They picked up Magu and drove to the Dona Marta Belvedere. It was a beautiful day. Magu was a serene presence. Bishop was grateful because, even though Magu was working on the Aterro like everyone around Lota lately, at no time did Magu talk about seedlings or manure or tanker trucks. They spent the day playing truant. When they got home, Joana's shrewd eyes saw something.

"My, my. What's happened here?"

NANÁ LIKED OPENING the door and seeing Lota. Since the tribulations of the Aterro had started, Lota had less and less time for anyone who wasn't an engineer, an architect, or at least a gardener, qualifications that Naná didn't meet. It was good to see her again, charming and well dressed, with that abundance of smiles.

Lota accepted the cafezinho, took her tortoiseshell cigarette holder out of her purse, and lit up a smoke. Naná observed that, as happens with some people, Lota had been favored by age. The contrast between the silver hair and her maté-colored complexion was very interesting. Lota had the noble air of a North American Indian.

"My dear, I'm very irritated with Sérgio. Don't worry, I didn't come here to get you tangled up in this mess. It's just that, since sooner or later he's going to come here crying the blues, I want to tell you exactly what happened. You know that I hate gossip."

Naná sighed. This was a problem she knew she'd have to face. The so-called work group was nothing more than a bunch of her old friends. Lota de Macedo Soares, Roberto Burle Marx, Sérgio Bernardes, Luiz Emygdio de Mello Filho. Everyone brilliant. Everyone a bit détraqué. For any paltry thing they'd raise the roof in that shed. And Naná would have to lend an ear first to this one, then that one.

"It's about the restaurant on the Aterro. Very well, after *months* of study, the group reached the conclusion that an adequate restaurant would be a grill, with a maximum capacity of three hundred seats. It would be a little building of only one story, about six hundred square meters. We thought of making an open grill and a very small kitchen, obviously. Evidently, it shouldn't even have had to be mentioned—but it was!—that to make the leasing easy, the plan should include simple installations, easy to maintain."

Lota paused to allow Naná to assimilate all this information. Naná prepared herself for what had to be coming. That way of talking, just as much as the Calder clasp in her hair, was Lota's official signature. Evidently. Obviously.

"Very well, I delivered the proposal to Sérgio, since Reidy and Jorge were already busy with other things. Naná, can you believe that Sérgio presents me with a restaurant with two stories, with thirty-six hundred square meters *on each floor*, and on top of that a tower or whatever the devil it is, about fifteen meters high? The kitchen alone is eight hundred square meters! And he still foresees an additional fifteen hundred square meters for what he calls an exhibition area. To compete with the Museum of Modern Art, no doubt."

"Imagine that, would you?" At heart Naná found it incredible that Lota had handed over a grill for Sérgio of all people to design, and then found the result extravagant.

"Now, what drove me up the wall is what he charged for the plan. Do you know how much? The mere bagatelle of fourteen million cruzeiros!"

"Imagine that."

"Naná, it had been agreed that the three architects would get seventy thousand cruzeiros a month to do the plans for the Aterro. It's clear that for architects of the caliber of Reidy, of Sérgio and Jorge, the amount is minimal."

A mockery, thought Naná.

"But everyone agreed, to help Carlos's government and also because of the beautiful work we're going to do. It's evident that Sérgio doesn't share the feelings that motivate the rest of the group. It's a pity."

"Lota, it's going to be difficult to force people to work for free," ventured Naná. "Not all of them have the, ah"—Naná searched for the right word—"the devotion that you have to Carlos."

"What, devotion, not even half a devotion! Naná, fourteen million! On top of the cost of the work! Let him go to hell."

Lota, Lota.

IT WAS THE LIMIT! Lota couldn't believe it. For lack of anything to do, Carlos simply named Sérgio Bernardes as adviser for Urbanization. And Sérgio had already begun to mess everything up.

Sérgio had been in Burle Marx's office with Lota, examining the group's solutions for the exits of the roads from the Aterro—this before his inexplicable promotion. Sérgio had applauded the solutions, especially the cloverleaf toward the airport. Now, Lota had come to hear from Carlos in person that Sérgio was going to eliminate the cloverleaf! Sérgio's rattlebrained idiocy was demoralizing the group in the presence of the governor. Yes, because the group had taken months to study the problems of traffic flow on the Aterro, and now Sérgio came into the game and in five minutes pulled a happy solution out of his vest pocket. No, my flower, things are going badly. Who's in charge here, after all?

Off went Lota to speak to the governor. Mamede had commented on the widespread mess resulting from Sérgio's interference with the traffic in Rio, with the population running in all directions in search of transportation. Lota passed on to Lacerda the warning that Sérgio was wreaking havoc. Carlos didn't like it. He said that the others only knew how to talk and did nothing. Lota struck back. Carlos said he had another appointment, and the two of them said good-bye coolly.

IT WAS AT THE END of the day. Bishop was reading others' poetry—João Cabral, Drummond, Cecília Meireles. This was a fecund time for Brazilian poets, inspired by an active connection to the land in which they were born. Bishop, meanwhile, couldn't write. Rio, Lota, Elizabeth, park, the slums—together they were a gathering of mistakes.

Cease your diligence and smile a little, recommended José Paulo Moreira da Fonseca, a Brazilian poet. Bishop looked at the sea and decided: she'd return to translating. Seeing that she was unable to make her own odd sonnet, an *estrambote melancólico* like Drummond's, she decided that translating was a way to anchor herself to creation. To begin, she chose "Travelling in the Family" and "The Table," poems of Carlos Drummond de Andrade that spoke of family ties. The father, the mother, the brothers, the tubercular cousins, the crazy aunt, she'd also borrow these from the poet. From then on, she turned herself over daily to the labor of rendering the Portuguese polysyllables into her synthetic language.

Another afternoon, it was Clarice Lispector's turn. Bishop found in her stories the capacity for fluency and the tone she herself was missing. How Elizabeth would have liked to have been the one to tell the story of the hen that flew onto the roof to escape turning into lunch and then, pursued, "in a pure fluster laid an egg"! Bishop was delighted with the sharp and transgressive humor of her neighbor in Leme. She decided to translate Lispector as well. Besides "A Hen," she chose "The Smallest Woman in the World," a creature of forty-five centimeters who belonged to a race of people who, relentlessly hunted, were always retreating, retreating into the forest. When she wrote "Brazil, January 1, 1502," Bishop used similar imagery to portray the Indians pursued by the white invaders:

> *they ripped away into the hanging fabric,*
> *each out to catch an Indian for himself—*
> *those maddening little women who kept calling,*
> *calling to each other (or had the birds waked up?)*
> *and retreating, always retreating, behind it.*

THE IMMINENCE OF Robert Lowell's arrival made Lota and Bishop more nervous.

Bishop circled around Joana, looking for someone to talk to. She explained in Portenglish that the large drainpipes on the beach in front had been donated by the U.S. government, as proof of friendship. Joana, very involved in the 1962 World Cup of Soccer, argued that the Brazilians put more faith in Amarildo, their center forward, than in Uncle Sam. This Bishop could see with her own eyes: on the days when Brazil played a game, all the domestics in the building, not at all interested in the large drainpipes, leaned over into the central courtyard of the building, attentive to the atonal narration on the radio. Suddenly, as if coming from a single throat, a demented cry rebounded down the corridors, and the women jumped, hugged, laughed, cried, gave thanks to God. Joana came to hug her:

"We won, Dona Elizabetchy! We won! Brazil! Brazil!"

Lota knew that the arrival of the important North American poet was going to overburden her. And he was coming with his wife and daughter, *bon Dieu*. She'd have to chaperone them here and there, and things on the Aterro were stalled. Everything was late; there was no fit between planning and doing. Only Magu was working feverishly; the rest went at a turtle's pace.

To cheer her up, the secretary of works, Enaldo Cravo Peixoto, showed interest in having the old locomotive that Lota wanted to move to the Aterro spruced up to carry passengers. This wasn't a very happy sugges-tion. The *Baroness* was an old museum piece, Lota explained, depressed. It would stay fixed to the spot, under a roof, to be seen by children. The vehicle that would take people around would be a little train pulled by a tractor.

"I'm going around discontented with God and the world," Lota summed up, to an alarmed Peixoto.

FINALLY ROBERT LOWELL (Cal to close friends), his wife, Elizabeth Hardwick, and his young daughter Harriet arrived. Lota left a note for the work group, telling them that she was going on a good will mission to Cabo Frio, taking the Lowelliad. She left worried that she would miss a meeting called by Paula Soares to study illumination on the Aterro. She left precise instructions that Peixoto be told *not* to go to the meeting, seeing that it would be a pure waste of time. And she left having already scheduled another meeting.

LOTA GAINED POINTS with Lacerda by introducing him to the celebrities, such as Robert Lowell, who came to visit Bishop. But the relationship between Lota and Carlos continued to be shaky. Lota tried to rise above her growing irritation, accepting invitations from Carlos to social events, such as going to the movies at Guanabara Palace. Invariably she returned to the apartment raving that she'd wasted her time with yet another stupid film. On one occasion, Lacerda asked her to attend a luncheon to appease Fontenelle, who was being heavily criticized for his innovative plans for Rio's traffic. Lota agreed with the criticisms heart and soul, but wanting to pass time, she went, dragging along Roberto Burle Marx. After they had sat through much boring speechifying, Fontenelle himself got up to speak. Everything he did, he declared, was to prove he was a man.

Lota was at the point of jumping up on the table and screaming: "What interest do your doubts hold for us?"

At home, the fights with Carlos on the phone were constant. Carlos, don't annoy me, she shouted, and slammed down the phone. She also called up departmental secretaries and other big shots and swore at them. Joana stayed in the background, waiting for Lota to order that lunch be served.

"Dona Lota, don't get so upset."

"Joanica, it's just that I want this garden to be really beautiful. I order it, and they don't do it."

Bishop was also intimidated by Lota's imprecations. It was more and more difficult to talk to her. To have a subject, she decided to read Lewis Mumford, an analyst of the evolution of the city in the West. Mumford emphasized the foolishness of destroying great areas of a city to build highways and parking lots. Reflecting on the role of the palace, he discussed how the extension of a panoramic park in the heart of the city had been the happiest contribution of the palace to urban life. To him, the essential functions of the city, which involved meeting, mixing, and mobilization, clamored for spaces in which many different activities could occur simultaneously. Heavens, that was exactly Lota's idea; she would like reading this.

Lota already knew Mumford's thinking, and this wasn't the time for sociologists. Her head was full of worries. To begin with, she wasn't having any luck selling lots in Samambaia.

"The Franciscans decided not to buy Alcobaça. Since we've decided to live in Rio, we've lost the rent on this apartment. The situation is serious, Cookie. On the Aterro, everything is going marvelously wrong in a thousand ways. I'll tell you, judging from the resistance that they're offering me in Carlos's government, you can already see how the next government could pervert what we're doing. I need to sketch the outlines of an autonomous foundation, one that doesn't depend on the state, to administer the Aterro. If not they'll build the most preposterous things there, you can be sure. Imagine, Peixoto said that Adolfo Bloch had the nerve to say that if a Trevi Fountain were built on the Aterro, he'd pay! Let him pay for the puppet theater, which will be decorated by Bianco. That reminds me, I have to call Napoleão Muniz Freire to study the puppet theater. Bianco is coming up to Samambaia next weekend, now that I think of it. And the damn cesspool, which still has that same problem, shit all over the place."

Bishop looked at the woman she admired so much. Probably this Peixoto was teasing her about the fountain, knowing the horror that monuments and statues in her garden inspired in her, but Lota was losing one of her riches, her sense of humor. Everything now was serious and menacing and exasperating. Lota was at war. Heroic? Or a crackpot?

BIANCO DROVE UP with Lota to lunch at Samambaia. At the wheel, Lota had the assurance of a man, thought Bianco with approval. Bianco also appreciated Lota's magnetic conversation and the vigor of her intelligence.

Arriving at the house, they found Bishop in an apron in the kitchen. Bianco didn't know her. He felt her to be domestic, needing the physical safety of a stove.

Lota and Bishop took up their relationship with a wholesome naturalness. Nevertheless, Bianco thought that he perceived a situation similar to that of a woman submitting to the personality of a very strong man. There was in Bishop a feminine fragility; in Lota, that savage thing. In intelligence, they were twins. But as personalities, Lota was infinitely more fascinating.

Bianco had known Lota since the early days, when she frequented Portinari's atelier, where Bianco worked daily. He was happy when, so many years later, Lota invited him to work on the Aterro. He saw once again in this gray-haired woman that petulant young woman with a man's haircut and eyes gleaming with passion, fiercely engaged, still flying the flag of the modern. Lota posted herself as watchdog of the aesthetics of the Aterro. She became furious with the enshrinement of bureaucracy and would not yield to those who wanted to interfere with her dream. It was magnificent to see.

Now, savoring a cafezinho in that refined house, Bianco reflected on Lota and Bishop. Lota should feel extremely gratified, because she was a South American Indian who had furiously enchanted a great poet from the first world. But Bishop's aquatic eyes seemed to be scrutinizing her future alongside that feverish entrepreneur. What awaited her? To be a good cook for an executive who was making a garden in an underdeveloped country? To be buried at Samambaia taking care of the dogs? Bianco thought that Lota was inattentive to Bishop's aquatic eyes. Finally, how to know? Woman is a mystery, thought Bianco.

"WHAT A HARD PERSON to track down, eh? I've been trying to speak to you for days."

"Yes, my dear, I've been on a merry-go-round."

"But it's not just that Dona Lota hasn't been at the Shed. Didn't Joana give you my message?"

"She did, Vivinha. It's written down here in my appointment book: call Vivinha. It's just that this month. . . . Just a minute, my dear. . . . There, it was just that shitty tow truck again. Now then . . ."

"I called because I heard that your ladyship got decorated. What an honor, eh! It's not every day that a woman gets a medal in this country."

"Right. But it wasn't a medal that this woman wanted. I just wanted Carlos to take a bigger interest in the Aterro. It's very tiring working like this, having to fight for every little thing."

"Hey, what happened to the Indomitable Lota? Did she get married and move?"

"I wish I had. Did you know that the Lowells were here? It was an uproar; since July, up and down with them. And then Nicolas Nabokov came, and right after him Raymond Aron and wife, and, as if that wasn't enough, John Dos Passos. All of them with rights to dinner, introductions to the governor, etc."

"Everyone in September?"

"Everyone. Cal seemed very on edge and ended up having a breakdown in Buenos Aires, after he'd left Rio. I had to arrange from here for his return to the United States, speaking to this one and that one, with Elizabeth extremely wound up because he was all alone; his wife had already gone back to the States with their daughter. As Edileusa put it, it was Pan-Demon-ium."

"Okay, and what can you tell me that's good?" Vivinha was irrepressible.

"Good? I can tell you that Monica is a little dear. You'd have to see her disposition when she sings Fall, fall, balloon. She's a sweet thing in my life, a very welcome little person."

"Okay then, dona grandmother, I won't waste any more of your time."

"Vivinha, you know how much I like to talk to you. If there's anyone who doesn't waste my time, it's you."

And she broke out into talking about the Aterro.

After she hung up, Vivinha sat thinking about her friend. In other times, Lota would have loved going around with these celebrities. Now she seemed to be looking exclusively at the park. There was the danger of Lota confusing herself with the Aterro, turning both into one thing. This would be a calamity, because in public life no one owns the work. Daughter of mighty Zeus, isn't it enough for you to seduce powerless women?

# PINK DOG

"CARLOS — stop being an idiot, Carlos!"

Major Osório, Carlos Lacerda's aide-de-camp, had never heard anyone address the governor like this.

"Carlos, making a garden out of gravel at the price of two hundred million is throwing money away. When it rains hard, the gravel is going to run and mix with the earth, aside from forming pools of water all over the place, because of the impermeable spots there are on the Aterro. Along with the wild grass that will grow. You want to throw money away? Spending two hundred million on a garden of trees and mud and wild grass is a lot of eccentricity to my taste. It would be better to just leave the soil as it is and save two hundred million."

"Lota, grass is very expensive."

"No sir. Grass is still the cheapest and most lasting kind of cover. The grass isn't picked, it's simply cut with big machines. It needs much less maintenance."

"I still say it's very expensive."

"The cost is going to be cut in half if we do the planting ourselves, instead of asking for bids."

"Lota, do you think things are that simple?"

"Carlos, the grass cover isn't a luxury. It's a necessity. It's not for nothing that *all* the parks and gardens in the *world* have a grass cover!"

"Lota! I'm telling you that *there will not be* grass on the Aterro!"

"And I'm telling you that *there will be* grass on the Aterro!"

"*Lota! I'm the governor!*"

"*Carlos! I'm the president of the work group of the Aterro!*"
"Holy cow," muttered Major Osório.

ELIZABETH HARDWICK, who had been in Brazil with her husband, Robert Lowell, wrote to Bishop suggesting that she send a piece on Brazil to the recently founded *New York Review of Books*. This gesture of collaboration was intended so that Bishop could publish (and get paid for) something. Bishop didn't write. The Ford Foundation promised some funding if she'd write a piece. Bishop refused. It's not 'cause I wouldn't. It's not 'cause I shouldn't. And you know it's not 'cause I couldn't. It's simply because . . .

Bishop's life went on in this dull sameness. Another February 8 came, and Bishop turned fifty-two. She suffered. At times the pain was desperate, and she needed to drink. But faithful Joana emptied the bottles of scotch into the sink and filled them with water. Bishop drank perfume.

A GRINGA, red from the sun, peeling, trotting shakily down the streets in Leme.

> *Oh, never have I seen a dog so bare!*
> *Naked and pink, without a single hair . . .*
> *Startled, the passersby draw back and stare.*

> . . . . . . . . . . . . . . . . . . . . . . .

> *Didn't you know? It's been in all the papers,*
> *to solve this problem, how they deal with beggars?*
> *They take and throw them in the tidal rivers.*

> . . . . . . . . . . . . . . . . . . . . . . .

> *Carnival is always wonderful!*
> *A depilated dog would not look well.*
> *Dress up! Dress up and dance at Carnival!*

Bishop was composing loathsome poems, she wrote Lowell. She wanted to go beyond the horror the way the Brazilians did, with their sambas and Carnival tunes, but she couldn't. The humor came out macabre. "Pink Dog" went with the others, into the drawer.

A CITY SHOULD BE built for the convenience and satisfaction of those who live in it and for the great surprise of strangers.

Lota picked this reflection by Sansovino, a sixteenth-century Italian architect, as an epigraph for her piece on the Glória-Flamengo Aterro, published in the *Revista de Engenharia do Estado de Guanabara*. The article opened as follows: "The biggest enemy of the beauty and comfort of a big city is the automobile."

Lota knew that her views would disturb many people but wrote that the Aterro dared to offer to the pedestrian—the pariah of the modern age—a share of the peace and leisure to which he had a right.

Well now, Lota was seen as a gatecrasher by the readers of the *Revista de Engenharia*. All the other pieces were signed by engineers. Indignant denunciations rained down.

The most serious came from House member Carvalho Neto, who used nothing less than a speech from the podium of the Legislative Assembly, during the session of May 22, 1963, to bring down the hammer on the urbanization plan for the Aterro, on the work group, and above all on its president, whom he branded as a terrible influence on the governor.

As always, Lota became furious, and wrote pages and pages to make amends, emphasizing the fact that she was working for free. Finally, she decided on a short piece, clarifying that the views expressed in the article echoed those of the most famous English and American landscape designers of the day. And that the president didn't have the importance that the House member had so generously attributed to her. Her only merit had been to have chosen the most capable, most honored, the best work group in Brazil.

WHILE LOTA WAS BUSY with urbanization in Rio, Bishop was on the verandah looking through binoculars at the slum of Babylon. One day she followed the hunt for a bandit and, unusual for her, sat down and wrote forty verses at one stroke.

When Bishop showed "The Burglar of Babylon" to Flávio, Lota's nephew was thrilled. The poem was fluid and infectious like popular poetry, and the accurate observations of the slum, the bandit, the military police, the poor people and the rich were all on pungent display in the poem's ingenious structure. Closely consulting Bishop, Flávio translated the poem and ended up publishing it in the *Cadernos Brasileiros*.

> On the fair green hills of Rio
> There grows a fearful stain:
> The poor who come to Rio
> And can't go home again.

. . . . . . . . . . . . . . . . .

*Micuçú was a burglar and killer,*
*An enemy of society.*
*He had escaped three times*
*From the worst penitentiary.*

Bishop narrated the actions of the military police:

*The soldiers were all over,*
*On all sides of the hill,*
*And right against the skyline*
*A row of them, small and still.*

. . . . . . . . . . . . . . . . . .

*But the soldiers were nervous, even*
*With tommy guns in hand,*
*And one of them, in a panic,*
*Shot the officer in command.*

until the end of Micuçú:

*It was early, eight or eight-thirty.*
*He saw a soldier climb,*
*Looking right at him. He fired,*
*And missed for the last time.*

*He could hear the soldier panting*
*Though he never got very near.*
*Micuçú dashed for shelter.*
*But he got it, behind the ear.*

The next day, the police were back:

*This morning the little soldiers*
*Are on Babylon hill again;*
*Their gun barrels and helmets*
*Shine in a gentle rain.*

*Micuçú is buried already.*
*They're after another two,*

*But they say they aren't as dangerous*
*As the poor Micuçú.*

In July, Lota had to be hospitalized suddenly. No medication had worked. Intestinal occlusion, emergency surgery. Lota spent two weeks in the hospital. Bishop was terrified at seeing Lota brought into the room unconscious, as if she were dead. All her fears rose to the surface. She had never thought of life without Lota. After so many carefree years, she saw the precariousness of her arrangement. Everything could change. Everything could end. Again.

Mary also went to the hospital, to take care of practical things and to calm Lota.

Lota would barely open her eyes, and she had visitors. People came all day to talk and laugh loudly, as if there were a big party going on in the hospital room. When the nurse came in on her rounds, those present would move out into the corridor, but they didn't go away. Bishop and Mary took turns entertaining them. Then they'd all come back to Lota's side and talk about illnesses, about people who almost died in surgery, or about the Aterro. Bishop got angry, but she didn't have the nerve to throw them out. Mary seemed to be all right with it. And Lota showed herself to be the same clown as usual.

When she got out of the hospital, Lota ignored the convalescence period and went straight back to work. Weeks later, she began to burn with fever. Bishop became very frightened; Lota's temperature didn't stop climbing, and her headaches were terrible. Typhoid fever, the doctor diagnosed. From rats. It was inconceivable that Lota would become ill like this, Bishop thought. She was the sick one. She began drinking steadily.

Joana became desperate, running from one to the other. The doctor had ordered absolute rest for Dona Lota; everything had to be taken to her by hand. And Dona Elizabetchy took advantage of Joana being so busy, drank like a fish, then lay in bed screaming, singing, crying, heaping afflictions upon Dona Lota.

When Dona Lota could travel, she and Joana went to Samambaia. There Dona Lota would have some relief. Dona Elizabetchy checked herself into a clinic and sent word that she had gone to get some rest.

*I got ramblin'*
*I got ramblin'*
*all on my mind*
*Hate to leave you baby*
*but you treats me so unkind*

Robert Johnson's nasal voice twanged out of Bishop's hi-fi. Bishop loved the shameless passion of the blues.

"Who's that?" Lota had just come in.

"Robert Johnson. He's *good*. He died, poisoned by a rival when he was just over twenty."

Lota sat down, not very impressed. She put her hand out, all spotted with the needle pricks for glucose, and picked up a magazine. With a sigh, she began to leaf through it. They'd been at Samambaia doing nothing for a few days, to see if each could recuperate from her ailments. Bishop had come there directly from the "rest clinic" and was very happy. She wanted her and Lota to return to their house in the middle of the clouds and for everything to get back to normal. But from what she could see, this would not be easy. Lota was furious at being sick because she never got sick. She was impatient to get back to the hurly-burly, to fight with Carlos and the whole upper echelon of the government and then come back to the house exhausted, to find Bishop exhausted from fighting with herself.

*Well, it's hard to tell, it's hard to tell*
*when all your love's in vain*
*All my love's in vain*
*Oh oh oh oh oh oh*

AT THE END OF SEPTEMBER 1963, Carlos Lacerda was in the United States, telling the *Los Angeles Times* that the military were going to intervene in João Goulart's government and were even thinking of ousting him.

Elizabeth Bishop was in the apartment in Leme, reading *The Group*, by her old classmate from Vassar, Mary McCarthy.

Joana dos Santos was in the kitchen of the same apartment, checking the stock of candles, because the power was being cut off every night.

Arnaldo de Oliveira was looking at an apartment in Flamengo that had been advertised in the Sunday paper; he was thinking about moving from the north zone.

Adrienne Collins was in her room in Seattle, reading Walt Whitman.

Vivinha was in her apartment in Botafogo, listening to her niece Do Carmo tell her how young people all over the world were preparing to change the destiny of the planet. Do Carmo had enlisted in the student movement and guaranteed, eyes burning with faith, that in Brazil there would be no more illiterates, or the rule of the colonels, or misery.

Lota de Macedo Soares was in a wooden shed on the Aterro, urging Sursan to pay the sixty contos to Reidy, which were late again.

WHEN BISHOP HEARD of the publication of *The Group*, she froze. She was terrified that Mary McCarthy had included her as a character, seeing that they'd been contemporaries at Vassar. When she finished reading it she was sure that Lakey, the character who spends a long time in Europe and reappears accompanied by a short and stout baroness, was her. The baroness, of course, was Lota. Mary McCarthy had gone out with Lota and Bishop two or three times, when the two of them had been in New York in 1957. Hannah Arendt, who had been enchanted with the brilliance and sense of humor of the Brazilian, had spoken highly of her to McCarthy. For this reason Bishop resented the characterization of the baroness as a masculine woman, not very intelligent, ready to use her revolver against anyone who got near the inscrutable and highly intelligent Lakey. Also, the fact that *The Group* considered this relationship abnormal disturbed Bishop. The vulgarity with which, in the book, the other woman friends thought about the physical relationship between the two women revolted her. Bishop did not make her distaste explicit to Mary McCarthy. She simply cut off relations. Meanwhile, when she heard, indirectly, the reason for Bishop's distancing herself, Mary McCarthy denied outright that Lota and Bishop had inspired her characters.

THAT NIGHT MARY MORSE, who was living in the house below, as her house had come to be known, heard a car coming up the hill headlong. Had Lota decided to come up to Samambaia in the middle of the week? Could she be sick again? Lota, that hard head, was working more than she should. But it was strange that she hadn't stopped in to see Monica.

Mary decided to go see what was happening. What if it were burglars? Better to get reinforcements. She got into her Beetle and went to Manuelzinho's house.

"Manuelzinho, someone is in Dona Lota's house. Come with me."

Immediately Manuelzinho, who was in his underwear, put on his straw hat and picked up a stick.

When they got to Lota's house, Mary saw flashlights playing over the terrace and the kitchen light on.

"Come on, Manuelzinho," she said, without thinking of the risk they were taking.

Under cover of darkness, the two of them went into the house.

"Who's there? Who's there?" Mary yelled.

Immediately they were surrounded by armed men. While Mary imagined what Manuelzinho was going to do, someone whispered:

"Morsey! Have you gone crazy?"

Appearing out of the dark, with his eyes wide behind his glasses, was none other than the governor of the state.

"Carlos! What are you doing here?"

"I've already spoken to Lota, Morsey. She said I could spend the night here."

"But why didn't you call me? Why'd you scare me like this?"

Lacerda called off the bodyguards with a signal.

"Morsey, I'm hiding here. They're trying to catch me."

"Ah."

Mary never knew who "they" were, nor did she want to. She knew times were tense and that it was likely that even the governor's life would be at risk.

"Then I'll go see if the guest rooms are made up," said Mary.

Mary knew perfectly well that the rooms weren't made up. When she opened the door to the first one, she saw a machine gun on the bed. She turned half around.

"Carlos, I'll give you the pillows and bedclothes, and you fix things up. Do you want anything else?"

"Scotch, please."

Mary knew there was no Scotch in the house because of Bishop. She went to her house and got a bottle.

"Thanks, Morsey. Look, no one can know I'm here. My life's in danger. They tried to kidnap me. Please don't tell anyone you saw me here."

"Why would I tell anyone? Don't worry."

The next morning, the gardener remarked casually to Mary:

"Lacerda was here. I saw his bodyguards in the kitchen. Buying flowers at the florist's next door, for sure, eh?"

"LITTLE JOANA, let's light a candle."

Lota seemed to accept the light rationing without resentment. Maybe because she always came home extremely tired and dying to fall in bed, so the quality of the illumination made little difference to her.

Joana lit a candle. She resented that the power failed exactly at the time of the soap operas, my Lord, her only distraction. All those lines wavering across the screen tired out her eyesight. Just as well to go to sleep too.

Bishop also resented the lack of electricity. Night was the only time the two had to see each other, talk a little. Bishop was very uneasy about the general political situation in Brazil, frightened by the threats of a coup that she heard, now from the right, now from the left. Still, Lota came home, as the Carnival music of that year put it, spitting fire. Bishop became all fingers and thumbs.

"Cookie, I didn't have time to go by the bakery. Please, my love, go down and buy us a few rolls, would you?"

When Bishop got back, Lota was already asleep. Bishop wasn't tired. She began to write.

> . . . Beneath
> our rationed electricity
>
> the round cakes look about to faint —
> each turns up a glazed white eye.
> The gooey tarts are red and sore.
> Buy, buy, what shall I buy?

Early morning and Bishop hadn't been able to get to sleep. If there was power in Leme, Bishop would greet the dawn listening to Billie Holiday.

> I go to bed
> with the prayer
> that you'll make love to me.
> Strange as it seems.

VIVINHA'S HAPPINESS KNEW no bounds. Sweet mother of Christ—Lota had called her, after a long time. Vivinha had decided not to call anymore, because Lota always gave the impression that she was anxious to hang up, with extremely urgent things to do. Vivinha missed Lota greatly, the funny Lota, always with an opportune outburst. Lota was the ultimate example of the capacity of intelligence to show itself through humor.

However, after the Aterro, Lota seemed to have developed a peevishness, an irritability that intimidated Vivinha. Even so, Lota maintained her charismatic influence, Vivinha had to admit. Only Lota would have the personality to force Rachel, Rosinha, Magu, and who knew how many others to stick themselves into that pigsty of a shed, in horrific heat, to work without earning a penny. Rosinha told her that they took a bottle of water, sandwiches, and a little fan and worked like slaves under the rule of a tyrannical chief, and they still thought that the cause was worth the sacrifice.

"Lota, my love, how good to hear your voice."

"Dear creature, let's go out and talk."

Having a milkshake at Bob's, Lota enumerated all her setbacks. Vivinha tried to cheer her up.

"It's because you don't collude. And also because you're a woman. Men aren't accustomed to it; they feel uneasy. Didn't you see that the winner of this year's etching prize at the Paris Biennial was Anna Letycia? And Edith Behring won the etching prize at the biennial of Mexico. Things like that get men all upset, poor things."

Lota had to laugh.

"I'm up to my neck with annoyances to resolve. Call me."

"I will. But speaking of annoyances, how is Cookie?"

This was taking up time. Vivinha was so sociable, so mischievous, but when it came to Elizabeth she became intractable. When Lota complained, Vivinha said it was just that Bishop was, without doubt, so-o-o-o intellectual.

"Vivinha, go fuck yourself."

"The same to you."

Damn.

# THE MERDOT

NOVEMBER 13, 1963. Carlos Lacerda got to his private office early. He needed to check on how negotiations were proceeding for the arrival of four U.S. generals who were coming to meet with the military, with the governor of the state of São Paulo, Ademar de Barros, and with Lacerda himself. The last month had been very tense, with the threat of a state of siege and the attempt to arrest Lacerda. The best time of day to deal with this kind of subject was . . . Lacerda spotted the letter in the middle of the table. It was a pile of papers with the Sursan stamp. "Governor." A bad sign: no "my dear," no "my sweetheart," not even "Carlos." Lacerda leafed through the pages. There were five of them, and another numbered 5½. Lacerda took a deep breath. Here came a blast.

"I don't have the patience, I don't have the time, I don't have the vocation, I don't think it's the tiniest bit funny to be left hanging on the phone, jumping from Guanabara Palace to your house, sending messages, trying to speak to you.

"I'm not asking you for favors, I don't like *power*, I don't like getting pissed off, I don't like living in Rio. Unfortunately one of the ways of working efficiently is to speak to you.

"It doesn't seem to me that I've wasted your time by passing on gossip or giving you the high and low temperature in Caxias. I think this attitude you have of 'credit in the bank' is extremely annoying—the less asked for, the less there is.

"I find it extremely annoying that Sérgio Bernardes manages to get the most immoral permission to build monstrosities on top of Pasmado or roly-poly hotels thirty stories high on the busiest street corner in Copacabana. What does it matter if he ruins Rio's beauty and gets a few million for himself.

". . . while Reidy has so much trouble getting his sixty contos a month from Sursan that he's already threatened to leave them there as a present and say he's never been invited to work on any project for this government. . . .

". . . while you've never given a damn thing to Bertha either, who by consensus is one of the best things there is in Sursan, with integrity and intelligence. . . .

". . . while, despite all that I told you about Mamede's splendid work in Copacabana, he was replaced by a dimwit who to this day hasn't realized that it's *useless* to fine the cars that park on the sidewalks because he doesn't have the means for it (no crane, no place to keep the cars, no guards). The only answer is to throw the cars into the ocean, which would be an idea. . . .

". . . and that this same Mamede, despite being loyal, intelligent, and active, is twiddling his thumbs, because he 'appeared too often in Ibrahim Sued's column' and despite always having served this work group. . . .

"It's evident that the members of this work group deserve a grade of Zero—Zero in prestige—Zero in requests.—It's pathetic—and it's hilarious!"

On page 5½, Lota added:

"While Roberto Burle Marx is making gardens in Paris, Vienna, and Algeria, where he is right now, a group of innocents is building a Noah's Ark in Penha (the idea of this Paulinho is to plant three trees of each species). . . .

". . . and to the selfsame Roberto no more work has been assigned in Rio, to the point that his office is closed for lack of money. . . . (Sursan hasn't paid him yet for the Outeiro garden, made more or less a year ago!)"

This was a massive indictment. Irritated, Lacerda scrawled on the back of page 5½:

"Lota, I hope that as you reread this letter you will reflect on the real injustices and the gratuitousness of your wrath. I will avoid analyzing, point by point, because what's more important is the general *tone* of the letter. Something's going wrong. It's not, I'm sure, my friendship or my appreciation for your work. Find out what it is and tell me when . . ."

He ran out of space. Lacerda turned the page and wrote laterally, around his own text:

"we can talk—without letters, and without fighting over details and leaving out the main event. Or do you think that Helio Mamede is my only concern? Hugs."

Not remembering the date correctly, Lacerda wrote: 10.11.63. And ordered that the letter be returned to Lota.

AFTER THE HOLIDAYS at the end of the year, Lota and Joana returned to Rio and left Bishop alone at Samambaia. Lota admitted this would be better for both of them.

Within the cycle that characterized the relations between the two of them, Lota was suffering a relapse in her connection with Carlos. He had been particularly subtle in writing, on the back of November's condemnatory letter, that he'd wait for her to say when the two of them could meet. And when she said so and they met, Carlos reminded her that he was combating the agents of international communism in Brazil and was in the thick of the presidential race, so he counted on Lota to attribute any deficiencies that escaped him to the trials and tribulations of a Savior.

Lota didn't make more trouble. In the first days of January 1964 she composed the first letter of the year in the capacity of adviser to the state, on delicate blue paper.

"My Dear Governor,

"Happy Holidays and above all best wishes in the final race. I'm only sad that Brasília is so far from here.

"Meanwhile let's get to a few problems.

"Have a good look at the Catholic Church, which is striving for some more building lots in Santo Antônio. Law 14, weakly designed, is giving it the opportunity, along with its hold on the lot of the Cathedral (which is a monstrosity), to claim 'areas for auxiliary buildings.' As long as that vacant lot is there, the requests are going to be tremendous. Is it possible that billions will be spent so that afterward the same mistakes can be made due to lack of planning, and an area vitally important to the correction of the deficiencies of the city center will be fragmented? *You still have the time to make a plan*, blocking the idea of selling lots and putting the area to better use.

"I think it's gross to take the fig trees from Paris Square and replace them with palm trees. Take out the *court* in the form of animals and chairs, yes, for a more classical form. The beauty of a city comes in part from the rigorous conservation of elements from different centuries: the Public Walk from the eighteenth century—Paris Square from the nineteenth century—and the Aterro, the twentieth century—despite Paris Square having been built at the beginning of this century, it's designed as a nineteenth-century garden and should be maintained that way.

"The situation of Urbanization is getting more and more shaky; I think it's going to be necessary to throw out all those people and start over again. Nobody does anything there. *They don't even go to work.* . . . Let's put a round table together and see if we can't get out of this impasse.

"I've heard with *horror* rumors about a cemetery in Lage Park and a hotel in Pasmado. To destroy a very beautiful garden that's already grown and whose reconstruction is easy and economical is barbarism. The argument that it would be a cemetery garden isn't viable, because you don't plant corpses beneath trees (it's not good fertilizer!), and the American formula for garden cemeteries is to plant trees among the corpses and *not vice-versa!*

"Urbanization, if it were working properly, would already have chosen two large areas—north and south—for cemeteries, and not let itself think of an area (Lage Park) that's too small and that will be full of corpses in ten years. There should be a work group created to take care of the problem, which is simple: (1) the renovation and cleaning of the garden; (2) its intensive utilization, with areas for children and adults (there's space, without touching the trees); (3) utilization of the Bezanzoni house as a cultural center, which would be the only one in a densely populated district that doesn't have a movie house! In this house there could be an auditorium for concerts, conferences, etc. etc. The residents could contribute as if it were a club, a lending library, a games room with ping-pong etc. Outside there's room for basketball and things like that. This garden would be alive and visited above all at night, because nothing like this exists in the district of the Botanical Gardens."

LACERDA INTERRUPTED HIS reading of the letter. Lota was right! He still had time to make a plan for the city! A housing plan had been designed, and Sandra Cavalcanti was in charge of transferring the slum dwellers to the recently built group housing. The waste disposal system was being expanded. The water supply was going to be regularized with the construction of aqueducts. Rebouças and Santa Barbara tunnels and the road plan were going to unsnarl the traffic. But that wasn't enough. He had to make sure that there was a master plan for Guanabara, a plan that would guarantee its orderly growth. When Lacerda suggested hiring Konstantinos Doxiades to design a global metropolitan plan, there was an uproar. The Engineering Club was indignant. But now Lacerda had decided. He was going to hire the Greek, even if he had to ram it down their throats.

Lacerda also decided to ignore the warnings of his political advisers about the dire consequences of vetoing installation of a cemetery in Lage Park. Very powerful interests would be thwarted, and Lacerda would lose some fundamental support. But Lota's arguments were irrefutable. And her dream of a vibrant park, maintained in collaboration with the area residents, its users, was innovative and ingenious. Like Dona Lota.

BISHOP SAT DOWN in her studio and shut her eyes for a few minutes, listening to the noise of the water flowing down below. How she missed that quiet. Only here did she feel at home.

She was finishing a poem she'd begun over Christmas. For years, Lota and Bishop had spent Christmas at Manoel Leão's house in Cabo Frio, which fascinated the poet with its wild beauty. However, this last time she noticed with distaste that the beaches of Cabo Frio had been "discovered" and that people were trying to spoil them as quickly as possible.

And Ouro Preto, was it still that bucolic little town, the mules carrying bundles of firewood and the women chatting by the fountain? She wanted to see the sky over Ouro Preto again. She wanted to see Lilli again.

Bishop looked over the envelopes of the letters she'd received. One of them drew her attention. It was from the University of Washington, in Seattle. Bishop opened it. The university was inviting her to assume the late Ted Roethke's chair, teaching poetry.

Bishop fell back in surprise. Lately she'd been feeling so shabby that the idea of being considered to join the ranks of an American university filled her with gratitude and relief. In Brazil, she was just the friend of Lota de Macedo Soares. Perhaps a respected maker of jam. But in the United States she had a reputation; she was the poet Elizabeth Bishop.

If the invitation had arrived some three years ago, Bishop wouldn't even have considered accepting it. First, because she didn't believe that you could teach anyone to be a poet. Second, because she was far too shy; she couldn't even think of herself in front of a group of twenty-year-old highbrows waiting complacently for her to say something they didn't already know. Third, because what would Lota do in Seattle?

But at that moment she saw Seattle as an alternative. The next year Lacerda's mandate would end, and with him, Lota's mandate. There would be a presidential election, and Lacerda would probably win. Very probably, Lacerda would invite Lota to work with him. Then things would have to be rearranged. Bishop wouldn't want to stay in Brazil any longer, if it was to prolong the demented life that she and Lota were living now. On the other hand, maybe Lota would want to move, to disentangle herself from the frenzy she had ended up in. Bishop wouldn't decide right away. Time would dictate the course to take.

ONLY AFTER HAVING pulled strings so that DOPS, the feared political police, would seize the primer *To Live Is to Fight*, approved by the Brazilian Catholic Church and edited by the secretary of education to teach reading and writing to the peasants, did Lacerda finish reading Lota's letter.

Now the onslaught was against building a hotel on Pasmado Mountain. Lacerda knew that for Lota, the elements of landscape were the citizens' birthright, part of the cultural heritage of a city, and therefore inalienable. But the interest of an international hotel chain in Pasmado Mountain could represent millions of dollars to the state. It was something to consider.

In the letter Lota argued that given the beauty and diversity of Rio's landscape, it was barbarism, stupidity, and a crime to "decorate" its mountains with whatever was going. She reminded Lacerda that it was not democratic to destroy the patrimony of the many to favor the few. And she anticipated the argument that this could be a "necessity" with a phrase of William Pitt's: "Necessity is the plea for every violation of human freedom. It's the argument of tyrants."

Lacerda threw the letter on the table. Lota knew how to ruin his day.

DO CARMO, Vivinha's niece and a law student, was among the two hundred thousand who attended Jango's rally on March 13, 1964, to demand immediate solutions to the problems of the many poor Brazilians who made up the majority of Brazil's population, and she went hoarse from yelling so much.

Maria Amélia, daughter of a general and a practicing Catholic, traveled to São Paulo to participate in the March of the Family with God for Liberty on March 19, and adopted as her own the words of Amália Ruth Schmidt Oliveira, who, speaking in front of the Metropolitan Cathedral of São Paulo, referred to those who participated in Jango's rally as the hired rabble.

Joana, ignoring what the two sides were doing to guarantee her rights, cried copiously in front of the television at the soap opera "The Right to Be Born," which unveiled the disgrace of an unmarried young woman who got pregnant and had to hide in a convent, after having smuggled her baby into the hands of an old black maid.

Bishop wrote to her friends that *Le Monde* was wrong to say that a right-wing coup was being orchestrated in Brazil by Standard Oil. A million people marched against communism under a torrential rain. Heck, they couldn't all belong to the rich reactionary wing of the country.

Fig. 1. Painting students, 1935. At left, kneeling, is Lota wearing a jabot. Behind Candido Portinari, who is sitting in the front row in a white jacket, are Roberto Burle Marx, in a dark suit, and Mario de Andrade, the tallest in the last row.

COPYRIGHT JOÃO CÂNDIDO PORTINARI

CARLOTIA IMPUDICA
da familia das DUBIACEAS

Fig. 2. Lota, caricatured as an impudent flower by Carlos Leão, 1949.

Fig. 3. Lota at forty: beautiful hands, rolled-up sleeves.

COURTESY OF ZULEIKA TORREALBA

Fig. 4. Samambaia: the start of
construction of the house.
COURTESY OF ZULEIKA TORREALBA

Fig. 5. Samambaia, still under construction: house, open house.
COURTESY OF ZULEIKA TORREALBA

Fig. 6. Samambaia: the house in the woods, beneath the magnetic rock.
PHOTO: AERTSENS MICHAEL. COURTESY OF ZULEIKA TORREALBA

Fig. 7. Bishop at Samambaia, after winning the Pulitzer Prize, 1956.
COPYRIGHT, THE O GLOBO AGENCY

Fig. 8. Tobias in his tuxedo.
COURTESY OF ZULEIKA TORREALBA

Fig. 9. Bishop beside the iron stove. Samambaia, 1956.

Fig. 10. Samambaia. A nook of the house with the stove, three paintings, and the Calder mobile.   COURTESY OF ZULEIKA TORREALBA

Fig. 11. Samambaia. A watercolor of the same nook shown in figure 10, painted by Bishop.   COPYRIGHT ALICE METHFESSEL

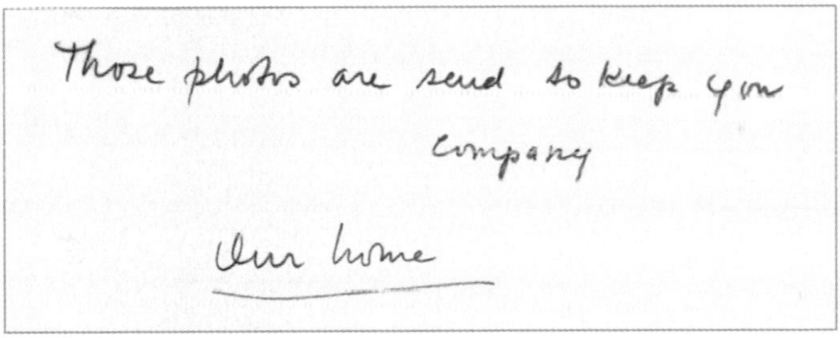

Those photos are send to keep you company

Our home

Fig. 12. On the back of a photo, in Lota's handwriting: "Those photos are send [sic] to keep you company. Our home."

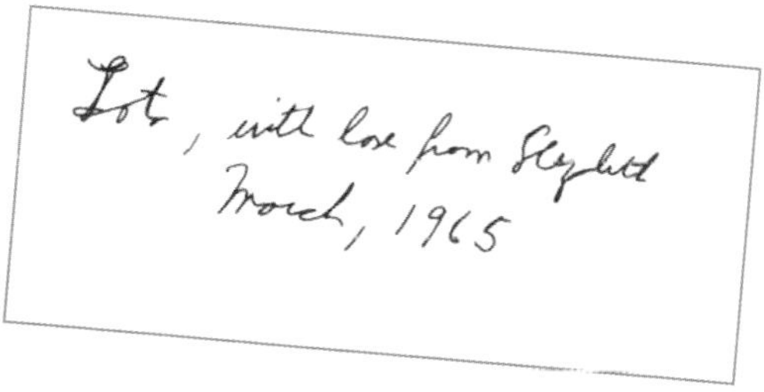

Fig. 13. Dedication from Bishop to Lota, on the opening page of Gertrude Jekyll's On Gardening.

Lot, with love from Elizabeth March, 1965

Fig. 15. The Aterro, urbanization finished.
PHOTO: CUSTÓDIO COIMBRA

Fig. 14. The Aterro, at the beginning of landscaping and construction, 1961.

Fig. 16. Lota and Affonso
Reidy talking on
the Aterro.
PHOTO: MARCEL GAUTHEROT

Fig. 17. Elizabeth Bishop gets ready to take a picture of Ashley
Brown. Salvador, 1965.

COURTESY OF ASHLEY BROWN

Fig. 18. Rachel de Queiroz in her apartment, in 1994, with
the statue of Saint Benedict that Lota left to her in her
will.

Lota was worried about the fourth centenary of the city in 1965, because the park needed to be finished by then, in time for the big commemoration scheduled by the government. Her head was absorbed with minitrains, bandstands, theater, beach, garden, playgrounds, lampposts, and washrooms. Lota had succeeded in getting rid of Paula Soares, but she was already feeling uncomfortable with the replacement, Marcos Tamoyo, who said that *he* would take charge of the Aterro. Who gave him the right to say this? If it was you, Carlos, don't stand on ceremony. We'll all go back home, from which, evidently, we never should have left.

LOTA FELT RELIEVED. Jango had been toppled. She genuinely believed that with the "intervention" of the military, the health of the economy would be restored and corruption eliminated from government. Soon the elections, which Carlos had an excellent chance of winning, would be held. Carlos would be a civilized president, and he would lead the country out of that humiliating third worldism.

Carlos thought the same. On an afternoon of hugs and compliments, the governor decided that Lota should have some holidays bestowed on her. To Bishop's joy, Lota had the good sense to accept. Bishop had received a check from *The New Yorker* for "The Burglar of Babylon." They decided to make the dreamed-of trip to Italy and bought tickets for May 13.

Lacerda also had a scheduled trip. He was going on an official mission to Europe and the United States, to explain to friendly governments the so-called revolution that had taken place in Brazil.

In reality, Lota thought it wasn't a good time to be away from work on the Aterro. She'd decided to go for Elizabeth's sake. The two of them had been very distant, and Lota knew how important the trip was to her companion. Barefoot in the snow goes the one who would serve love, as Camões said. Lota left very worried; if under her hundred-eyed vigilance the Sursanlets behaved like robots, without doubt they'd really have the time of their lives in her absence.

So, even at that moment, Lacerda was not spared an assault from *semper idem* Lota. Here came another long letter, opening with praise for his speeches and his family and then setting out in the direction of recommendations amid shouts of warning.

"Show some kind of friendliness to Reidy, who is very ill, but he's a gentleman and has shown the greatest dedication possible. Don't commit the stupidity of turning over to the Glória Hotel the parking places planned to serve the garden!"

She skidded into the usual blast. "*Everybody* has something to say about traffic and urbanization. The only ones left to consult are the sisters of charity and the statue of Manneken Piss. It's enough to say that one of the persons giving orders is one Dilson, the boy of the four roadways. It was with him that we fought for *months*! I'LL BE DAMNED!"

BISHOP WAS LOVING THE TRIP. From Milan they went to Florence, and from Florence they were going to Urbino. They'd rented a car, which Lota drove with the same flair as always. The weather was perfect.

On the way to Urbino they passed through Arezzo. On the central piazza, they bought a lovely loaf of bread and some Parma ham, made a sandwich and ate it like avid teenagers. When they got back to the mountain, they were surprised by a hard rain. Bishop looked out the window and saw some white spots on the road. Was it possible? Lota stopped the car and Bishop went to check: yes, it was snow! Snow, Lota!

Later they stopped in Anghiare, a medieval city, and walked through its tranquil alleys.

After some very beautiful valleys, they got to the walls of Urbino at the end of the day. There was some sort of conference going on, and it was difficult to find accommodations. Finally they had to settle for a malnourished hotel, to Lota's distaste.

A nearby bell tower chimed every fifteen minutes. The bed had a mattress with plaintive springs. Some time toward dawn—by Bishop's calculation, judging from the number of times the bell had performed its musical score—Lota had forgotten all the marvels of the day and was asking herself what she was doing there.

In the morning, sleepless, they went to visit the Palazzo Ducale. For the first time, Bishop saw Jesus suckling peacefully at the breast of Our Lady. In front of magnificent works of art, Lota's mood improved. But Bishop saw that she was restless.

*Is it lack of imagination that makes us come*
*to imagined places, not just stay at home?*

"HEY, DONA LOTA, are you back already? Where is Dona Elizabetchy?"

Lota hadn't been able to stand her anxiety about the Aterro and didn't continue the trip with Bishop. Bishop went to London, as had been planned, and Lota returned to Rio.

She had barely given Joana her presents when she ran off to the Shed.

"Hi, my butterfly, how are you?"

"Dona Lota!" Fernanda got a big hug. "People, look who's here!"

Everyone came to greet Lota.

"And Reidy?"

"He didn't come today, Dona Lota."

Lota got worried. Sérgio Bernardes had been dismissed after the fiasco of the millionaire project for the popular restaurant, and Jorge Moreira had withdrawn from the project due to a car accident, so the triumvirate of architects had been reduced to Affonso Eduardo Reidy. Lota considered Reidy an irreproachable professional and admired him profoundly for his probity and courtesy. When Reidy had called to tell her he had lung cancer, Lota was devastated. Meanwhile Reidy, characteristically, suggested to Lota that she recruit some young architects, who could work under his direction while that was still possible.

Lota called Reidy and he came to the phone himself, calming her. He'd be with her the next day.

Within minutes Lota was informed of the new events. There was nothing new. The planting was still suspended, waiting for installation of the sewage system. The construction of the tunnel for the sewage system was suspended, waiting for Lacerda to return from the United States.

LOTA HAD BEEN familiar with the French language since childhood. She would make up new words in French whenever she wanted something unpleasant to sound elegant. So she referred to the sewage system—that conductor *de merde*—as the merdot.

She had had thunderous discussions with Lacerda about the merdot because the engineers had said that, for economic reasons, it would have to cross the Aterro, bisecting it from top to bottom. In view of this problem, Lota refused to begin planting the grass, because she thought it conceivable that they might have to redo the whole garden afterward. The paralysis meant a delay that put the plans for the Fourth Centenary at risk.

Lota went to talk to the secretary of works.

"Peixoto, this merdot is not going to go through the garden. Let's create a beach in Botafogo and the merdot will go through the beach."

Peixoto frowned, opened his eyes and mouth wide.

"Lota! The merdot . . . how so? . . . *create* a beach?!"

"It's decided."

"Lota! But . . . And the governor?"

"I'm the governor."

Two weeks later Peixoto went to speak to Lota.

"Lota, Carlos found out in the newspapers that they're making a beach in Botafogo. The man is a wild beast. He called in an absolutely feral rage."

"Aw, little Peixoto, did he give you an ass-whipping, a tongue-lashing?"

"Lota, he's possessed! I *told* you this story was going to make the shit hit the fan."

"I know that Carlos is wild. Leave Carlos to me."

Finally Lacerda returned from his diplomatic mission. He got Peixoto and went to see Lota's maneuver. Arriving in Botafogo, he met a throng of people holding banners and posters. Thank you, governor! The residents of Botafogo thank Governor Carlos Lacerda! Thank you for the beach! Much applauded, Lacerda signaled to the small crowd and gave in to Lota, the organizer of the spontaneous demonstration.

Afterward he promised that he was going to order a statue built for the Aterro. Lota would be standing, feet spread, hands on her waist. As a label, her favorite phrase: Don't piss me off!

CARRIED AWAY BY HER SUCCESS, Lota decided to formalize the demand that absolutely all of the projects planned by the work group be realized. The Sursanlets, claiming a lack of funds, wanted to cut this or that piece, provoking aesthetic nausea in Lota. What a pissoff! Lota was sick of wasting her breath on the lack of discernment of these guys. If only the pavilions were covered with marble, or other fantasies! For the last time, she explained to Sursan that the elements of the plan were interconnected and that the Aterro *would have* a bandstand, a dance floor, libraries, restaurants, marinas, and everything that had been planned. Period. Salutations.

Peixoto called Lacerda.

"Leave Lota to me," said Lacerda.

ON JULY 22, 1964, the military government decided it was early to think of elections and determined that the mandate of Marechal Castelo Branco, the leader of the conspiracy that had toppled João Goulart and head of the military regime since April, was to be extended for another three years. It was a blow to Lacerda's hopes. To Lota, it was a warning that the political situation in Brazil was still like happiness to the poet Fagundes Varela—a nebulous dream.

Having the park declared a national heritage site by the Department of State Property moved to first place on Lota's list of priorities. It would be an event sui generis, given that Lota was claiming this status for a park not yet finished. For Lota, it was the only way to protect the park from the greed aroused by an area of inestimable value as real estate, as well as from what she called the frivolity of the people who managed the country. She sent her formal request to the director of the department, her friend Rodrigo Melo Franco de Andrade.

Second place on her list of priorities was the question of lighting. Studies indicated that eighteen hundred conventional lampposts would be needed to light the Aterro. However, Lota would not accept, after all their landscaping effort, seeing the park transformed into a pile of toothpicks. Discouraged about finding a better solution in Brazil, Lota asked Reidy to consult with his North American friend Phillip Johnson. Although very weakened, on August 5 Reidy wrote to Johnson asking him for a name.

Johnson replied promptly, saying that the person in his country who understood the most about illumination was Richard Kelly. Reidy died before the letter came.

*Presentiment—is that long Shadow—on the lawn*
*Indicative that Suns go down—*

*The Notice to the startled Grass*
*That Darkness—is about to pass—*

Bishop read Emily Dickinson. Presentiment—could that be the persistent thing she was feeling? Was she returning home? Was Rio her home? After so many years in the Tropics, she admitted to herself that she had liked seeing snow again, raspberries, oaks.

She closed the book. One of the good things about traveling by ship was to read like this, on the deck. She was returning by ship, slowly, the way she liked. The way Lota detested.

How different the two of them were! She was almost always bewildered, blaming herself for her mistakes. Lota was always secure; she always knew exactly what needed to be done and then did it. Could it be that in Lota's soul there were no dark places?

She was returning to Lota. Touring Italy, they had gone back to laughing together, to sharing the languor of the end of the day the way they hadn't done for a long time. It was true that Lota hadn't stayed on through the end of the trip. But who knew if now they couldn't re-establish their daily routines, as they had in Samambaia, saving time for themselves alone.

When the ship anchored in the port of Rio, Bishop descended the stairs with a bold heart. Lota would be waiting there for her without doubt. They'd go home together, to put an end to their longing, *matar as saudades*, as they say in Portuguese.

Lota really was there waiting for her. With Mary Morse and that little stinker Monica at her side.

# BRIGHT MOONLIGHT

ONE NIGHT IN AUGUST 1964, Ashley Brown was in one of the box seats at the Municipal Theater of Rio de Janeiro for a performance of the American Ballet Theater. Brown had just come to Brazil as a Fulbright scholar, and that night he was the guest of the U.S. cultural aide George Bohrer and his wife.

Brown ran his eyes over the sumptuous interior, from the rich stage curtain and the parade of celebrities to the immense crystal chandelier in the middle of the room. Suddenly, his eyes were arrested at a box on the other side. A woman was sitting with her profile to him. She was an august figure, with such an air of nobility that Ashley lost himself in it. A young man leaned over with elegant solicitude to speak to her. It was a scene from a nineteenth-century romance.

At the end of August, Ashley Brown called Elizabeth Bishop. They didn't know each other, but he had a letter of introduction from Flannery O'Connor. They arranged a meeting for the following evening at Bishop's apartment. When he arrived, Bishop introduced him to the lady from the box seat.

Lota was dressed with elegant simplicity. She had her hair done up in a topknot, held with a rare clasp. She treated him very affably and asked that she be excused for withdrawing early; she had to be at work at seven the next morning.

Bishop asked many questions about O'Connor. She'd very much wanted to know this southerner personally, this physically frail woman who raised peacocks and wrote fascinating stories. In 1957, when she was going back to Brazil with Lota, Bishop had called O'Connor from Savannah, wanting to go and visit her, but there hadn't been time. Nor would there ever be again, because O'Connor died just at the time when Brown was moving to Brazil.

Bishop told Brown that she and O'Connor had maintained a sporadic but gratifying correspondence. In 1958 Bishop had sent O'Connor a copy of her translation of My Life as a Girl, which had led O'Connor to reflect that perhaps in a Catholic country whites and blacks could live together more easily. On another occasion, speaking of Lourdes, she concluded that the great miracle of the Sanctuary was that no general epidemic had broken out, since all the sick drank from the same bottle and used the same hospital gown to bathe in.

Bishop sent her photos of the Amazon region and also a bottle containing an altar, chalice, missal, and candlesticks, and a wooden cross with a ladder and the instruments of crucifixion, with a rooster at its top. She called it a crucifix. O'Connor adored the present but, as a practicing Catholic, thought that Bishop did not understand very much about crucifixes.

After the introduction, Bishop and Brown began to see each other regularly. Bishop was delighted to have someone to talk to about contemporary poets such as Tate, Auden, and Lowell. Brown was impressed to see how Bishop kept herself up to date, not only by subscribing to the most important literary periodicals but through an assiduous correspondence with the pre-eminent figures of North American intellectual life.

It was rare for Lota to be present at these meetings because she was engaged, body and soul, in the creation of the park. Still, on some weekends Brown risked his life crossing the city in Lota's minuscule car and went up the mountain. He came to like Lota very much; she maintained an incredible sense of humor, even when she was tense.

Once Lota came to the apartment in Leme in the afternoon. Bishop and Brown were talking, and Brown was having a drink. Lota got very angry and reprimanded him severely, saying that Bishop didn't know how to drink and he shouldn't tempt her. Brown became very uncomfortable. Bishop remained mute.

LOTA TOOK UPON herself the task of resolving the problem of how to light the Aterro. She sent Phillip Johnson all the available information. In September, Johnson confirmed that the only man in the world capable of properly lighting such a park was Richard Kelly. Lota invited Kelly for an appraisal in loco, and he accepted. Lota wrote an official letter to the president of Sursan asking that he send to New York a first-class return ticket on Varig Airlines, reserve a room at the Glória Hotel from the 4th to the 10th of December, and make provisions for payment for professional services equivalent to two thousand dollars.

BROWN ONLY LEARNED the extent of Bishop's alcoholism when, arriving at the apartment one night, he was informed by Lota that dinner had been canceled. Bishop was completely drunk.

Next it was Rachel de Queiroz's turn. Because they both cooked very well, Rachel had challenged Bishop to a cooking tourney, with shrimp as the theme. On the day scheduled, shrimp and seasoning in hand, Rachel got a phone call.

"It's not going to work, Rachel."

"Why, Lota?"

"A binge."

When Bishop resurfaced in a condition capable of hearing her, Lota would tell her clearly how disappointed she was at Bishop's heavy drinking. One day she said: "Elizabeth, you want me to be indulgent with you. I won't be. To me, indulgence is a lack of esteem, a sign of disdain."

After Lota went out, Bishop reflected. She went to the verandah, looking out at the ocean in front of Leme for a long time. Afterward she sat down and wrote to the University of Washington accepting the position.

WHEN LOTA FOUND out she was beside herself.

Lota asserted that Bishop didn't have the least qualifications to be a professor, that it was evident this was a mistake! A gross idiocy! Bishop tried to calm her down, saying that she wasn't going to begin immediately, and only for the first semester of 1966. That was more than a year away. Before then, many things could happen.

Lota didn't know what else could happen. Things were getting out of control. For example, the formation of a foundation to run the Aterro was paralyzed because Lacerda was never in Guanabara anymore. He was all over Brazil proclaiming himself a candidate and making public his disagreements with the military government. He was one of those who had made the "revolution." Then an interminable amount of time was lost with ill-fated bids; with inflation, the prices quoted became obsolete long before the bids completed their passage through the bureaucratic channels and were approved, so everything had to be done over. There was interference of every kind with the construction. Now the navy wanted to move the statue of Admiral

Barroso to the Aterro, claiming that he was too far from the sea. Why would Barroso miss the sea, retorted Lota, when he owed his reputation to a battle fought on a river?

> *It happened that my heart went cold*
> *And our love nest is empty*
> *If I could still fake loving you*
> *Ah, if I only could . . .*
> *But I don't want to, and I shouldn't*
> *This doesn't happen*

Bishop listened to Cartola sing in the midst of the stir of customers.

Brown's friendship had opened some wonderful doors. Lota had never been an aficionado of popular music, and after the Aterro she was never available at night. Brown, on the other hand, was always ready to go out. The two of them often went to the Zicartola, on Carioca Street. They also went to Zum-Zum, in Copacabana, to hear Vinícius de Moraes. Bishop never drank; she really went to hear the music itself.

One time, however, Lota joined them. The three of them went to a show called *Opinion*, considered vaguely subversive at the time. For Bishop, who was curious to see the composer from the slums, Zé Keti, as an actor, it was a disappointment. It was as if she were seeing one of those school productions again from the thirties, with miners from Kentucky shaking their fists in protest. Lota found the piece boring and Nara Leão's voice screechy. Bishop also preferred Clementina Jesus's magnificent voice a thousand times over.

"What a drag, eh," grumbled Lota when they got home. "I won't fall for another one of those hoaxes."

RICHARD KELLY CAME.

For Bishop, this meant new sessions of services rendered in the category of resident American. She lent her Anglo ears to tedious discussions about the height of posts, the lasting power of bulbs, visual comfort. She had to do simultaneous translation of technical terms she didn't know well. Damn, how do you say *ballast* in Portuguese?

For Kelly it was unbelievable. The opportunity to illuminate that absolutely dazzling seashore was unique in the life of a specialist. From the window of his room at the Glória he could see the light coming to the park, throwing the outlines of the vegetation into relief without revealing the light source. Immediately he began to design a system that would illuminate the park as if on a night of bright moonlight.

For Lota this meant promoting the convergence of a passionate technician with a spectacular idea. Posts of the greatest possible height and the smallest possible number to support lamps of the greatest possible power. Put another way, just 112 posts forty-five meters high, each supporting a battery of six projectors, would substitute for the eighteen hundred posts previously planned. The projectors would be equipped with one-thousand-watt mercury vapor lamps and covered with antiglare cylinders. Yes, she'd fight tooth and nail for this project. Nothing on the Aterro would be banal.

## BULLETS CAME FROM ALL SIDES.

Brazilian industry wasn't ready for Kelly's posts. No one made these mercury vapor lamps, which would have to be imported from the United States at astronomical prices. Nor were there posts that tall ready to go. They'd have to be specially built. Those who loved the roadways said that that tiny little light, moonlit, would provide terrible visibility for drivers. Those who understood maintenance said that to change one of those lamps it would be necessary to mount an operation that would almost involve national security. In short, Lota's solution was extremely expensive, complicated, and prejudicial to national suppliers, who were vociferously united behind the idea of the eighteen hundred posts of normal size with normal lamps.

Lota didn't want to hear about it. The park into which the Aterro had been converted was a work in the vanguard. The illumination would also be in the vanguard.

Without mincing words, Lota declared to the press that Brazil did not have architects who specialized in the technology of illumination. Richard Kelly was at the summit, with a long list of finished projects that included Washington International Airport, Lincoln Center, and various other spaces for urban living. It would be a waste to allow the technological backwardness of Brazilian industry to annul the possibility of using his conception of an ambience of diffuse and soft clarity.

It was the cost that was the devil: 1,408,043,440 cruzeiros, aside from Kelly's honorarium of thirteen thousand dollars. A billion and a half cruzeiros! But in defense of the project Lota argued convincingly that, considering the size of the park, any solution would be expensive. It would cost an equivalent fortune to build an appalling pile of toothpicks.

Lota also expounded on the plastic senses of illumination. Illuminating wasn't simply to clarify, she explained to the admiring Sursanlets. The technology had to be responsive to the sensitive and creative gaze of the artist. She reported on the recent works she'd read on the subject as well as on her direct observation in the big world centers.

To the allegation that she was an adherent of U.S. imperialism Lota reacted with an outburst. Yes, she wanted the technological resources already available in other countries to be accessible to Brazil! What was despicable was that the same Brazilian companies that also had sites outside the country were inundating the local market with limited and even obsolete products— products that constituted the only options for the talents of a Brazilian artist.

Lota's firmness, based on a passionate commitment and at the same time solidly grounded, silenced the nationalist Luddite-technocrats. The project was approved, with the condition that it be divided into two stages. In 1965 seventy posts would be installed, and the rest would remain for the 1966 exercise.

Exultant, Lota dove headlong into getting the plan under way. She asked the federal government for a favorable sign that they'd allow the importation of the mercury vapor lamps duty-free, since this was for the Fourth Centenary. She consulted Emilio Bauggart about the foundation for the towers—should it be solid or ribbed? She provided technical details to the State Energy Commission, which would execute the plan. She asked for estimates for the building of the towers from a Brazilian company, Fichet and Schwartz-Hautmont, and a Swedish one, Uddeholms Aktiebolag. She took care of the smallest details. She reasoned like a specialist. It is going to work, she wrote Kelly.

BISHOP NOTICED THAT there were no indications that her imminent departure represented a real fact to Lota. Lota remained faithful to her new passion and practically lived on the Aterro, now turned into a park. Discouraged by the hope of waiting for any change between the two of them, Bishop went to Ouro Preto with Ashley Brown.

# A B°°B°°B°° IN THE B°B°B°

IN THE FIRST WEEK of January 1965, Lacerda went to Cabo Frio to relax. That's what he meant to do, but a letter from Lota arrived. Lacerda read through the pile of sheets and immediately set about replying, point by point.

"First, the literary amenities. The film about Sir Thomas More (How much would a statue of him—one of those big ones—cost for the Aterro? For a reasonable price, I'll get the dough . . .). Shakespeare (I'm finishing the outline of the translation of *Julius Caesar*—by hand!). Elizabeth Bishop (I didn't answer, but I liked the ballad. I was falling-down tired, combat fatigue). Eliot (send the telegram in my name, on the palace account).

"Now, with your permission:

"The issue, Lota, is not as y. put it. It's not just that y. write to Cabo Frio complaining about the ring for model airplanes, which I've been complaining about myself for a long time. What's the deadline? What's the contract? You should complain to Tamoyo and Peixoto and tell me what they say—or tell them to talk to me. Complaining for the sake of complaining is enervating and doesn't lead to anything.

"Finally, for a change, you start getting gross. Lota, if y. have trouble there, learn, once and for all, that I fight troubles everywhere, including there.

"It's false that there's $ to build the restaurant. I want to finish the Aterro, your works, pomp, and glory. *I don't want to build the restaurant or the libraries.* I don't have the $ or the time to make them. To rent the restaurant, I'm fed up with hearing, many will show up. But who pays the bill? I know what I can and w. I can't do.

"I'm going to call Peixoto *now* and charge for the work on the Aterro. Monday I'll deal with this personally.

"I don't believe y. have moved things ahead much by assaulting me here with this subject. But I believe y. haven't seen yet, amid yr. criticisms, that we've performed a miracle, but the $ has been stretched thin. Right now I'm taking $ from Sursan in 65 re: finishing hospitals we began. Stay with w.'s already planned, let's get down to it and finish this. The site of the restaurant will be clean and ready for y. to find, in 66, a governor more capable, more dedicated, and more energetic to do w. y. want.

"Don't be like this, Lota. Help me to be patient, which is what I lack. I have more than enough impatience. Hugs."

WHEN BISHOP RETURNED from Ouro Preto, she found Lota on strike. Lota had decided to stay at Samambaia for one week, in protest against the discrediting of her work, to which Carlos had referred disparagingly in the context of "pomp and glory." The protest was extended to the governor's lack of interest in creating a foundation to run the Aterro.

Bishop was surprised but doubted that the retaliation would last a whole week. She was right. Before the deadline was up, the striker returned to the Shed.

Bishop stayed at Samambaia. She'd come back from a pleasant trip, on which she'd come to know a perfect little town, Tiradentes. She felt well. She wasn't going to put everything at risk by going back to Rio. She was going to take advantage of Samambaia's tranquility to take some waterfall showers and write an article that had been commissioned by the *New York Times Magazine*. The subject: Rio de Janeiro. Who knew whether, in the quiet of her study, she'd be able to write a piece free of the aversion she felt for the Marvelous City.

Bishop was ripening her idea of making her piece evolve from the lyrics of the sambas and marchinhas of Carnival. This was a virtue that Bishop admired in Cariocans: the capacity to make social critiques through music. She remembered the samba that signaled the frustration with the Aterro on Flamengo beach:

*Ai, ai, your excellency,*
*What am I going to do with my bathing suit?*
*Flamengo beach is finished.*
*(What a bummer!)*

That year, the target of one marchinha had been Fontenelle's naughtiness:

*Hey, guy, don't cry,*
*Hey, guy, don't whine,*
*Everybody fills it up*
*And Fontenelle empties it out.*

When the passage came that said "it was a bomb that exploded," everyone yelled BOOM! throwing their arms up, in the greatest happiness. In this way, they exorcised the urban terror instigated by Lacerda's director of traffic, who, on the sly, emptied the air out of all four tires of cars parked in the only space available for anyone to park in Rio de Janeiro—the sidewalk.

Determined to fulfill her commitment to the *New York Times*, Bishop imprisoned herself in her study. The problem was that Tobias imprisoned himself, too.

Tobias, who had been abandoned in Samambaia while his owner scrutinized Guanabara Bay through her binoculars, decided to reclaim his rights. He was already thirteen years old, and with age he had become sluggish and irascible, even for a cat. While Bishop fought hand-to-hand combat with the blank paper, Tobias rubbed her leg voluptuously and batted her with his paw, asking for a few tickles. Bishop bent down and scratched behind his ears. You are an "animal of esteem," as they say in Portuguese, thought Bishop, finding the expression funny and already veering away from her work to think of more funny expressions. Tobias insisted: more tickles.

"Tobias! I have to work."

Oh yeah? Tobias withdrew, grandly cloaked in his imperial cape, but not without first letting her have a good sharp nip.

"Pest!"

When Lota called, Bishop told her the story.

"Drown that cat. Poison him. Strangle him," she suggested, having taken an instinctive dislike to that castrated kitten from the start.

*The ballroom was all lit up*
*On the night of the coronation*
*There in the splendor of joy*
*The townfolk shouted their acclamation*
*Vibrant with feeling*
*The luxury, the richness*

*Reigned with magnificence*
*Beauty showed her presence*
*Bestowing honor on independence.*

The samba school Império Serrano came along the avenue singing its samba, "Five Traditional Balls Recounting the History of Rio." Every year, each samba school had to present a samba on a historical theme at the carnival parade. The official theme for the sambas of 1965 was the Fourth Centenary, so the samba writers had to cudgel their brains to get four centuries of history into their lyrics. The result was surreal. All that satin, that shining, that dignity, that irresistible rhythm—even Lota tried out a few small steps—crowned by a moving lyrical ingenuity.

Bishop couldn't aspire to write about Rio without having been to a samba school parade. She and Ashley Brown persuaded Lota to go. The first time that Lota and Bishop had gone to a parade, there had been a monumental delay of four or five hours before the first school entered onto the avenue. When the roquefort sandwiches and the coffee in the thermos were finished, Lota got up and left, swearing, without having seen any of the "great" schools. Bishop, of course, left with her.

Now the American let herself be swept away in the craziness that came along the avenue. A black couple with white wigs, dressed like European nobility, danced an exquisite pas de deux. Indians and marquises, counts and baianas, Princess Isabel and Saint Sebastian swung their hips in time with the story. Lá lá iá rá lá iá rá, sang the crowds, deliriously.

Yes! Yes! Bishop's heart pounded awkwardly.

THE ARTICLE ON RIO followed the trajectory of all the literary commissions that Bishop had accepted for money. It got stuck, she wanted to give up in the middle, and she wound up sending in the text at the last minute, after a lot of dexedrine and strong coffee. It was published in the *New York Times Magazine* on March 7, 1965.

When Bishop received her copy, she was dismayed. She disagreed with the selection of photos. And the title wasn't what she had written! The editors had appropriated the theme of one of the Carnival songs that Bishop had translated for the article, the samba "Juvenal," sung by Angelita Martinez:

*Marshál, Illustrious Marshál,*
*Consider the problem*
*Of the suburbs on the Central!*

*I'm sorry for poor Juvenál,*
*Hanging in the old Centrál*
*All year long. . . .*
*He works in Leblon*
*And lives in Delight*
*And gets to work mornings*
*Late at night.*
*Oh, Marshál!*

Bishop quoted the samba in a context that exemplified, with the drama of the user of the Central Brazil railway company, how the poor Cariocan expressed his feelings about life's hardships through music.

The district of Encantado, in the translation into English, turned into Delight. That wouldn't have been so important if it hadn't been precisely this word that the editors had picked out for the title they'd invented: "On the Railroad Named Delight." The title of the article suggested that Central Brazil transported its passengers to a place of glee, delectation, pleasure. The opposite of what the lyrics said. Bishop found this unacceptable.

LOTA COULDN'T ACCEPT it either. She had invited the press to cover Kelly's talk at the Museum of Modern Art. She opened the paper, and the piece began like this:

"Richard Keller, hired to plan the illumination of Flamengo Park . . ."

They couldn't even get a proper name right!

What shit. What shit!

BISHOP THOUGHT THAT people were treating her strangely. It was a belated commemoration of Lota's birthday, and there were the old friends as always, Rosinha, Magu, Naná, Ismênia, the very annoying Maria Amélia I-don't-know-what of I-don't-know-what, and, alas, Vivinha. Joana circulated with hors d'oeuvres. Could she be mistaken? Bishop went for a smoke on the verandah. Coming back into the room, she caught a wisp of conversation: ". . . a real hodge-podge. She took it on herself to speak about *everything*, inflation, the JK government, the Jango government, the revolution, carnival, the press, the slum dwellers, the communists in Castelinho, the show *Opinion*, Central Brazil—even Lindolf Bell without socks got into the story."

Bishop went to find Lota at the other corner of the room.

"Lota, what's going on?"

"Look, dear, an abusive piece about your article came out in yesterday's

*Correio da Manhã*. I didn't say anything because I don't think it's even worth it for you to get upset. Something from some two-bit journalist. Just let it go."

Bishop didn't want to let it go. It was horrible. Accustomed to being praised in the United States as an important poet, if not a very productive one, Bishop felt herself scorched. The full-page article by Ferdinando Castro, "Paternalism and Anti-Americanism," was crushing. Bishop was vitriolic, racist, and ungrateful to the country that had given her shelter. A false friend. Concluding that the Brazilian reader would not have access to Bishop's text, Castro quoted from it excessively, to demonstrate to the Brazilian people the negativity and lack of empathy in this foreigner. He reacted indignantly to Bishop's comments on the poor taste of the costume parades in the Municipal Theater and on the bad habit of Brazilian men of standing at the doors of corner bars at ten in the morning, watching the women go by. He felt himself wounded in his patriotic susceptibility when Bishop glanced at the large number of translations of North American playwrights and the small amount of material produced by Brazilian playwrights. The photos chosen had, for Castro, the hidden intention of showing Brazil as a country of niggers. And Bishop's racism showed through clearly in the way she dealt with a billboard on which a little black maid kissed her white boss, radiant with happiness because the lady had bought a new stove. What did Bishop know of the soul of a Latin American democrat? Pieces like this only served to strengthen the conviction in the average U.S. reader that outside of his own country there flourished an immense desert of underdevelopment, waiting for the paternalistic assistance of the United States government. Heck, Mrs. Bishop didn't need to amplify the misinformation of her countrymen, who ignored the fact that the Alliance for Progress wasn't a philanthropic expedition but a financial investment. As far as the Rio slums went, had she forgotten what the housing in Harlem was like, in the heart of New York? Now, the biggest offense, the quatrocentenary offense, lay in the correction that Bishop had made in the epithet for Rio de Janeiro:

"Rio is not a Marvelous City; it's merely a marvelous setting for a city."

Castro sent a curt and gross message to Mrs. Bishop, "stalking on the crutches of her condescending racism": Monkey, mind your own tail!

Bishop was sickened. To be insulted like this, in public! To be branded as prejudiced, colonialist, petty, even dumb as a donkey! What drove her to despair was that the Brazilian reader didn't know her text, full of ironies and understatements, but only the abusive reading of it that this Castro had done. Oh, certainly—she should have praised the play *Do You Have a Boo-booboo on Your Bobobó*. And she had also complained about the choice of photos. She had written in protest to the *New York Times*. Now, to argue that in the name of being a good neighbor, you couldn't say anything about there being illiteracy, ignorance, and misery in Rio: come off it. And on top of everything the damned title wasn't her own.

Lota translated Bishop's defense into Portuguese. The *Correio da Manhã* published it a month later, in the Letters to the Editor section.

"ELIZABETH IS IN terrible shape. I'm going to send her to you, all right dear? Things are all screwed up around here, and I'm in no shape to take care of her." Lota spoke on the phone to Lilli. "She's mortified by that cursed article in the *Correio*. . . . Yes, still. She's down in the dumps, and then you know what happens. . . . Thanks, sweetheart. A few days there in Ouro Preto will do her good."

"Lota's in terrible shape," Bishop wrote to her therapist Dr. Baumann. "Carlos Lacerda has disappointed her all the way down the line. She's exhausted, fighting like a lioness to finish the park. She's at the last degree of exasperation. Last night, while Ashley and I were talking in the living room, she pounded the wall of the room, shouting that she wanted to sleep. Please don't criticize Brazil in your letters. Lota reads my mail."

# THE FOUNDATION

PEOPLE WERE TIRELESS in their praise. What Lota had been able to do in so little time was spectacular. From the rubble, lawns had appeared, and trees, walking trails; fields for pick-up soccer games, a dance floor, and a bandstand; a ring for model airplanes, overpasses, underground walkways; a tank for model ships, pavilions, and a puppet theater. And a beach.

Lota had already succeeded in having the park designated a national heritage site. However, perceiving the transitory nature of power, she decided that it was fundamental that the park be free from the arbitrariness of politics. It was necessary to guarantee that the work be finished and that it could never be disfigured. For this, she was convinced, there was only one way: the Foundation.

The Foundation would be an autonomous entity, provided with funding to conclude all the work and to administer the park in perpetuity.

"The problem is that the Foundation has to be approved by the Assembly," Lota explained to Vivinha, "and Carlos won't lift a finger."

Lota began to persuade people to champion the Foundation.

"First, it will eliminate the bureaucracy," she said to Rachel de Queiroz. "These days it's like this: you arrive at the Shed and find the secretary having a fit. 'But what's happened, dear?' 'Dona Lota, I'm in disgrace, we're out of carbon paper.' You know, without carbon paper life is impossible, everything is in innumerable copies, one copy to secretary so-and-so, another copy for department this-or-that, another copy for the board of directors of I-don't-know-what, another copy for the archive, another for the whore who dropped him. 'But dear, send what's his name across the street to buy the damn carbon paper from that store in front.' 'Dona Lota, have you gone mad? Don't you remember that we have to send an official statement to Sursan, requisitioning the carbon paper, and then after going here and there the request will go to the bidding department, and then we have to wait until the result is published in the *Diário Oficial*, and only then can we have the carbon paper? Oooooh, how did I let the carbon paper run out?'

"What we're going to simplify is not just the purchase of carbon paper," Lota continued. "It's the actual need for carbon paper. Today, for the park to function smoothly, more than a dozen sectors have to intervene. It's Parks and Gardens, it's Urban Cleaning, it's Water and Waste Disposal, it's the Police, it's Works, it's Education, it's the devil squared. Each one more gussied up than the next. With the Foundation, all of that would be over. Only the Foundation would be in charge."

"But will the Foundation have enough people for all these functions?"

"Of course not, my dear. It will hand over the services to third parties. The Foundation will only supervise the execution of the services. We already tried this system in the garden, with Ceres, and the result was fabulous. Now we're going to do this in all sectors. The Foundation itself will have a severely reduced number of functionaries."

Persevering, Lota succeeded in gaining the manifest support of a large number of artists and intellectuals for the idea of implementing a Foundation of Flamengo Park: Pascoal Carlos Magno, Rubem Braga, Lúcio Costa, Manuel Bandeira, Tonia Carrero, Pongetti, Nelson Rodrigues. She unleashed a tenacious campaign and got various editorials written in favor of the Foundation. She sent a petition to the Legislative Assembly with 12,400 signatures.

Now all that was missing was for Carlos to present it as a bill to the Assembly for approval.

MARCOS TITO TAMOYO DA SILVA, interim secretary of public works, asked whether everything that had been done here didn't deserve the title Park of the Century.

The engineer Walter Pinto da Costa, executive president of Sursan, said that the illumination would be the most perfect in the world, which was why the services of the greatest world authority on the subject had been contracted.

The judge of the Court of Appeals, Garcez Neto, acting governor, thanked God he'd lived long enough to be present at the scene before his eyes.

Hundreds of people applauded.

Lota could have bitten herself. It was inconceivable that, at a moment like this, Carlos would think he had more important things to do, sending the substitute for the substitute to inaugurate the works in the park. Carlos, you are hurting me in a way I don't deserve. You're humiliating me.

That night, Carlos called. Lota dear, I was in Niterói. The president of the UDN was going to be elected—the president of my party, Lota. Do you see, Lota dear?

JUNE HAD ALREADY ARRIVED, and the UDN candidate for state governor had not yet been named. The elections would be in October. Lota was uneasy. The work in the park wouldn't be finished by the end of Lacerda's mandate, that was for sure. The lucky stroke would be if Carlos named his own successor.

Lota thought about writing a letter to Carlos alerting him to the apocalyptic consequences of this indecision. Meanwhile, a remark of Joana's that morning (it's you who should be governor, Dona Lota) decided her on another tone. Sitting in the Shed after lunch, she brooded. Then, on an impulse, she wrote:

"Sir Governor,

"I beg leave to propose my candidacy as your successor in the government of the State.

"I don't know if I am presenting myself a bit late, but as your choices have already been many, and your criteria extremely eclectic, and since self-declared candidates are abundant, in these months that we still have maybe my turn will come.

"Permit me to show you the qualities that make me aspire to this 'position of sacrifice,' etc.

"I am as well born (or better; it's no use being modest at this point) as Rafael, and I am just as terrified of the masses as he is . . . and like him, I don't give a damn about anyone.

"If Sandra is a woman . . . I am too. Unhappily, I don't have her imagination. I can't see a federal case in Flamengo Park, nor in the minitrain a solution to all the problems in transportation.

"I have the same temperament as Helio Beltrão; I'm also disbelieving of the prospect of becoming governor . . . and unfortunately I don't know how to play guitar.

"I have two advantages over Flexa. I have a horror of being a teacher and my art collection is better than his. (I'm jealous of the sons he has . . . but I don't think this should enter the discussion. . . .)

"I don't know as much about work projects as Peixoto. In compensation, I have much more hair. . . .

"Permit me to present you with my manner of governing. Naturally, I won't have a government like yours. I'll do much better; this is, of course, what we candidates think.

"I will have an austere government. That is, I'll go to Europe and the States several times a year, for reasons of State, to find money for research, studies, some purchases, and so that I can bring my successor from there. But I won't do as Yr. Excellency did, which was to go up with one and come down with another; that created a certain confusion among us.

"I also promise you I won't fight with the Assembly. Politics is the art of conquering. After five years in government I hope to have all the members of the House, if not on my side, then at least incapacitated and impotent.

"I promise to finish all of your projects, except for those that don't please me. I am going to study this subject in an objective and profound manner, and then I'll send you a report.

"I will order that all statues of thin women put in place by Yr. Excellency be changed for statues of fat women (from the Giacometti phase to the Marino Marini phase). I find the thin muses an unpatriotic allusion to the state of our underdevelopment; furthermore, all the fat women will look like me.

"Inheriting your post, I will also inherit your Palace and your vassals. Considering that the white paint in your palace transformed it into a colossal and ridiculous wedding cake, I intend to paint it in polka dots or stripes, or I will consult the Patrimony . . . (in this case it would be cheaper, because with the delay of the Patrimony it'll be my successor who pays . . .).

"As far as your vassals go, all of them will wear an elegant band aid over their mouths, in order to diminish gossip.

"With my highest, my very highest sentiments . . .

"Another candidate."


BISHOP CAME BACK from Bahia in good spirits. She loved to travel. She had wanted Lota to go as well, but when Ashley invited her Lota replied:

"I only travel in first-world countries, my dear."

At that moment, in the elevator, Bishop thought of nothing but seeing Lota again. She hoped she'd be home. How she missed that hardhead! Bishop wanted to open the door and fall into an embrace. Then tell her all about the trip, inch by inch. She wanted to tell how she'd met Jorge Amado and the sweetest woman, Zélia, but they hadn't talked at all about literature. She and Ashley had arrived at Jorge's house in the middle of a candomblé ceremony.

Bishop opened the door.

"Lota, I'm home!"

Lota was on the phone. With the hand that held a cigarette, she gestured vigorously for Bishop to wait. Bishop put her suitcase on the floor and waited.

Lota continued to talk on the phone. She paced from one side to the other, letting loose with vehement blasts and underlining the words with binary sweeps of her hand, a gesture Bishop knew all too well. She didn't address Bishop again, not even with a summoning gesture. When Lota crushed her cigarette in the ashtray and got ready to light another one, Bishop picked up her suitcase and retreated to her room.

The next month, August, Bishop got a ride with Lilli to Ouro Preto.

LACERDA DIDN'T NAME his successor. On the 5th of October, Negrão de Lima, an adversary of Lacerda's and ex-mayor of the old capital city, was elected governor of Guanabara.

Lota was in despair. Carlos hadn't pushed the idea of the Foundation with the members of parliament, and now the president of the Commission of Finances of the Assembly, the member Levy Neves, had formally declared himself against the project. Among the various absurdities he saw in the project, declared the member, was the fact that the nominated directors would have terms of six years, which would take away from Governor Negrão de Lima the prerogative of indicating who his choices were for these posts.

Lota's friend Gustavo Corção used his space in the *Diário de Notícias* to move his readers: "It's necessary to have the magnanimity and the patriotism to ask, even to beg Dona Lota de Macedo Soares to stay with her admirable team for the sake of continuity."

But dissenting voices also began to be heard, like that of Pomona Politis: "The creation of a Foundation means taking away land that was rescued from the ocean by the efforts of the whole population, which paid heavily for this. Beneath the apparent interest of preserving this project there exists, in reality, the intention of the current directors of perpetuating their positions with absolute power."

Lacerda, having lost the election, knew that with the opposition of the president of the Commission of Finances he would be defeated again. He didn't push it.

TEN DAYS AFTER the elections, Lota took advantage of the Week of the Child to put on a large party on the Aterro. The various sections of the park had each been inaugurated when they had been finished, but this would be *the* inauguration. Lota put Carequinha the Clown on the bandstand, the flutist Altamiro Carrilho on the dance floor, and got the great comedian Grande Otelo to lead a *bumba-meu-boi*, a traditional dance with a cast of characters. There was a kite-flying championship—Bishop's idea. Soft drinks and cotton candy for everyone. Toys dropped from an airplane for the kids. All the newspapers featured the party, and the *Jornal do Brasil* took up the whole first page of section B with pictures of radiant children taking possession of the miniature city. Lota cried with happiness. Bishop couldn't share this moment of glory; she stayed on in Ouro Preto.

NANÁ WAS SHOCKED. On the morning of the 20th of October, as she did every morning, she had breakfast and then read the newspaper. Suddenly she came upon a long letter from Roberto Burle Marx addressed to Lota. The transcription of the letter was headed by the title: "Despotism in the gardens of the Aterro leads the landscape designer Burle Marx to break with Lota de Macedo Soares." Break! Naná knew that Lota and Roberto had been brandishing swords, which was nothing to worry about with two passionate people. Roberto had called, saying that Lota was intractable, Naná could ask Jorge. But a break between old friends in public, in the newspaper, was very painful.

Apprehensive, Naná read Roberto's letter.

"You deliberate without any respect, any consultation with the expert responsible for the landscaping project, as if you were the author of the project. Perhaps it would be opportune to remind you that having the good taste to pick out a spoon or a Finnish kettle does not signify that you have creative talents."

That was hitting a sore spot. The man knew how to be vicious. He accused Lota head on of perverting the whole plan of the Aterro with her despotism and consequent intervention in technical subjects for which she had no competence, such as illumination and playgrounds. Specifically, he said:

"There's the result . . . the spaces give the impression of concentration camps . . . the wall of Flamengo made use of in a vulgar and badly understood manner. The playgrounds are devoid of fun or fantasy and are incoherent. They follow the orientation of you and this other woman, your adviser on the subject, always very concerned with the sexual life of four-year-olds . . . a woman who could be a fine teacher, but has appallingly bad taste.

"The plan for the plants, aquaria, and cages that I saw in the Shed is poorly designed and simply bad."

Roberto recognized Lota's efforts and dedication to bring the park into being, but no more than that. The Aterro "was created by me and my office of experts, with the decisive support of Governor Carlos Lacerda and the worthy collaboration of the ex–work group over which you preside."

Worthy collaboration! Ex–work group! Naná felt mortified for Lota's sake.

The letter came at a very delicate moment, in the power vacuum caused by the indecision over the Foundation. Meticulously, the letter tried to demystify the positive image of the omnipresent Dona Lota, presenting in its place a despotic and pretentious Macedo Soares.

"It's a pity that things have come to this point, but I can't help but declare my profound disappointment at seeing the ruin of a project that represents my biggest contribution to this city.

"Let the Foundation come, but not with you at its head, which seems to be your great desire. Forgive me, Lota, but I detest your despotism."

Naná was floored. The unimaginable had happened. Someone, and worse, Burle Marx, had given voice to the hypothesis of the Foundation existing without Lota. Of all the hostility in the letter, perhaps this item was the most unpalatable for Lota. Spoons, Finnish kettles! It was unjust that Lota should be depicted in this way, as an unskilled person who stubbornly insisted on imposing her will indiscriminately, firing wildly into the air. Even if the accusation came from a genius of landscape design. Who, by the way, like Lota, did not have a university degree.

BURLE MARX'S CRITICISMS and letter from Mrs. Lota de Macedo Soares to O Globo:

"Dear Editor in chief:

"Using the right of reply that the law permits me, I ask that, in the face of the declarations made by Mr. Roberto Burle Marx in today's edition, October 10, 1965, of this prestigious newspaper, the following clarifications be published:

"Mr. Roberto Burle Marx never belonged to the Work Group for the Urbanization of the Aterro. He was nominated by me, accepted by the governor, and contracted by Sursan to create the gardens for Flamengo Park. This project of making the gardens has nothing to do with the other projects in the park. The diverse and extensive trips of Mr. Roberto Burle Marx during these last five years, to North America, Algeria, England, and Venezuela, naturally did not allow him to know of these projects.

"As far as the 'despotism' of the president of the work group goes, manifested, naturally, after the elections, this comes from the fact that when consulted by Sursan, at the beginning of this year, I opined in an official statement that they should look for other companies to furnish grass for the park, because Roberto Burle Marx Ltd. had proposed astronomical prices per square meter. This 'despotism' saved the state more than one hundred million cruzeiros, which naturally changed the opinion that Mr.

Roberto Burle Marx held of my temperament, so appreciated up until now."

Ismênia fetched the album. There were several clippings to paste, all of them, unhappily, involving the exchange of asperities between Burle Marx and Lota. As she pasted the clippings, Ismênia dated them in her tiny handwriting, in the upper right-hand corner. First the letter from Burle Marx. October 20, 1965. Then Lota's reply. October 21, 1965. Following that, Burle Marx's retort. October 23, 1965. Ismênia reread this last one.

Burle Marx said that Lota, unable to contradict the positive arguments in his letter, tried maliciously to place him in an unpleasant situation in the court of public opinion, as if he were motivated by personal or political interests. In the case of the grass, he alleged that there was no public bidding, so that there was no comparison made of the prices quoted. It would be difficult, therefore, to verify whether or not there were any savings in awarding the work to the firm that did it.

The letter went on to reaffirm that it was in the single and just intention of protecting his professional name that Burle Marx protested work done on the Aterro with which he disagreed.

How so "with which he disagreed," Ismênia asked herself. Was Roberto installing himself as the owner of the park? Did he think, then, that Reidy, Jorge, Ethel, all should subordinate themselves to him? It was true that the aesthetic unity of the park was provided by its gardens; otherwise, it wouldn't be a park. But it was also true that Burle Marx was one of the specialists working under Lota's supervision; it did not fall to him to lay claim to authorship of the Aterro. Lota was probably very annoyed. Even accusations that lack any foundation often corrode the heart.

NOTWITHSTANDING THAT the specific target of Burle Marx's attacks was the candidate for the president of the Foundation, the professionals involved in the projects on the Aterro thought themselves justified in replying, because they had been described by the landscape designer, in a generalization, as "mediocre and incompetent."

Ethel Bauzer Medeiros was "this other woman" accused by Burle Marx of being overly preoccupied by the sexual lives of four-year-olds. In an interview, Medeiros emphasized that making gardens was one thing and planning a park for children's and adolescents' recreation was another, for which it was not enough to have good taste; it was also necessary to have specialized information. As a word to the wise is sufficient, Ethel added that furthermore, no one ignored the fact that sexual problems deserve attention not only in infancy but also throughout life.

The architect Júlio Cesar Pessolani Zavala recalled that the "poorly designed and bad project" for raising plants was the development of a sketch drawn up in the office of Burle Marx himself. And that the wall used to protect the children who were on the playgrounds, "made use of in a vulgar and badly understood manner," was planned by Affonso Reidy, with Burle Marx's knowledge.

Even Governor Carlos Lacerda, although spared the landscape designer's bad temper, wrote Burle Marx to remind him that professional status does not exempt one from the necessity of displaying some decorum.

Lota didn't want to talk about the subject anymore.

ON OCTOBER 27, the military government instituted Law AI-2, in effect canceling direct election of the president. The next day Lacerda created the Foundation for Flamengo Park by decree. He named a council, and he named Lota as executive director. He left to his vice governor Rafael de Almeida Magalhães the business of placing them in power. He was not going to finish his mandate; he was leaving.

# GREAT EXPECTATIONS LEAD TO GREAT DECEPTIONS

❦

FROM HER HIGH WINDOW IN OURO PRETO, Bishop could see people and animals gathering to drink at the fountain.

> . . . *Women in red dresses*
>
> *and plastic sandals, carrying their almost*
> *invisible babies—muffled to the eyes*
> *in all the heat—unwrap them, lower them,*
>
> *and give them drinks of water lovingly*
> *from dirty hands, here where there used to be*
> *a fountain, here where all the world still stops.*

She felt able to write poetry again. And what was better, she liked what she wrote. She had finished a poem and sent it to *The New Yorker* in this same period, without finding that she had to carry it up and down to modify it here and there, as had happened with the odious poems she'd written in Rio.

The poem was dedicated to Lilli Correia de Araújo, at the beginning simply a commissioned hostess but now a generous friend. Lilli didn't mother her; on the contrary, she put on her glacial Scandinavian demeanor when Bishop brooded and went looking for easy happiness in the bar. When Bishop sobered up, Lilli, who was always sober, turned into a wonderful companion; the two of them laughed, talked about art, understood each other.

Perhaps because of the massive walls of Lilli's house, perhaps because of Lilli's calm voice, perhaps because of the blue of that sky; perhaps because of the fundamental reality of the mountains; perhaps because of the languid sensation conveyed to her by the town with its hills from another century to be climbed without hurrying; perhaps because of all of this at once, Bishop uncharacteristically gave in to an impulse. She bought a big eighteenth-century house that was falling to pieces.

Instantaneously, she became as excited as a child. She thrilled at the view, the avocado trees, the crooked walls made from mud and wattles, the design of the roof, the stone wall covered with moss. It didn't matter that the house was falling to pieces. Bishop was going to spend six months in the United States, and during this time Lilli would look after restoring it. After so much time in a daze, without knowing what to do with herself, Bishop made plans. She needed to plan to cover the expenses of the restoration. She had a future: she had a house in Ouro Preto.

Bishop had gone to Ouro Preto in August to stay for about two weeks, as always. They were already in November!

She missed Lota a great deal—the Lota of Samambaia. But the tranquility of Ouro Preto heightened Bishop's fear of going back to the Lota of Rio, and she postponed her return.

That day, when Bishop came back from a walk in the middle of the afternoon, her heart stopped. Lota's car was parked at the door.

"Lota!"

Bishop came running in.

"She just got here," said Lilli. "She's upstairs."

Bishop began to climb the stairs. Hearing her, Lota left her bedroom and began coming down. The two of them met on the landing and embraced.

"I came to get you."

Bishop nodded, and they went to the bedroom.


AT NIGHT THEY came down to have tea with Lilli. The painter Carlos Scliar was there. Lilli had transformed the basement of the Chico Rey Guest House into a studio for Scliar, who used the town as a theme for his work.

Scliar knew of Lota's troubles with Burle Marx and was qualified to understand them. He himself had gone head to head with the temperamental landscape designer, and the two of them had fought irremediably. Nevertheless, Lota didn't touch the subject.

Lota knew Scliar's political position. Scliar knew Lota's social position. Meanwhile, the meeting went very cordially. Lota admired the passion with which Scliar dedicated himself to art. Scliar saw this woman's determination, impatient at having to wait for a decade for people to begin to fathom what she was doing. Lilli followed the discussion between the two of them with satisfaction. She admired their intelligence.

*For Lota de Macedo Soares*
*. . . O dar-vos quanto tenho e quanto posso,*
*Que quanto mais vos pago, mais vos devo.*
—Camões

Lota went back to reading the opening page of Bishop's new book. She wasn't prepared for the straightforward dedication: "to give you as much as I have and as much as I can/The more I pay you, the more I owe you." Lately, talk between them had faltered, and at times Bishop's missing replies had become a litany of silences. This public declaration, without subterfuge, utterly disarmed Lota.

*Questions of Travel*. My little sailor . . .

For the first time in a long empty stretch, they were alone in Samambaia. They talked quietly on the sofa in the living room.

Bishop was amazed at what had happened in her absence. Lota had been laconic in Ouro Preto, but now she gave her a complete report. Everything had been turned upside down. Lacerda had lost the elections in Rio. After Law AI-2 had been instituted, he had gone from a promising leader of the nation to a political renegade. The fabled work group had been destroyed; Bertha and Jorge were no longer able to work with Lota—they had become incompatible. Burle Marx had undone a decades-long friendship in a bloody way. The Foundation had come about, finally, but in the worst way possible, because the decree had not been approved by the House. Now the funding of the Foundation would depend on the good will of the next governor.

What shit!

"Lota. Things are bad. Who knows, if you distanced yourself a little, if you came with me to Seattle . . ."

"Cookie, you know what? I'm going to wait for Negrão to take power. If I see that things aren't going to work out, I'll resign and leave this country with you. It's decided."

BISHOP'S RELIEF WAS FLEETING. On December 5, Negrão de Lima took power as governor of Guanabara and already by the 10th the Assembly had annulled Lacerda's decree that had instituted the Foundation. There was no Foundation.

The all-important members of the Assembly decided that Negrão would create an entity subject to the funding and governance of the state to take care of the park. It was time once and for all to finish with this endless whining that only the grand man Carlos Lacerda is capable of doing things; we're going to show that we can do much more for the park than what he did, proclaimed Minister Levy Neves.

Lota was angry.

The frenetic goings-on began again, this time around the legal counselors. Opinions diverged. On one hand, Lota fastened onto the thesis that the annulment of a decree from the chief executive by the legislature was an invasion, a violation of provenance. Going against the counsel of friends that she spare herself new grief, Lota sought an injunction. She called the press and said that this squabbling was minuscule in the face of the importance of the park, already internationally recognized. She showed them the most recent issue of *Time* in which Santa Claus appeared, descending by helicopter, for a crowd of one hundred thousand people in Flamengo Park. She told the press that the Foundation was a reality.

On December 13, 1965, the Foundation was given provisional status. During that entire day and night, a pilgrimage of people came to show their enthusiastic support for a radiant Lota. Bishop could barely hide her consternation.

FOR BISHOP THE SITUATION was very clear. Clear and desperate. Lota would never be able to live again without a state of war.

Bishop had hoped for a change. On Lota's last birthday she'd given her the book *Gardening* by Gertrude Jekyll. Bishop saw that Lota and Jekyll had a lot in common: a refined aesthetic sense, a profound knowledge of botany, an inflamed temperament. Jekyll was an example of someone whose late-in-life devotion to a specialty had turned out right. Jekyll published her first book at fifty-six and with such success that she wrote innumerable others and participated in the planning of hundreds of gardens. Bishop thought that in this way she could encourage Lota to seek other opportunities for herself out of the Aterro.

How foolish. Lota didn't pay any attention at all. Maybe at heart Lota liked this whole massacre.

That night, during the scant half hour that they saw each other at dinner, Lota lost control. Again she'd come home exhausted, wanting nothing more than a little peace, and found Bishop in a deplorable state. Lota went to the bathroom and got the box of Antabuse. It was almost full. Elizabeth wasn't taking the medication that could keep her away from drinking! Lota came back to the living room with a pill in her hand.

"Take this!"

Bishop refused.

"Take it!"

Lota grabbed Bishop's face in anger and forced her to swallow.

EVER SINCE BISHOP had announced her appointment as a professor in Seattle, Lota had proceeded systematically to discourage her. First she argued that Bishop had no vocation for teaching, which required that people speak easily in public. Then, because Bishop was in fact drinking heavily, she fixed on the issue of alcoholism. Now she submitted Bishop to a hideous caricature. She took the briefcase that Bishop had bought, made of authentic Brazilian alligator skin, and acted out a perverse little scene.

Miss Bishop directed herself, staggering, toward the table. She held her beautiful new briefcase to her chest. She tripped over the dais, letting the beautiful new briefcase fall. Badly closed, the briefcase fell open, spilling the papers on the floor. Miss Bishop got down on her knees and began to gather them with trembling hands. Hobbling, Miss Bishop succeeded in getting up and putting herself behind the table.

"Mumbo jumbo," she mumbled, always holding on to her dear briefcase.

Bishop hated Lota for this.

"Stop that!" Bishop tried to grab the briefcase from Lota.

"Mumbo jumbo!"

"Stop! Stop!"

"You stop! Can't you see that this is just what it's going to be like—your triumphant entry into the classroom?"

"Give me back my briefcase."

"Elizabeth, don't go. You will regret it bitterly if you go."

"Give me the briefcase."

"Take it! Shit!" Lota threw the briefcase into Bishop's hands. "Elizabeth, think a little."

"You're hurting me too much, Lota."

"Don't go," Lota pleaded.

"Why won't you come with me?" Bishop pleaded.

"What the hell, I've already explained millions of times that at this exact moment I can't leave. I've got a suit in court; I'm waiting for the result! You're the one who can cancel your commitment, because you still haven't started anything. Is it possible that you can't get out of your little world and see what's happening with me? Just *once?*"

"How about if you have a look at what's happening to *me?*"

The rancor made them raise their voices and lash out at each other with italicized words. Joana came into the living room.

"Listen here, what's all this yelling?" She spoke with the authority of the longtime servant.

"Don't butt in, Joana."

"I will butt in, my lady. I want to know what's going on here."

"Joana!" Lota ground her teeth. "Dona Elizabeth and I are talking, that's all."

"Then I'm going to call Dona Mary, to translate what you're saying for me."

"Joana, *please.*"

Joana gave in and went back to the kitchen. Her intervention, however, changed the soul of the dispute. The two of them stayed parked in the same places, Lota with one hand on her hip, Bishop holding the preposterous briefcase. Bishop began to head toward the bedroom.

"Elizabeth."

Bishop looked at Lota. Her gaze was very sad. Lota's gaze was very sad as well.

"What?"

"Think better."

Bishop gave an unconvincing nod. If there had been other words, perhaps she would have thought better. Lota didn't have the right words.

BISHOP TOOK THE PLANE to Seattle on December 27. The farewell was awful.

Lota was impassive. She kept her hands tightly closed over crossed arms and looked at the floor in a dark silence.

Bishop felt herself breaking down. She wanted Lota to understand how it was hard to separate; she was leaving full of fear and doubt.

The first call for the flight was made. Bishop thought it useless to prolong the suffering.

"I'm going."

Lota made a gesture of disagreement.

"Lota, who knows if soon you won't be going too. I'll be waiting for you."

Lota opened her arms and hugged her with the desperate hug of departures.

"Have a good trip, dear. Call as soon as you arrive."

During the whole trip, which was very tiring and full of stops, Bishop brooded over her despair at going away. All her insecurities emerged, and she got ready for an asthma attack. At the Seattle airport, while she waited for her bags on the carousel, she felt an acute moment of regret. Only by a hair did she avoid going directly to the counter to buy a return ticket for that same day. She reminded herself, however, of the arguments she'd given herself while she was packing: she needed to leave Rio. She needed to get involved in something. She needed to make money to pay for the restoration of the house in Ouro Preto.

When she closed the door to her hotel room, Bishop sat down and cried like Saint Peter. She felt remorse at having abandoned Lota at such a pressing moment. She felt angry at not having known how to resolve the situation in a less lacerating way. She felt sorry for herself. After so many years, she was back in a hotel room, completely alone. Soon the rooster's crowing would surprise her as at so many other times in the past—a little girl crying at dawn.

# A BOLT FROM CAMÕES

BISHOP'S SOLITUDE in the hotel room was absurd. She was terrified at the idea of teaching classes. You will regret this, Lota had said. She was right. What was she doing there? Nothing was worse than the solitude of that room.

The days dragged themselves by, null.

On New Year's Eve, a reception was organized for Bishop. She didn't want to go. She wouldn't be able to drink or she'd already be starting her new career disastrously. She knew absolutely no one. It would be torture.

On top of everything, New Year's intensified her missing Lota. For fourteen successive years she had spent the turn of the year with her companion. Dressed in white, they walked barefoot through the fine sand of Cabo Frio, making plans for the upcoming year. Lota's absence threw everything off course, made the recent past seem remote, the new year bitter. Bishop was dying of loneliness. She didn't have anything to celebrate.

At the last moment, however, absolutely incapable of coming up with an excuse, she put on the black dress that she'd ordered from Esmeralda, put on high heels, put on the mask of the respectable Miss Bishop, and went.

From the first minute she received uninterrupted reverence. Ungracious men and arrogant women took turns submitting her to tedious shows of erudition. These people didn't have the least idea of who she was, thought Bishop bitterly. They accepted her imposture as a respectable lady with relief.

"Should we have stayed at home and thought of here?"

Bishop turned, surprised. A young woman with an irreverent smile was at her side.

"Questions of Travel," explained the young woman. "I also read your book. Only I know more about it than anyone in this room."

"Hm. More than I, without doubt?"

"*With* doubt." The young woman widened her smile. It was a generous smile. Bishop liked it. "But not one that can't be clarified," proceeded the saucy thing.

She must have been just over twenty, the age of Bishop's prospective students. She fixed her lovely eyes on Bishop. Bishop felt a chill at imagining a dozen of those facing her in the classroom.

"For example, the quotation from Camões," resumed the young woman, pronouncing the name of the poet laureate with a horrible accent. However, the hostess approached them and, with a quick nod at Miss Knowitall and an enchanting smile for Bishop, drew the professor away to meet another colleague.

The rest of the night was the same kind of harangue, ornamented with much bowing and scraping. Bishop was exhausted. She wanted to take off her shoes. She wanted to be at peace with her bottle of gin. Would it be impolite to ask for a lift already?

Finally Bishop found herself walking toward the door.

"Happy New Year, see you soon!" she said, wanting never to see these people again.

She found the lovely pair of eyes.

"Good night, Miss Bishop."

"Good night, . . . ?" She didn't know the young woman's name.

"Adrienne. Adrienne Collins."

A sweet name, unexpected.

"Good night, Adrienne."

Back in her hotel room, Bishop pulled off her coat, dress, shoes, and mask. She threw herself on the bed and opened the bottle.

THE FIRST LETTER that Lota wrote in 1966 was to Roberto Marinho. Carlos Swann had included in his column in *O Globo* the note:

### The Reason

*Many have asked themselves and to this day have not been able to explain the reason for the attachment of D. Lota de Macedo Soares to the Aterro Foundation. To some it seems, as well, that this lady works without remuneration. In truth, about two years ago Lota was hired by Sursan with earnings equivalent to eight minimum-wage salaries per month. During this period, she made four trips to Europe at Sursan's expense, one of them lasting for four months, all of them with per diems paid in dollars. It's very understandable, then, that Dona Lota demon-*

*strates so much tenacity and so much energy when the subject of the Aterro is involved.*

SHE STILL HADN'T been able to pull herself together after the attacks of her ex-friend Burle Marx. She was still laboring under the impact of the contingency of having to administer the Foundation while it only had provisional status. And now she had to defend herself against the accusation of wasting public money?

Lota felt like Giordano Bruno: But, for being a designer in the field of nature, for being concerned about the nourishment of the soul, interested in the culture of the spirit, and dedicated to the activities of the intellect, the ones I have aimed at threaten me, the vigilant ones assault me, the wounded ones bite me, the unmasked ones devour me. And it's not just one. They are not few, they are many; they are almost everyone.

Making use of the Law of the Press, which guaranteed her the right to reply, Lota complained and got her refutation published:

"I didn't go to Europe four times. *I went once on the job.*

"I went in November 1962 to New York for forty days, to review the page proofs of the book that E. Bishop wrote on Brazil. Sursan did not pay for anything, and I was not on salary at that time.

"I was in bed fifteen days with typhoid that I picked up on the Aterro. Those were the holidays that I took during 5 years: two work trips and fifteen days in bed. . . .

"I worked nearly three years without remuneration, or better. . . . I paid to work. I began to receive in August 1963 the *extravagant* quantity of one hundred and fifty-eight thousand a month. Today, with the normal discounts, I get four hundred and sixty-three thousand, five hundred. I had and continue to have the greatest financial liability with this 'tenacity' for the work in the park. I abandoned my house and my business affairs in Samambaia and I stopped getting rent on my apt. on Atlantic Ave. when I began to use it to stay in Rio. More important than any sacrifice was to leave the peaceful and independent life I'd already chosen for thirteen years—and to which I am anxious to return.

"I only reply to this note because as executive director of the Flamengo Park Foundation I feel obliged to give the public satisfaction, and to defend the ex-governor Carlos Lacerda against the lie implicit in the note, which is that he spent public money to benefit his own friends."

NANÁ, LIKE LOTA'S other friends, was concerned at seeing these sorts of constant disparaging comments in the newspapers. It was inconceivable that, at that point in her life, Lota would have to waste her breath to protect her reputation. For the first time Naná saw Lota make an inventory of what she had lost with the Aterro. To all of that should be added, without doubt, the drawing away of Bishop. Could it be that Lota was signaling to Bishop the recognition that she wanted to resume the tranquil life of Samambaia? Naná took Lota's declaration as an indication that her friend was fed up with objections and aggression and inclined to end her public life.

LOTA TRAVELED TO Brasília on January 8, with Rachel de Queiroz, a childhood friend of President Castelo Branco. Queiroz was able to get Lota a meeting with him, despite the hostile relations between the military government and the Lacerdists. On the way, she talked to Rachel.

"You know, Rachel, I am sure that the president is going to give us the support we need." Lota was totally wound up. "I brought the numbers, he's going to be impressed. Just think—in the past year the minitrain carried nearly 450,000 people, aside from the 38,000 poor children who rode for free. Along with the people who came to the beach and the gardens, more than one million people visited the park. That's a hell of a number, we have to agree."

"And what exactly do you hope that the president is going to do?"

"Simply, I want him to admonish Negrão, so that he sends a message to the Assembly asking for the creation of a law that bestows resources on the Foundation. Negrão could indicate, for example, that 2 percent of what Sursan collects goes to the Foundation. With this, all our problems would be over."

"But is it that simple?"

"Actually it is, because there's already a precedent. One percent of what Sursan collects goes to the metro. It would be a precisely equivalent mechanism."

Rachel admired Lota, seeing how prepared she was for the interview. Her request for institutional support was substantiated by precise facts. However, it was also a precise fact that the current wasn't running in the direction of the Lacerdists. Rachel hoped that Lota's luminosity would penetrate the dark attics of politics.

NOW THERE WAS NO further doubt. Lota had been absolutely right. Bishop didn't have the least aptitude for teaching. At the end of the first week she was certain she would have made a better choice if she had gone and raised pigs in the Himalayas. The students were futile and conceited. They had no poetic sensibility. Above all, they had no manners. The tone in which they spoke to her was exasperating. They said that her white streak was coo-ol, or they pontificated fatuously on Bishop's own poetry. The classes were too long. Bishop didn't have anything to say, so she proposed themes to be versified. At night, in the hotel, she regretted all this to her very soul. She had this pile of work to "correct," and, heavens, how to correct it? Bishop cursed herself. However, since Lota insisted on remaining cold and disinterested on the telephone, Bishop did not admit to her that she was having a terrible time.

JOÃO AUGUSTO MAIA PENIDO, secretary of works, finished reading Lota's letter. The lady underestimated him, without a doubt, thinking she could succeed in snaring him with idle talk and obsequiousness. Maia Penido had been the vice chief of Juscelino Kubitschek's civil cabinet, and he judged himself well prepared to perceive snake-like attitudes. "Come and see the shed in the garden, learn about the projects that Your Honor will bring to life." All that rigmarole about a small group of altruists working so that he, Maia Penido, could shine, was bullshit. In truth, Dona Lota was trying to escape the imbroglio that was her invention: the Foundation. Dona Lota spoke of "entailment" and "intimate collaboration" between the Foundation, as planner, and Sursan, as executor. But what she was proposing was an odd relationship, in which the secretary of works would be subordinate to an autonomous foundation, the Flamengo Park Foundation, which would decide which works were to be executed. Only in the head of Dona Lota de Macedo Soares could this idea have been hatched.

Dona Lota was spoiled. She'd received as a gift a position of trust, which she didn't have to reach by climbing, in the same way that her surname assured her of a social position for which she hadn't had to fight. She had always been disdainful of the experts at Sursan. Now that she'd lost Lacerda as a rearguard, she drew near, hoping to entice him.

Right, Dona Lota. It's like Ibrahim Sued says, in society everything is known. I know that your ladyship went around trying to turn Castelo Branco against me. Be careful. Your Foundation doesn't have a nickel. All the technical equipment and workers are on Sursan's payroll. I can easily, in a routine act, reallocate everyone and instantly empty out your ridiculous Foundation. And then all that easy-as-pie stuff is over.

THAT SAME DAY, Bishop was leaving the classroom building, awkwardly carrying the crocodile briefcase, two books full of page markers, and two thick envelopes full of student exercises, which she hadn't been able to fit in the cursed briefcase.

"Hi!"

"Hi," Bishop replied, bending her legs, throwing her hips backward, and waving her hands like a baton twirler.

To no avail. Bing, bang—the two books fell wide open, and the pieces of paper that had served as bookmarks were scattered all over the floor. What a disaster. She'd have to find all the pages again.

Adrienne collected the papers and the books and put them under her left arm with natural ease. Bishop was about to excuse herself and thank her, but Adrienne had already offered:

"Let me take your briefcase."

She took the briefcase gently.

"Where are we going?"

The question rolled around in Bishop's head. Where are we going?

"Where are you living?" insisted Adrienne.

Ah, yes. Bishop gave the name of the hotel. They started to walk.

"Do you prefer to live in a hotel?"

Bishop said that on the contrary, she hated it. But the houses that they had arranged for her were far from the university and she didn't have a car.

"Ah, I see. Even so it's a good ways to walk in this cold."

It was, Bishop thought, seeing that it was cold.

They walked a while in silence.

"Listen, how about a hot chocolate?"

Bishop had thought of going to her room and drinking a can of Metrecal, but when she came to she was sitting in front of Adrienne in a peaceful place, drinking a tasty hot chocolate, while the young woman spread circles of thick syrup on top of a pancake.

Adrienne was very bright and loquacious. She was twenty-six, married, and at the moment unemployed. She had a way of looking persistently at Bishop that disconcerted her. Bishop, however, tried not to show it.

As they said good-bye, Adrienne offered herself to ease Bishop's life as far as possible, since she knew Seattle like the back of her hand. Bishop said many thanks and went up. Coming into her room, she didn't go running for a drink. She had the good taste of chocolate in her mouth.

LOTA'S FIRST AUDIENCE with Negrão wasn't to speak about Flamengo Park but about Lage Park. Lota and Rodrigo Melo Franco de Andrade went with Lina

Bo Bardi to protest the government's leasing of rooms in the Lage mansion to three different entities. For Pete's sake, Lage Park had also been turned into a foundation, of which Lina was the executive director, and Lota considered Negrão's intervention an act of contempt.

It happened that Secretary Maia Penido was present at the meeting. After a while, Lota and the secretary began to disagree over Lota's premise that it wasn't the prerogative of the governor to choose his auxiliaries. Soon Lota began to yell at Maia Penido that he was harassing her and to demand that the governor go to the park to verify the truth of her accusations. Maia Penido began to yell too. This created tremendous unease among the others. Negrão had to use all his diplomatic skills to placate the antagonists. The issue of Lage Park was put off. In compensation, Lota left with a date scheduled for the governor's visit to the Aterro.

The quarrel between Lota and Maia Penido made the headlines in all the papers. The secretary gave several interviews, saying that Lota had become annoyed because three water tankers had been taken from the Aterro. The secretary explained that, because he thought that people were more important than grass, he'd taken the tankers to attend to the hospitals that had been damaged by the big flood in January. Maia Penido took the opportunity to declare that the Foundation was illegal and that it wouldn't survive without Sursan. As far as the story about Lota yelling at him was concerned, Maia Penido denied it energetically, saying that this could never happen, because Lota was his subordinate.

LONG-DISTANCE CALLS were frustrating. The connection was usually terrible, with both participants spending a large part of their time with eh? and what?, each wanting what she didn't hear to be what she wanted to hear.

But each time Lota began to speak, again she stampeded into talking about the Foundation. Bishop, hurt, began to relate her pedagogical clumsiness:

"And how is it possible that they've never read Herbert or Donne or Blake? . . . whereas I've never seen so many haiku in my life . . . hai-ku . . . *hai-ku!*"

After they hung up, the dejection.

Alone in her moldy room, Bishop watched the snow fall outside. She talked to herself. Lota, Lota, what will become of us? She opened the bottle of bourbon and drank to missing her.

Lota looked around the room. On the side table, the book Bishop had dedicated to her. *Questions of Travel.* Joana came closer, worried. What's the matter, Dona Lota? Where was that crazy Dona Elizabetchy, my Lord. Joana took Dona Lota to her bedroom, stayed there sitting in the dark, in silence, until she went to sleep. Dona Lota could only sleep by taking medicine.

ALL THE NEWSPAPERS were invited to cover Negrão's visit to the Aterro. Dona Lota made a point of having journalists accompany the inspection. This way everything that she showed the governor would be documented. After a certain amount of commotion, the governor, his retinue, executive director, photographers, and reporters finally were settled into the mini-train. Oh, the vicissitudes of things! In the middle of the trip the popular vehicle had a fit and wouldn't move! Everybody off! Annoyed, Dona Lota guaranteed that the minitrain, which had already carried hundreds of thousands of people the previous year, had never broken down. It's Negrão who's bad luck, the reporters teased. Negrão, who knew that crew very well, remained as serene as a lord despite his hostess's corrosive scowl. Finally the mechanic tinkered successfully and they proceeded, even if at slow speed ahead.

"It doesn't matter, this way you'll see better."

As the minitrain crept around the park, Dona Lota pointed out the effects of the new secretaries' perfidies. The governor was uncomfortable with the sun beating full on his face, but he made his hand into a visor over his eyes and looked. Garbage and debris, weeds growing in the grass, dead trees, paralyzed work. At each calamity Negrão pulled a scandalized face and promised immediate remedial measures. He listened like a gentleman to Lota's unfamiliar ideas on debureaucratization and subcontracting, and asked that she send him a complete report on everything. They said good-bye cordially.

Lota became excited at the prospects. She thought she had the two highest authorities on her side, the president of the republic and the governor of the state. Still missing, however, was the larger force: the people. She needed to bring the population back to the park. She needed to do something big, a happening.

One afternoon, Lota went with Magu to inspect the saplings. Magu was worried about the Malayan *Bombax malabrium* and the Mexican *Pseudobombax ellipticum*. When they got back to the Shed, Lota had an inspiration.

"Magu! But of course! Of course! The pickup soccer fields! Mother of a whore, the soccer fields! Let's go, Magu!"

And there they went, Magu trotting behind Lota's eureka. Getting to the Shed, Lota exploded:

"Fernanda, connect me right away with Mário Filho, of the *Jornal dos Esportes!*"

ADRIENNE BEGAN TO WAIT for Bishop regularly after classes. This strayed from Bishop's rigid code of discretion, but Bishop gave in because Adrienne's solicitude and energy were very welcome to her spirit at that time of day. The routine began to include a cup of tea in Bishop's room.

That afternoon, Adrienne greeted her with an even more assertive smile.

"You have a new home."

"How so?"

Adrienne took her to an apartment nearby the university. It was only a bedroom–living room with bathroom and kitchen, but Bishop adored it. It was the right size for someone who did not want to spend a stretch of time in a hotel room.

"It's reserved for you."

"It's perfect, but . . ."

"But nothing. I've already arranged things with the group. Each is going to bring some old thing from home to furnish it. You can leave it to me; I'll take care of everything."

Bishop didn't have to do a thing to help. Adrienne took care of the lease and on the day of the move sent Bishop far away, so that people could swear at will. When she triumphantly entered the new apartment, Bishop found a bed, sofa, pots and pans, even paintings. Adrienne had involved some of Bishop's students in the move and there they were, smiling and proud, lined up for Bishop's inspection. Bishop hated herself for once having thought ill of these loves and shook each one's hand with sincere thanks.

Later, on her first night in her new home, Bishop began to feel happy again, even if only a little. It was much better than feeling very unhappy, as she had been feeling recently. She looked over the disparate furniture, the dubious taste. It was a restrained ambience; there were no chairs made to size, nor any stylish lines. But it was hers. And put together, besides, with generosity and devotion. Bishop had never been revered in Brazil. It was marvelous to receive a warm welcome from her American students, even if she were a, hm, beginning professor.

So many nights in Rio had been an Antarctic for her. Now, she felt sheltered in Seattle in midwinter. The memory of Adrienne's vivid eyes warmed her. Sweet and unexpected Adrienne. She remembered Camões's quatrain:

Venceu-me o Amor, não o nego;
Tem mais força que eu assaz;
Que, como é cego e rapaz,
Dá me porrada de cego.

Love has won, most unkindly;
Resisting him would be frivolous.
For as he's blind and ravenous,
Love keeps striking me blindly.

# URBAN CLEANING

DONA LOTA was always punctual. But lately she'd begun arriving ahead of time, so it had been arranged that as soon as she arrived at the gate, Fernanda would ring the bell to alert the group. Whoever was outside in the fresh air discussing soccer came running in and sat down at the drawing board. Dona Lota always arrived in a good mood, said hello to everyone, and went to her table, in the bigger room, which was also where the table for meetings was. On her table there always stood a delicate crystal vase with a fresh rose bud.

The group knew that Dona Lota was under great pressure. The visit of Governor Negrão de Lima in February had not changed the dismal condition of the park at all. The secretaries maintained their general boycott, and there were even some acts of apparent harassment. Trucks from the state threw some rubbish into the park from a mudslide that had come down on Santo Amaro Street, and a buried person's arm emerged, pointing gruesomely skyward. Urban Cleaning started to systematically spread debris on the area already cleared. The press began to call the Aterro the New Garbage Dump.

Meanwhile, Dona Lota didn't let up at all. On the contrary, she kept herself surprisingly active. She maintained contacts with the *Jornal dos Esportes* to put on a pickup soccer tournament. She scheduled the opening date for the puppet theater. She checked Fernanda's arrangements for the cocktail party to launch the sailing center. And she still attended to the reporters who came to ask whether the appearance of a shed signaled the beginning of an Aterro slum, or whether she knew that Cariocans found that the lampposts on the Aterro didn't light up very much at all, so that they deserved the nickname of Belo Antonio, Lovely Anthony, from the film starring Marcello Mastroiani—big, but falling short. Who wouldn't get irritated?

But on that morning, March 10, 1966, Dona Lota, modest as a nun, met a reporter from the "Rio from Neighborhood to Neighborhood" section of *O Globo*. Dona Lota wanted the residents of Flamengo at the forefront of her battalion of allies, since, as neighbors of the park, they would be the ones most immediately interested in its preservation. Dona Lota's strategy was to emphasize the good will of the governor, attributing the abandonment of the park to a few secretaries and the Legislative Assembly. It would amaze readers that since Maia Penido had taken away the water tankers, the park had gone twenty-eight days without irrigation. Sixty percent of the grass had dried up, and hundreds of rare and expensive trees had died, including fifteen melaleucas acquired in Lorena, São Paulo. Acts of vandalism and an invasion of homeless people had resulted from the total lack of vigilance. Because of the director of urban cleaning's lunacy, garbage was accumulating all over the park. It was already time enough to stop with this craziness, declared Dona Lota, urging the residents of Flamengo to support recognition of the Foundation.

Dona Lota was satisfied with the interview. Except that, instead of "melaleucas," the press printed "melaloucas"—or, "crazy" mela, a misprint that made her accusations seem hilarious, as if trees from the sapotaceous family were called saponaceous. Who wouldn't get irritated?

"GOVERNOR, SIT DOWN right there, Governor!" ordered Dona Lota, as in old times, pulling Dr. Negrão by the arm. The man had come late and still spent time saying hello to this one and that one, leaving the admiral standing there in front, waiting for him to settle down.

Then Admiral Saldanha da Gama could make his speech, praising the idea of the creation of a sailing school. Finally attention was being paid to the sea, he exclaimed, after centuries of metropolitan civilization. The admiral himself explained the project, which was going to cost a billion cruzeiros. He was loudly applauded.

Dr. Negrão also made a short speech, remembering that it was he who began the Aterro, during his mandate as mayor of the federal district. Days before, Secretary Maia Penido, in an interview, had remembered that the Aterro had been *his* idea, when he was president of Sursan.

Aside from having taken up a section in all the major newspapers, the cocktail party had another immediate effect. With her usual eloquence, Dona Lota left the whole navy indignant at the negligence with which the state government had been treating the park. The Aterro had been turned into a place for beggars and vagabonds. And wasn't it a scandal that they took baths in the pond for model ships? Everyone noticed that during the party, various military authorities talked somberly with Negrão.

The next day, eighty policemen from the Brazilian air force, with guard dogs—including Tanucha, who guarded the presidential plane—swooped down on the Aterro. Fifty people were arrested.

Dona Lota felt it was time to write the admiral. She reminded him that the Foundation needed to be recognized and receive the funding to which it was entitled. It was essential that measures be taken to win this war as soon as possible. She indicated explicitly that it was up to the admiral and the other directors of the Naval Club to ask for an audience with the president of the republic and explain the project to him, so that he in turn could order the governor into action.

Something went wrong. It looked like the admiral was for sailboats, not wars. The fact is that the sailing center, which in the admiral's speech was going to be the maracanã of sailing, meaning the largest in the world, disappeared completely from the news.

SLOWLY AND GENTLY, Adrienne began to enter Bishop's life. She shopped for her at the supermarket. She typed up her lesson plans. She went to the bank.

That afternoon, in Bishop's apartment, they were sitting at the table after a meal. Bishop had made chicken fried in corn meal, one of her dishes that Brazilians adored. They'd had some red wine. Adrienne fixed Bishop with one of those long looks. Bishop dissembled, tapping the cork mechanically on the table. Adrienne cut the silence abruptly.

"I'm in love."

Oh-oh.

"Is that so?" Bishop kept tapping the table with the cork.

Adrienne held the hand with the cork, interrupting the motion.

"You *know* it's so."

"Adrienne,"

Bishop created a pause, but didn't add anything.

"I want you."

A fine blade grazed the skin. A spark ran crazily through her body.

"Look—." Bishop wanted to tell her that she was just passing through, that she wasn't available, but, dizzy, said only, "I'm a very complicated person."

"My specialty!"

Impudence had always fascinated Bishop. Still, she tried:

"But . . ."

"But, nothing."

Adrienne didn't pay attention to buts. She got up and came close. Bishop knew what would follow. She let it.

AND THE DAY that the swings and seesaws showed up on the playground at Widow's Hill?

Dona Lota jumped out of her Interlagos (she had bought a new expensive sports car). She was like a loaded gun.

"Let's get these rattletraps out of there, and I mean *now!*"

Dona Lota sent the mothers and children home and didn't move a foot until all of the playground equipment had been taken down. There were some protests. A lot of people gathered to watch. Reporters came.

Dona Lota wasn't interested in knowing who was or was not the author of the deed. She replied to a reporter that this was a stupid idea from an ignorant mind. To put seesaws, etc., between roadways, without the least protection, in a place where major accidents had already happened, could only be the work of a lunatic. The work group had planned two playgrounds surrounded by stone walls, with gates, teachers, and guards. The toys would be put in these playgrounds. If the parents of Widow's Hill wanted toys, they should demand that the governor get on with the work on the Aterro.

She finished with the inevitable "besides which":

"Besides which, Flamengo Park is a Foundation. Its location has been declared a national heritage site. Nothing can be put here without the express permission of the Foundation."

The uproar had begun. The ignorant lunatic who had ordered the playground equipment installed was the director of parks and gardens, supposedly on the order of the governor, supposedly in response to the request of the residents of Widow's Hill. None of that made Dona Lota ease up. She was very firm when she was right. And she was always right.

A few days later, the governor confirmed that he was receiving innumerable letters and telegrams complaining about the removal of the playground equipment. Dona Lota retorted immediately. Those letters and telegrams were fabricated. There were bound to be many more complaints about the lack of seats on the swings, the filth of the toy city, the generally bad conditions of the whole park. She took the opportunity to reveal that 617 clubs, totaling approximately nine thousand players, had entered the pickup soccer tournament.

BISHOP APPRECIATED PUNCTUALITY, and Adrienne was punctual. That's why Bishop found her lateness that afternoon odd. The wind blew flakes of snow against the facade of the building where Bishop was standing. The students, she thought, greeted her with an insolent look. She was already getting ready to go when Adrienne arrived, out of breath. They dragged Bishop's bad mood with them all the way to the apartment. After warming up and having a cup of tea, Bishop demanded:

"What's up?"

Adrienne answered with her usual spontaneity. She was pregnant.

JOANA DIDN'T KNOW what to do anymore. From the minute that Lota opened the door, it was just one long sadness. She'd sit down, mute, in her favorite armchair, her eyes shut.

"Would the lady like a little something to eat?"

"Would the lady like a little tea?"

"Would you like me to get a little bath ready?"

Nothing helped. She was waiting for the phone call. Which also wouldn't help anything, because generally the connection was terrible and she'd be yelling things in English that Joana could well guess at.

The sadness seemed to get worse afterward. Joana tried everything. She told her what was on the radio; she sang. She even danced.

Sometimes that American came, a very nice man, Echebrow. From who knows where, Lota would find a normal face and would simply look a little tired. The two would have dinner. There would be a certain formality to it, and then they would talk. But only a little. Soon she'd excuse herself: she had to get up early the next day.

Then it depended. There were nights when she'd stay up reading in the living room. Joana would watch television in the maid's room. Every little while Joana would come in to see how she was. She took medicine to get to sleep; many times she slept in the armchair. Joana would come and carry her to the bedroom. Other times, she'd go right to bed. Joana would carry in a little bench and sit down beside the bed.

"My Joanica, they want to destroy what I made. I'm in a war."

"Sleep, Dona Lota, sleep."

BISHOP NOTICED THAT every time she mentioned the University of Washington, Lota became sour. Lota thought that Bishop was playing at teaching. She didn't have the patience to hear long-distance accounts of Bishop's tiny victories over her insecurities. Perhaps because she couldn't admit the possibility of Bishop surviving a single day without her, Lota brooded over Bishop deceiving her. Clearly Bishop could only be spending her days drunk, incapable of getting out of bed to go to the university. That story about spending her nights reading students' haiku was a tall tale.

Lota's hostility turned Adrienne's company into something more and more revitalizing. Adrienne was rapturous, a quality that Bishop had been missing a lot, since for a long time the only raptures that Lota had felt were for the Aterro. Adrienne showed herself to be enchanted with Bishop and showed it with ardor. Sometimes Bishop would open a book in the middle of a class and find a note full of little messages. At other times, Adrienne would go to the far side of Seattle to find an ingredient that Bishop wanted for her cooking adventures. Bishop admitted that she needed this reaffirmation of her capacity to interest another person.

After the first minute of displeasure, Adrienne's pregnancy never interfered with the relationship. When it became visible, it acquired another function: it threw people off the track.

LOTA'S LETTER THREW everything into disarray. Dropping the tone she adopted on the telephone, Lota wrote a letter with her defenses stripped. For the first time, after so many years, they were going to spend their birthdays apart. It was like an amputation. In the letter, neither the partners nor Lota's adversaries in the Flamengo epic intervened. The letter was only about Elizabeth and Lota. It recalled savory details of living together, spoke of their house as our house, proposed a renewal of vows. Fatefully, the letter took longer than usual to arrive. It had been written for the occasion of Bishop's birthday, at the beginning of February, and it was already March, almost time for Lota's birthday.

When she finished reading, Bishop met Adrienne's celebrated pair of eyes; she was installed in an armchair in front of her. What an imbroglio, my God. Bishop felt doubly guilty. She was an idiot; she did everything wrong. Because she couldn't succeed in simply evaporating, disappearing, she asked Adrienne to go. She wanted to be alone.

At five in the morning of the following day, she called a taxi and went to the hospital. She thought she was having a heart attack. She was in the hospital for a week. The doctors said it was the Asian flu. Adrienne took care of her.

Bishop needed to absolve herself. She wrote a desperate letter to Dr. Baumann, wanting to schedule an appointment in New York, but in the letter, she explained that she had lived five years in hell; that it was more and more difficult to live with Lota; that she had let Lota order her around for years and suddenly couldn't stand it any longer; that, because she didn't know how to protest, she kept swallowing and accumulating resentments. She was deteriorating day by day. She thought she needed to distance herself a bit, and really it had been a good idea. Nobody in Seattle could compare with Lota, but they treated her much better. She hadn't known such tenderness in a long time.

# N° TIME F°R L°GIC

LΟΤΑ WAS CΟNVINCED that the sabotage was orchestrated by Maia Penido, against whom the president of the republic hadn't lifted a finger. The park survived haphazardly. One day Magu discovered that the sprinklers had been stolen, without doubt to be sold as junk iron. In fact, all of the manhole covers had already been stolen for junk iron. Another day, it was Shell that plastered all its gas stations alongside the park with fripperies and trinkets, which had been strictly prohibited in the contract. Actually, Shell had caused one of Lota's biggest frustrations. The company had won the bid to develop the stations alongside the Aterro because it had committed itself to installing and maintaining a little traffic school in the park. Lota thought that education about traffic was essential for children. But now Shell alleged that it couldn't pass on the money to a foundation that was being contested. Let it be decided to whom the Aterro belonged, and then, yes, investments would come from Shell.

Even though she faced hostility on all flanks, Lota refused to retreat. On the contrary, she decided on new attacks.

First she wrote a formal letter to President Castelo Branco, explaining that war had now been declared. On one side the Foundation, which wanted to assure the suffering people of relief in their daily struggle, and on the other the government of the state of Guanabara, captained by Dr. Maia Penido, which wanted to make a pork barrel project out of the park and a mine for private swindles. Let Marshal Castelo Branco practice his heroic politics in Rio as well.

Next, it was Dr. Alcino Salazar. Faced with the slowness of the judiciary in establishing the legitimacy of the Foundation, Lota saw that the government of Guanabara was going to dismantle everything before the Supreme Court showed up. Imperious, she wrote to her friend:

"Winning in Justice is a slow process and doesn't depend on one word from President Castelo Branco, as in the case of the message to the Assembly. The logical thing would be to win first and ask for the message afterward. But we don't have time for logic—the problem is really to 'put the spirit into the body' and try the law in the Assembly *now*."

"Put the spirit in the body," sighed the attorney general of the republic.

BELIEVING IN THE reinforcements that would be sent by these powerful allies, Lota decided to attack her first cousin, José Eugenio de Macedo Soares. Since he had taken power, the director of urban cleaning had never freed up a functionary even to remove the garbage from the park. Dr. José Eugenio based his position on one argument: the Department of Urban Cleaning was only to clean public spaces. Heck, didn't Dona Lota continually claim that Flamengo Park was part of some Foundation? Then let the Foundation clean it. This time Lota decided to get radical and sent an ultimatum to her cousin: she gave him a deadline of eight days to clean the park. If the deadline was not met, the Foundation would take the legal measures it thought necessary.

And following that she sent a little note to Dr. Alcino Salazar: what to do with Urban Cleaning if it didn't clean the roads in the park in eight days?

APRIL, THE CRUELEST MONTH. Bishop was close to a breakdown.

She was being confronted by some students who disagreed with her suggestions for improving their poems, preferring them "the way they were before." Others swore they'd made substantial revisions, as indicated by her, but Bishop insisted on saying that they'd given her back the same poems. In general, Bishop felt that, with the exception of one or two students, the young poets thought her a bit too eccentric in asking them to versify on the prosaic things she took out of a supermarket bag—a fork, a pack of seeds, an eggbeater. They wanted to write poetry about something big—pain, madness. There was one in particular who pleased himself by terrorizing the class. When Bishop asked that each one read his favorite poem, the imp read out a tedious list of obscenities, hoping, perhaps, to offend the white hairs of the mistress. Coitado, poor thing, sighed Bishop in Portuguese. The real obscenity was the trash they wrote, calling it free verse.

Seattle, for its part, revealed itself to be dangerous to Bishop's susceptibilities. Lots of rain, lots of humidity—the asthma attacks were constant.

Adrienne was the balm. Soaked, she waited for Bishop with a bunch of flowers in her hand. Lota's letters, claiming Bishop's presence, upset the thimbleful of serenity that Bishop had managed to collect. Bishop got angry with Lota for having left her so vulnerable to this new attachment. She was angry with herself for deceiving Lota. She started drinking. She started missing classes.

LOTA COULDN'T BELIEVE IT. She paced from one side of the living room to the other, holding her neck in her hand as if she'd been wounded in the throat.

The whole first page of the second section of the *Correio da Manhã* on that Thursday, April 14, 1966, was devoted to Flamengo Park. But the substance was an exercise in the defamation of Lota de Macedo Soares. She reread, for the umpteenth time: "Burle Marx declares: intemperate commands will bring about the Aterro of absurdity."

As before, Roberto had come to throw stones. He returned to his charges against Kelly's project, saying, spiritedly, that instead of illumination for the Aterro, there was an Aterro for illumination. He called the posts Lampshadeland. He said that the gigantic lampposts oppressed people and that their ugliness during the day didn't compensate even slightly for the supposed moonlight that Dona Lota proclaimed so often. And of course, he attacked Ethel's playgrounds again.

Everything was Lota's fault. Burle Marx assured the readers that, from an apparent initial humility, Lota converted herself, little by little, into a little dictator, deciding everything by herself. Now she demanded and countermanded. Having liked the honoraria, she moved heaven and earth to remain in charge. The fight for the Foundation was nothing more than the only way for her to protect her position after the end of the Lacerda government. Lota blamed others for the mistakes and imprudences she committed and tried to persuade the public that without her the poor little children would have nowhere to play, nor the people anywhere to entertain themselves. He ridiculed Lota, saying that it was grotesque to see her try to transform herself into a Joan of Arc of the Aterro.

In the article, Roberto Burle Marx attributed the general plan of the Aterro to himself, even though the caption for one of the photos stated that the general design was by Burle Marx and Affonso Reidy. Roberto resumed his insults of Lota, saying that artistically, the woman was no better than a rotten egg.

Lota took the phone off the hook. She didn't want to receive condolences from anyone. Roberto didn't have the balls to tell her about her "countermands" face to face. He attacked her through the newspapers. He unsheathed his sword when he saw that she was disarmed. My heart roars, and I howl.

IT CAME OUT IN Léa Maria's column, in the *Jornal do Brasil*: Dona Lota spends her weekends in Petrópolis now. She climbs the mountain at the wheel of her Interlagos with the exhausts wide open and in a big hurry to get to her destination.

Hardly had she arrived at Samambaia when Lota would stop at the house below. Monica was already in her nightgown. Lota didn't care. She gave Mary's daughter a tight hug and said:

"Shall we go see the owls, my love?"

Monica gave her little hand to Lota and they went. Mary yelled:

"Lota, it's her bedtime! Let her go, Lota!"

Lota and Monica paid no attention. They went on tiptoe to surprise the owls, which took flight when they saw them. Every time it was exactly the same. Every time it was just as electrifying.

Monica waited anxiously for those moments with her "grandmother." Every Friday she came. Sometimes Lota didn't even go up to her own house; she slept there. In the morning, hardly awake, Monica ran to Lota's bed and snuggled up in her embrace. Then came the solemnity of the combing. Loose, Lota's hair came almost to her waist. Monica adored combing it. She ran a large comb through the gray hair, which she smoothed with the other hand. Then Lota would make a banana *coque*, take that clasp she liked so much, and presto.

Joana would come in with a tray, with hot eggs, toast, coffee. Lota always had breakfast in bed. After breakfast, Lota and Monica would go for a walk around Samambaia. Lota liked to cross the river to pick guavas. The water was cold. Sometimes Monica would see enormous crabs headed in her direction, but she wasn't afraid with Lota beside her. After the crossing, the two of them went into the forest, carrying baskets. Lota would disarm the bird traps set up by the ragamuffins and free the birds that had already been caught. When they came to the guava trees, Lota would hold Monica on her shoulders so that she could pick the fruit herself. It was delicious.

One day, Lota bought Monica a new dress, took her to the Aterro, and put a little white dove in her hands. At the moment when Monica set the dove free, the puppet theater would be inaugurated. But who said that Monica would let the dove go? For nothing in the world. The little thing was a present from Grandma Lota, which she was going to take to Samambaia. She only opened her little hands when Lota explained that the dove was like those birds they let out of the traps; it had to fly. The next week, to Mary's despair, Monica's bedroom was full of guinea pigs.

LOTA AND NANÁ MAINTAINED an ashen silence. Naná couldn't remember seeing Lota like this, except for the time when everyone was talking about the situation with her father and Horacinho.

Naná sighed. My Lord, how to console her. Since the beginning of the year Lota had sought alliances with power, starting with the dictator, to guarantee the continuity of the park. What Lota had interpreted as acquiescence turned out to be nothing more than a conveniently gradual roasting. Organized and strengthened, the new bosses in the Guanabara government planned the park's orphanhood. With their vocation for puns, Cariocans had begun calling Lota's project the Foundering.

Not that Lota at any point had accepted any of this. It wasn't in her nature. Noticing that some tried to soothe her stubbornness with false diplomacy while others hit at her hard, Lota changed strategies. She arranged the soccer tournament with the *Jornal dos Esportes*, which made the Aterro daily headlines in the paper. Such were the repercussions of the event that the governor felt obliged to do a rush cleanup on the eve of the tournament, so that he'd look good in front of the people. It was a victory for Lota, but a short one, like winning an arm-wrestling match. The ungrateful crowds quickly took it upon themselves to make the park dirtier than it had been before. In addition, they spread the damage, bouncing balls on the grass while waiting to get on the field and parking cars in the gardens. On the streets next to the park, the residents of Flamengo hated Lota's idea. They couldn't sleep at night because of the players' yelling, punctuated by obscenities. Lota couldn't get the games to end on time, and eventually she had to ask that the lights be summarily cut off at eleven o'clock, whether the games were over or not. Ironically, the initial idea, which had seemed so wonderful, created a surplus of disfavor and disillusion, which led Lota into her current depression.

"Well," said Naná, "well."

"I'm not giving up, Naná."

It's not possible, thought Naná.

"But Lota, what else can you do?"

"What I'm *going* to do. The First Puppet and Marionette Theater Festival of Rio de Janeiro. I've already asked for Barbara Heliodora's support, from the National Theater Service. Oh, and the minister of agriculture wants to put a meteorological station in the park; we're going to install it."

"But Lota, is this allowed in a national heritage site?"

"No, but I'm going to ask for permission from the Heritage Sites board of directors, why not?" Lota elucidated, without time for logic. "And I'm also thinking about bringing the Municipal Symphony for a concert on the dance floor."

Could stubbornness be a virtue? reflected Naná.

"DONA LOTA, TELEPHONE."

"Who is it?"

"It's Dr. Negrão."

Negrão was hopping mad. Brigadier General Nelson Freire Lavanère-Wanderley, commander in chief of the armed forces, was beside himself. Lota had ordered that a plaque be removed, one about obligatory military service that the commander in chief had put up near the War Veterans' Monument in the park.

"Don't get annoyed, Governor, we'll get out of this one. Leave it to me; I'll take care of the problem with all the sweetness and diplomacy required. No, don't worry. The armed forces will be the first ones to obey the law, and the law says that in an area designated as a national heritage site, you can't put up posters. It's a federal law, Governor. Yes, I'll send a dispatch. Today, right away. Stay well."

If only he'd get this upset with the filth on the Aterro.

Lota wrote the document, citing the article of the law that forbade the plaque. Then she wrote to the beer company, Antarctica Paulista Ltd., asking that it contribute the prizes for the puppet festival. She wrote to the president of Philips asking for the photo albums of Richard Kelly's work on the Aterro, in which it should be written in English that Philips had donated the lights, not to the park, but to the Flamengo Park Foundation. She wrote to Dona Yolanda, the wife of the new dictator, President Costa e Silva, inviting her to visit the park. She called Fernanda, gave her the letters to type, and asked that someone be sent to buy her a chocolate milkshake at Bob's.

IN JUNE, Bishop's school term was over.

The head of the department had met with some students who complained about Bishop's attendance as well as about the marks that she'd given them. The department head asked the students for tolerance. Miss Bishop was going through a difficult time, with many health problems. Allergies. Asthma.

For their part, the professors in the department resented never having really been colleagues of the lionized author. Bishop behaved as if she had expected to find the finest blooms of the American Academy of Poets at the University of Washington. Her disappointment showed itself in her sardonic deprecation of the students and her glacial indifference to the resident gang of teachers. The only person with whom Bishop seemed to have vaguely succeeded in associating was another visiting poet, Henry Reed, author of the much-anthologized poem "The Naming of the Parts," in which the thoughts of a recruit wander off toward camellias and bees while the sergeant gives instructions about the parts of a gun. Like Bishop, Reed had a caustic sense of humor, aroused when he'd been drinking. In their worst moments, they made a mean pair.

Bishop thought she really wouldn't miss it. Seattle had been an interlude. Another city of passage. Her place was still Brazil. Or at least in Brazil.

She tried to get herself ready for her return. The Rockefeller Foundation awarded her twelve thousand dollars to write a book of travel pieces about Brazil. This would be the realization of an old dream: to travel a lot, learn the details of the Brazilian landscape, and take advantage of her travel notes. Bishop had always liked travel books, like Darwin's or Burton's. With the difficulty she'd had in writing poetry—absolutely nothing in Seattle—the project was a safe direction toward resuming her literary production. It would also be a motive to avoid Rio's turbulence, if Lota insisted on staying there.

Lota! Bishop felt distressed.

There was Adrienne. Adrienne had always known about Lota. It had always been understood that Bishop would go back to Lota. But now that the moment had come, Bishop was finding everything complicated and ambiguous. She didn't want to lose Lota, but she also didn't want to lose Adrienne.

Bishop decided to postpone her return. She sent word that she was exhausted and would take a few days to rest. She went with Adrienne to the San Juan Islands, near Vancouver Island. They read, walked on the beach, and arranged to maintain a correspondence via Ouro Preto.

Bishop returned to Rio on July 4.

# THE THIRD-RATE PARK

THE NEWSPAPERS began to report more fully on the number of people killed by cars on the Aterro. The traffic volume at rush hour reached seven thousand vehicles. It was impossible to cross the roads. Since the time of the Lacerda government, Lota had battled in vain to have traffic lights installed for pedestrian crossings. Many daredevils who tried to cross became victims. With a measure of foresight, Negrão ordered that screens be installed to cover the corpses.

It was then that the Marinho family, of the newspaper *O Globo*, sent a request to the Foundation that it cede a small piece of the Aterro on which an amusement park could be built, with the income to go to the Help a Child to Study campaign. Lota thought that this license would be worthwhile and also that it would be a way to encourage the orderly occupation of an area that had been abandoned. Therefore she authorized the installation of the amusement park on the piece of the Aterro that was by Widow's Hill, which hadn't yet been urbanized.

On July 14, 1966, *O Globo* announced that the biggest amusement park in Brazil was about to be built in Flamengo Park. Lota was happy. Finally, the newspapers were going to have something good to say about the park.

The trucks arrived with the amusement rides, and the first booths began to be erected. Then things started to go awry.

The newspapers denounced the terrible state of the equipment and the ramshackle quality of the stalls. It's sloppy, said one. It's a load of junk iron, said another. It's dismal, anti-aesthetic, it's a mockery, they all echoed.

Lota was dismayed. It hadn't occurred to her that she'd have to check on the quality of the damned little park before allowing it to be built, seeing where the request had come from. But the photos that the papers were publishing were chilling. Curses!

At the same time, the inappropriateness of the site chosen for the amusement park was raised. The innocent children, attracted by the Ferris wheel or the merry-go-round, would risk their lives trying to cross the highways. It will be a massacre, predicted the *Correio da Manhã*. It's the devil's playground, said the *Gazeta de Notícias*.

Lota found that defending the amusement park put her in a very uncomfortable position, because she herself had raised holy hell when the director of parks and gardens had tried to put in some swings and seesaws in the same area. On that occasion, as the director remembered very well, Lota had said that only someone ignorant or crazy would do such a thing.

The criticisms rained down. The stalls were gambling dens. Almost all of the iron structures were rusted. The sheds constructed to house the workers were making a slum on the Aterro.

Finally, to Lota's bitterness, the press labeled the little amusement park the "third-rate park."

For Lota's adversaries, this was music to their ears. Quickly Maia Penido emphasized that it had been the Foundation that had authorized the third-rate park, that Sursan hadn't even been consulted, and that personally he was against it, given its proximity to the highways. The Assembly member Mac-Dowell Leite de Castro started a public campaign to eject the third-rate park. The Lions Club of Widow's Hill was bemused that Dona Lota had approved the installation of this monstrosity, which disfigured the landscape and disrespected the destiny of the Aterro.

Lota suspected that the campaign was being mounted by the owner of an amusement park in the city's south zone who felt threatened by the competition on the Aterro. In any case, Negrão's team had taken wonderful advantage of the situation.

Finally, an editorial asked the governor for an immediate ban on the third-rate park, alleging that it was unjust that the Foundation consented to the destruction of a property that didn't belong to it but to all Cariocans, who had already paid ten billion cruzeiros for Flamengo Park.

Lota saw the woods begin to move.

WHEN BISHOP ARRIVED, they went to Samambaia. It wasn't good. Communication was difficult, and Bishop felt that Lota resented her having survived. It was forbidden to talk about Seattle. Lota's subjects were traps and treason.

Bishop hadn't been in Brazil two weeks when the third-rate park fiasco began. Bishop watched Lota fight the inevitable, rearing up and snorting like a horse that won't let itself be roped.

"Lota, this park is killing you. Why don't you let it go once and for all?"

"Imagine that you were writing a poem and your publishing house were sold. The new boss comes along and says that your poem is going to be finished by another person, chosen by him. Well, Flamengo Park is my poem."

Bishop didn't know how to cheer her up and didn't know what advice to give her. When Lota went to Rio, Bishop stayed in the Samambaia winter.

IN SPITE OF EVERYTHING, Lota thought that the Foundation should maintain its position and refute the editorials, branding the newspaper pieces as hack jobs. Because she was a bundle of nerves, she asked Hélio Mamede to speak to the press.

Very calmly, Mamede said that there was too much fuss being made right now. On the danger of pedestrians being run over, he said it was almost impossible, because there was an underground walkway. As to the poor state of upkeep of the equipment, he said that all of it would be inspected and painted. He also said he didn't see anything wrong with the park employees living in sheds, since the Foundation itself was also installed in a shed.

On July 22, Lota went to see the filming of *Nick Carter against Lady List*. The scene in which Richard Wyler takes off in a minicopter was being shot on the Aterro. Accosted by a reporter about the third-rate park, Lota admitted that the location wasn't ideal but that it was preferable to occupy the area with a park than to leave it to the vagabonds and prostitutes. As far as the aesthetics went, she suggested that one couldn't expect from a temporary amusement park the same standards as those of the permanent areas of the Aterro. The little park would only remain on the Aterro during the Help a Child to Study campaign. She insisted that there was an underground walkway to the little park and that the park would be surrounded by a protective railing. And she finished, acidly: "If anyone wants to die in spite of all this, that's not my problem."

That wasn't a kind thing to say. Prudence stops when patience ceases, as the marquis of Maricá puts it. The next day, Negrão revoked permission for the amusement park.

The interdiction, supposedly, was so that the claim of the delegate from Diversions could be investigated—that the installation had been done in a clandestine manner, without a license for the work having been requested. What work? wondered Hélio Mamede. This was only the installation of some recreational equipment. The Foundation therefore decided to send out a six-item statement explaining that installation of the amusement park avoided the greater inconvenience of the Aterro being occupied by garbage, including prostitutes and drifters.

Five days later, without an apparent motive, Negrão reversed himself and set the amusement park free. Lota considered herself victorious. She made a public announcement that the governor did not have legal support to stop the Foundation from putting up an amusement park on the Aterro. And she sent a new letter to the newspapers, justifying the position of the Foundation.

The next day, July 29, 1966, a court terminated the provisional status that had been given the Foundation in December 1965.

"Dona Lota doesn't rule!" proclaimed the headline of the *Gazeta de Notícias*.

BISHOP CALLED LILLI DAILY. She asked about the restoration of the house; she asked whether any correspondence for her had arrived. She wanted to go to Ouro Preto and to Lilli, but Lota was being made a martyr. Bishop simply couldn't abandon her in that situation, even though she could do nothing to ease it.

Finally, at the very beginning of August, Lilli told her that a letter had arrived. Bishop asked Lilli to open it and read it. Lilli opened it and began:

"Kisses, kisses all over."

Lilli didn't like that at all. She wasn't inclined to stay on the telephone reading that kind of thing. She was going to send it to Rio and Bishop could read it herself. No! No! Not here! Please, Lilli. Bishop really had to take care of the renovation of the house. She'd come to Ouro Preto.

The next day, Bishop took the bus and went.

AS WAS TO BE EXPECTED, the government got its checkmate ready. The secretary of works assigned three engineers to inspect the devil's playground. Lota already knew that the finding would be condemnatory, but she didn't agree with the arguments offered. The experts said that the park forced people to cross the two highways, despite the existence nearby of an underground walkway of doubtful efficiency.

Lota knew that to present counterarguments was to carry water in a sieve, but she could never manage to keep quiet. She wrote to the governor:

"Heck, this walkway of doubtful efficiency *was made by Sursan itself*, is fourteen meters wide, and has been serving thousands of people for more than two years. *It's identical* to two other underground walkways to the Aterro, which have, therefore, to be equally condemned."

Next, she wrote a dispatch to the Help a Child to Study campaign. She was withdrawing the cession of the area on Widow's Hill because Sursan's commission of inspection hadn't found the installations of the park safe enough.

Then she wrote a letter to the president of the Foundation council, Rodrigo Melo Franco de Andrade, asking that he replace her as executive director for twenty days. Under medical orders, she was going to rest.

THERE WAS A LOT of sadness at the Shed. What was happening to Dona Lota was unjust. Wasn't it true that the Assembly, excited at the cancellation of the Foundation's provisional status, had decided not to wait for the judgment on the injunction requested by the Foundation? The Assembly members confirmed the December recommendation that Lacerda's decree be revoked, and they promulgated Law 1.045, extinguishing the Foundation.

It didn't help at all that the lawyer for the Foundation had exclaimed that the Assembly members were subservient and politically motivated. The fact is that on August 20, 1966, the Assembly determined that there was no longer a Foundation.

Dona Lota brought the group together and said that she was turning the case over to the lawyers. She was going to withdraw for a few days, because she was tired and her health was weakened. She asked everyone to stay at their posts, because things hadn't yet been decided. She went away very sad.

LOTA WENT TO Ouro Preto.

Lilli didn't have much information about what was happening in Rio, since all that Bishop said was that it was a mess. She saw that Lota had arrived downcast, really unrecognizable, very different from the resplendent person Lilli was used to. Meanwhile, Lota avoided talking about questions of the Aterro, refusing to say a word. It was evident, however, that a belligerence had developed in relation to Bishop. Lilli had lived with the two of them through the years and witnessed Lota's pampering of Bishop, her almost maternal protection. Now Lota's tone was irritated, full of impatience at Bishop's furtive manner. Lota didn't swallow Bishop's story of buying a house in Ouro Preto.

ONE MORNING LILLI and Lota went out in the car. Lota was mute. She'd had a bad telephone call. Lilli had observed the scene from a discreet distance and seen that Bishop held her hands over both ears when Lota yelled. What a pity. Two fabulous women, two extraordinary intelligences; two people who loved each other, tearing at each other in that way.

Lilli also stayed quiet. Suddenly, who knew from where, a little Beetle appeared. Lota swerved violently. Lilli saw the world turn over and felt a flash of pain in her neck. When she opened her eyes she saw that she and Lota were ridiculously squeezed between the roof and the floor of the car, head down and legs up. Lilli wanted to free her shoulders and head from the weight of her body, but it was difficult in the space of the Interlagos. Lota seemed stunned. Help, help, Lilli repeated until some high-laced shoes came near and a deformed head confronted her own. Taken out of the car, they verified with relief that they weren't injured. Except for Lota's self-esteem; she couldn't accept the event. One of the things she prided herself on was being a splendid driver and never having had an accident in her life.

THE CURTAIN WAS flung open violently.

"Elizabeth! What does *this* mean?"

Lota brandished a sheet of paper. A chill came in through the open door, shivering along Bishop's naked body. What an intrusion; she was taking a bath! At least in the bathroom a person's privacy should be respected.

"Answer! What is this?"

It was appalling to be intimidated in this way, under the shower. Bishop closed the tap, came out and covered herself with a towel. She was trembling.

"This what?"

"Elizabeth, don't be an idiot! Who is this letter from?"

Bishop had taken every precaution to ensure this would never happen. How could the letter have ended up in Lota's hands? How? Bishop looked dejectedly at the sheet of paper with handwriting on it from top to bottom: "I love you, I love you, I love you, I love you, I love you, I love you . . ."

"Lota, you can see that this is just foolishness."

"Who wrote it?"

"It's one of those foolish student crushes for her teacher. It doesn't have the least importance."

"Who wrote it!"

"The letter isn't signed, is it? How am I going to know who wrote it?" The sagacious logic of a lie.

For an instant they stood like that, pathetic, Lota with the letter in her hand, Bishop wrapped in the towel.

Lota's eyes were filled with fury and incredulity, but Bishop met them with the icy blue of hers.

Suddenly, Lota half-turned and went out, slamming the door with all her strength in Bishop's face. She was left naked and dumbfounded in the middle of the bathroom.

WITHOUT PRIOR NOTICE to their hostess, Lota and Bishop put their bags in the car, said a flat goodbye to Lilli, and left.

Lota imposed a punitive silence all the way. They went straight to Samambaia, and there Bishop went straight to the studio. She felt stunned, like a bird that has flown into a windowpane.

Aware that she had no one to count on at that moment, seeing that the people she called friends were really Lota's friends, she decided to resort to Dr. Baumann. She asked her to write to Lota advising, no, prescribing a holiday trip. It was the only way out.

The shrubs had taken over the land by the pool, where the vegetable garden had been. The weeds grew all around. Bishop could hear Edileusa's tuneful voice singing "Beautiful rose of youth." What had become of her? What had become of them?

# SUNS GO DOWN

*I do not intend to torture myself, or you.*
*Why persist in asking? You will not persuade me.*
*No, I will not go on. Rage as you please.*
*How dreadful knowledge of the truth can be*
*When there's no help in truth!*
*You made me speak. I did not want to.*
—Tiresias, on being pressured to speak by Oedipus

"I want the truth!" Lota demanded.

Bishop used the subterfuges and the delays that cheaters use but ended up admitting the existence of Adrienne.

"You mean that while I was here in hell, at the most difficult moment in my life, you were going to bed with a young thing!"

Bishop disputed this. It wasn't as simple (or as ugly) as that. Adrienne was a shelter. More than that, Bishop had been lost and exhausted like one who had drowned, and Adrienne . . .

"Enough! Enough!"

Lota bent over, hugging herself. Bishop pressed her hands against her mouth. The inevitable comes like a cold dagger.

After fifteen years, the one who drew close, hugged her, and proposed a way out was Bishop. Lota was the love of her life. She could not imagine life without Lota. They should go away from there, go far away, things would have to be worked out.

Lota could barely hear over the noise of her pain.

LOTA BEGAN TO suffer from labyrinthitis. Bishop went back to drinking heavily.

Lota would arrive at the Aterro by taxi and noticeably stagger to the Shed. She told the apprehensive staff that it was the result of a car accident in Ouro Preto.

Although shaky, Lota went back to sending official dispatches from the Shed. When a private company announced with satisfaction that it was going to mount a National Festival for Children on the Aterro, without the Foundation having been consulted, Lota directed the lawyer to formally question the governor.

Negrão decided to cut the agony short. Attending to the disposition of Law 1.045, which had declared the Foundation extinct, he signed a decree summarily passing over everything that was the Foundation to Sursan.

Lota gave in then to Bishop's requests. She went away "on vacation leave" and on October 23 got on a ship with Bishop for Europe. Things would have to be worked out.

LACERDA ALLIED HIMSELF with his archenemies Jango and Juscelino Kubistchek. The current split was between civilians and the military, politicians and dictators. The Wide Front Manifesto, published in the Tribuna da Imprensa, was intended as a turning point in Brazilian political life. While Brazil boiled, Lota forced herself to find it fun to wander around Holland.

From Amsterdam they went to London, to an exhibition by Kit Barker, a friend of Bishop's. Lota and Kit liked each other very much. But Lota seemed to be having serious problems with her balance. And she found something wrong with everything they saw in London. Once Bishop went to spend the day alone with Kit and his wife, Ilse. It was very pleasant, and the Barkers thought that Bishop seemed relieved to be out of Lota's sight.

Lota and Bishop ended up having to plan an early return to Brazil, by the beginning of November. Magu went to get them at the airport. Lota was having a nervous collapse and needed medical treatment, explained Bishop.

"THAT'S WHEN THINGS got really messed up."

Joana was talking to Ismênia, who had arrived from Washington and had been surprised by the news that Lota had been hospitalized.

"Dona Lota was going to the psychiatrist, but it wasn't helping at all. She had to be put in the hospital. She had shock treatment; it was horrible. Dona Elizabetchy falling down drunk. It was Dona Mary who had to come to stay with Dona Lota. She sleeps at the hospital, poor thing."

"But what does Lota have?"

"Nerves."

Ismênia looked at Joana silently.

"Now my life is going to the hospital. Or does the lady think that Dona Lota eats hospital food? Not at all. I'm the one who brings food here from the house. And she's fussy about other things too. I have to bring the sheets here from home. Suddenly the phone rings: my Joanica, I want you to come wash my hair now. I go crazy. Dona Elizabetchy sick. Dona Mary downtown. Dona Lota calling. What should I do, my Lord. You can't imagine the rushing around."

Ismênia got very worried. What could be happening to Lota? She had to speak to the girls.

CHRISTMAS PASSED, New Year's passed, and Ismênia still hadn't been able to see Lota. She called Joana again.

"That's right, she had to be put into the hospital again. Look, speak with Dona Mary here."

Mary explained that unfortunately Lota had to take a new round of insulin shock.

"But that's a very violent thing, isn't it? Why is she taking shock treatment?"

"She's profoundly depressed. There is no other treatment."

"And Elizabeth?"

"Also interned. For detox."

"What a situation, my Lord."

Don't you tell me, thought Mary Morse. She had to redouble her efforts to care for the two of them. It was complicated, because Mary had already adopted three children. And the costs for Lota's treatment were very high. To save the companion's fee, Mary slept on the floor.

LOTA STAYED IN the hospital throughout January and February of 1967.

At the end of January, Bishop arranged with Lilli to go down the San Francisco River in a gaiola, a steamboat. Bishop went to Ouro Preto but became ill, and Lilli brought her back to Rio, to be interned again.

In March both Lota and Bishop were set free. Both felt a lot better. They went to Samambaia, to be like in the old times.

Immediately Bishop set herself up in the studio and began to write. Oh, it was good. How long it had been since she'd had the composure to be able to create. Bit by bit, strange personages began to appear on the page, animals that spoke of dissimulation and displacement. One was a giant toad, who announced that the protuberances on his back were not muscle, but sacs of poison that spread like wings on his back. I am an angel in disguise, he warned, beware. Then came the giant snail. The snail tried to give the impression that he moved with mysterious ease but said that really it was only with the greatest effort of will. He had a saying: withdrawal is always best. Finally Bishop created a stray crab. The text was flowing, a prose poem:

> This is not my home. How did I get so far from water? I believe in the oblique, the indirect approach, and I keep my feelings to myself. But on this strange, smooth surface I am making too much noise. I wasn't meant for this. If I maneuver a bit and keep a sharp lookout, I shall find my pool again. Watch out for my right claw, all passersby!

While Bishop spent her days holed up in her studio, in a creative burst, Lota remained immobile. She was a creature gone astray, like those that were rising off Bishop's page. House, rock, forest had lost their hold, and Lota's clouded eyes wandered listlessly over Samambaia.

THEY HAD TO GO down to Rio twice a week for Lota's psychoanalytic sessions with Dr. Décio de Souza. This chopped up the week and involved a great physical effort for Lota, who had gone back to driving. Lota didn't gather any more large bunches of wildflowers; she didn't want to read anymore. Her heavy silences asked the cruelest question: What for? When she did speak it was to blame Bishop for the "idiocies" she had committed in Seattle and for refusing to take Antabuse, preferring instead to remain an alcoholic. If medicine could resolve problems just like that, Bishop thought, with the boxes and boxes of pills that Lota was taking she would have already stopped crying every day and being a bundle of nerves.

But Bishop didn't reveal her feelings to Lota. She revealed them to Dr. Baumann and to her friends, to whom she wrote exalted letters, defending herself, explaining that she'd lived the ten happiest years of her life with Lota but that the last five years had been hell. And that although she felt guilty at wanting to distance herself from Lota, her presence with her was futile. Bishop thought about going to New York.

IN MAY OF 1967, José Eduardo de Macedo Soares died. Lota fell into despair. Lota and her father had spent their lives in friction, in admiration, hating and wanting each other, as is often the case with two ardent and explosive temperaments. Lota was proud of her father's fearlessness. She kept the hat with the bullet hole in it, proof of the risks he ran to defend his positions. Sitting in the bedroom of the apartment, Lota remembered the morning she had taken her father to visit the Aterro. The senator was trapped in a wheelchair, but he kept his bearing. Lota wanted him to be proud of her, showed him all the details. They didn't fight, but not everything that had to be said was said. Now there was no more time. Father! A dense tear formed. Lota closed her eyes. She wanted to stay in the dark.

BISHOP DECIDED NOT to postpone her trip on the San Francisco River any longer. She was getting money to write a book of essays on Brazil and it was already the end of May, and she hadn't done anything. She went to talk to Dr. Décio about the possible repercussions of her being away, since Lota's depression had returned. The doctor thought that, to the contrary, the separation might even be desirable. But he advised her to travel alone. Lilli's company would awaken Lota's jealousy and insecurities.

Bishop went and was happy to have gone. The suffering of the last while stayed behind. Bishop took notes diligently, certain that the material she was collecting would interest some American magazine. For example, at the start of the trip there were many animals on board. As the days went by, the chickens and pigs kept diminishing. Bishop found out that they were slaughtered and that it was their meat the passengers ate. For the American reader, no doubt, this would be exotic. Bishop was struck by the region's misery, but after the annoyances of her article about Rio, she was fearful of tackling it. Nevertheless, the experience helped to lessen Bishop's feelings of guilt. That really was a trip she had to make alone. Lota would have hated every minute of it.

WHEN BISHOP RETURNED to Rio, another squall had formed. A letter from Adrienne had arrived. Lota was completely beside herself:

"Elizabeth, you aren't thinking of bringing that woman here!"

Bishop didn't know what Adrienne could have written. She hadn't read the letter! The whole thing was a disaster. One thing was clear: Bishop no longer wanted to be in that situation. She didn't want to live like this any longer. In front of Joana's worried look, she opened the door and left.

DR. DÉCIO SUMMONED Bishop to his office. Lota was in terrible shape. Bishop was harming Lota, he said severely.

One year after her return to Brazil, Bishop took a plane back to the United States. Domum reditionis spe sublata. When hope is lost, return home. She was going to New York, to Loren MacIver's studio, the same place that she and Lota had stayed in 1961. Had there been a moment when I really chose all of this? I don't remember, but there must have been, Bishop reflected, casting her eyes around the small apartment, dusty and smelling of mold, closed up for two years.

WITH BISHOP'S NEW DEPARTURE, everything fell on Joana again. Joana felt pity for the condition of her mistress. After Dona Lota left the hospital, she stopped being happy. Always sad. But after Dona Elizabetchy went away, the tears came in a downpour. She took a lot of medicine; she became dispirited. She didn't get out of bed anymore. Joana brought the little bench in and sat near her. She never sat on the bed or in Dona Lota's chair. A person who respects herself knows her place. Joana knew how to come in and how to go out. From the little bench, she watched, she encouraged, she listened. We've wound up just the two of us, all alone, my little Joana. But I'll go and get her. I'm going to the United States too.

The days went by very slowly. Lota would call Magu, ask if she could stay with her. I'm in despair, Magu. Life isn't worth anything.

At night she'd speak to Naná, to Rachel. She was wounded. Elizabeth was right to have said that living in Brazil had become impossible. She wanted to go to New York, but she was afraid of finding that young thing there.

Ashley Brown also visited Lota. He always found her very sad and tired. When Ashley went to New York, Lota asked him to take some winter clothes for Bishop. Ashley spent a week with Bishop. He thought she was in good shape. One night they went to a discotheque; another, to a Spanish restaurant.

THE LAWYERS IN charge of requesting a new injunction against the decision of the Assembly said that they required documents and data so that they could draw up a report on Flamengo Park that would support the legal action. Lota called Rosy Peixoto to coordinate the organization of the material. Rosy had been hired by Lota to plan the libraries, during the time when she believed that there would be libraries on the Aterro.

Unexpectedly, Lota came out of her depression. Things weren't going to stay like this. The journalist Elsie Lessa met Lota in her convertible sports car, displaying the self-assurance of a professional race driver on Atlantic Avenue.

"You're ready for all comers, eh?"

"If you only knew what I hear behind this wheel. . . . 'Cool Granny' is one of the things I can repeat."

Lota got an audience with Dona Yolanda Costa e Silva. Praising the good will and the good humor of the first lady, she sent her a barrage of arguments in defense of the Foundation. She took the opportunity to name Flamengo Park as one more agent in the fight against communism, in the sense that it was a place where an adolescent could spend his energy in a healthy and educational way, instead of plotting conspiracies and street riots. She signed and dated it: August 18, 1967.

On the same date Lota signed another document of several pages: her will. She divided her works of art with scrupulous care among her friends. To Lilli she left the statue of Saint Francis Xavier, to Rachel the statue of Saint Benedict, to Oscar Simon the saint of Samambaia, Our Lady of Conception "or whatever they call her," and so on, a remembrance for each friend. She assured Joana a pension of two minimum salaries per month for the rest of her days. She left to her nephew Flávio all the goods that belonged to her family: her father José Eduardo's sword, the viscount of Itaboraí's pink wash basin, the flatware with the initials M.S. She left the Leme apartment to Bishop. Samambaia, the house and property, went to Mary Morse, who was also named as executor. To her sister Marieta she left a China duck.

IN SEPTEMBER LOTA decided that she would go to New York to meet Bishop, against doctor's orders. Dr. Décio thought that Lota was not in good condition to travel. All her friends—Naná, Vivinha, Rosinha, Magu, Rachel, Ismênia—one by one and in chorus they begged her: Lota, don't go!

Useless. Lota had decided. Joana packed many bags. Dona Lota said she'd be away for a couple of months and then she'd come back with Dona Elizabetchy.

On the eve of the trip, Rosy went to bring the big folder with the documentation on the Aterro. Lota didn't get out of bed. She leafed through the album, emotional, reviewing the chapters of the work that was her passion, from the mound of turned-over red earth to the advanced ideas of the Foundation. After, the legal terminology with which the lawyers attempted to bandage the cuts made by brute force: "intangible juridical act," "nonoperative revocation." She stopped at the terms that defined her: Brazilian, single, housewife.

Lota asked that Rosy go to the bank for her. On her return, Rosy found Lota looking like a corpse, as if she'd died in bed. Frightened, she called Joana. No, Dona Lota was just sleeping. But Rosy was deeply affected. Lota was emaciated, disjointed. The Park had finished this woman. The Dona Lota that Rosy had known was dead.

LOTA TRAVELED ON September 17. The plane was many hours late. Bishop was waiting for her at the airport. Moved, they embraced each other. Bishop could only imagine the determination of Lota to come to her: she was weaker than Bishop had ever seen her. They went to the apartment to drop off her bags. The apartment had the decadent air of places that stay shut up for a long time. Bishop thought it better to keep Lota out of the house. She took her to meet the neighbors, Harold Leeds and Wheaton Galentine. By chance, Emanuel Brasil was there. Lota was courteous, but she was exhausted. Bishop took Lota to a restaurant and then they went right home. They had a long talk until ten at night. They were both very tired. They each took a sleeping pill, gave each other a tight hug, and went to bed.

Bishop slept heavily. Near dawn, she was awakened by an indistinct noise. She turned on the light, got up and met Lota standing at the door of the kitchen. When she got closer, she saw that Lota had a bottle in her hand. Without a word, but with a terrible look, Lota fell. Bishop threw herself on Lota's inert body. A scream hung over Greenwich Village, as another scream had hung over Great Village, over a terrified girl.

NO ONE WAS prepared for the synoptic cruelty of the telegram:

LOTA SICK SINCE ARRIVAL. DIED TODAY. TRYING TO CALL. ELIZABETH. SEP-
TEMBER 25 1967.

Lota's friends had found the lack of news strange. Normally, Lota would have already sent a playful telegram, called. But, because she had traveled this time in the midst of a depressive crisis, they thought the weeklong silence understandable if worrisome. Bishop sent the telegram to Magu and Rosinha, who called the others. The news was a blow. All of them were revolted at Bishop. If Lota had been sick for a week, why hadn't she called to tell them? And what had happened to Lota, finally?

The body arrived four days later. Lota came in a black lace dress, all made up. She was buried in São João Batista, next to her father. Lacerda wrote an emotional note:

"Lota Costallat de Macedo Soares was the creator of Flamengo Park. She died without the Park, which was taken away from her by petty politics and chicanery. But what remains of the Park, if it exists, if it survives, all of it is due to the tiny and frail creature, all nerves, all light, who was called Dona Lota."

Bishop didn't come.

BISHOP ONLY APPEARED months later. She came with her arm in a cast, due to a fall after a binge. She looked for Lota's friends, hugged them, told them what had happened. She had found Lota on the floor with a bottle of Valium in her hand. She was in a coma. Dr. Baumann came running and put her in the hospital. Bishop hadn't told them because she didn't want to worry them unnecessarily; she had hoped that Lota would recover.

Ismênia felt full of pity, imagining what it must have been like for Bishop to find Lota dying on the floor. Afterward the panic, the hope, and then the despair in the face of the confirmation of death.

Vivinha didn't give an inch. What did you do to her that she wanted to die?

# RIO DE JANEIRO, 1994

LEAVING NANÁ'S HOUSE, Vivinha offered Ismênia a lift. She was the only one who still drove. She had a papaya-yellow Variant. Ismênia thought it risky but accepted. The album was heavy.

"That boozer orbited around Lota all her life and after her death was outrageous," resumed Vivinha. "She took a long time to show up, and then when she did it was to question the will."

"Vivinha, it wasn't quite like that."

"What do you mean it wasn't quite like that? So she didn't want to take the paintings that Lota left to Mary and Rosinha, saying that it was she who had bought them?"

"The climate was hostile, everyone very upset, and then on top of it Marietta having a lawyer contest the will."

"Of course the climate was very hostile," said Vivinha, running the red light at Santa Clara. "What did she expect? Lota shouldered her weight for her whole life, and at the only moment when Lota needed her she didn't have the generosity to shelter her. Oh, no, she was all puffed up because a little girl had fallen in love with her."

Ismênia remembered the little girl, a lovely young woman that sometime afterward Bishop had introduced as her secretary. At that point Bishop was already living in Ouro Preto. She'd sold the apartment in Leme and taken her things from Samambaia, after an ugly fight with Mary Morse. That is, Ismênia thought that the young woman was lovely. But Lilli, speaking to her on the telephone, said that she didn't know what Bishop saw in that little idiot.

"Instead of making a little food at home, no, she took Lota to eat out! And that story about after they'd talked she got irresistibly sleepy, come off it. Lota left here in shreds, went to New York looking for comfort, and the other one went to sleep! She lay down and went to sleep!"

Ismênia didn't reply. All of that was so bad to remember. Soon she'd be getting out, thank God; Vivinha was a terror behind the wheel. For no reason at all, the bending foliage of a sweet potato that Naná kept in a jar came to her mind. The foliage hung down for almost a meter. Plants didn't grow in Ismênia's apartment. All her African violets were artificial.

"We're here, Vivinha. Thanks a lot."

"Of course. Tchau."

Carrying the album awkwardly, Ismênia thought it easier to ring the doorbell than to fumble for the key in her purse. After a long time the janitor came. He took a look, recognized Ismênia, and pushed the button to open the gate. He didn't even think of helping her to carry the heavy package.

VIVINHA GOT TO her apartment a bit irritated. Maneuvering in the garage of her building was an ordeal. The neighbor on the sixth floor, who only had a right to one space, had two cars. And the light in the corridor had been burned out for days. She had to find the keyhole in the dark. Old buildings were deplorable. Old age was deplorable.

Vivinha went directly to open the window. At least the apartment had one good thing: the view. Vivinha watched the red traces of the car lights crossing the Aterro. Undisputable, the tall, tall lampposts still poured down their moonlight. She missed Lota enormously. To this day she couldn't accept what had happened. Bishop killed Lota, she repeated to herself.

THEY ALSO READ the piece about Lota in O *Globo* of July 2, 1994:

Arnaldo de Oliveira, retired businessman. Lived in Flamengo for thirty years and took daily walks on the Aterro, with other retirees. He had never dreamed that the Aterro had been made by a woman. He always thought it had been Burle Marx's project.

Do Carmo, editor, ex-exile. She remembered Lota as a representative of the rural, decadent aristocracy, friend of Aunt Vivinha, who adored her. She had that air of arrogance of the well born. She wore a very strange clasp in her hair, which made her look as though she had had surgery on her skull.

Monica Morse, married, two children. She had been dismayed at the revelations of the emotional life and the circumstances of her grandmother's death. She called her mother. What's past is best forgotten, said Mary Morse.

# BOSTON, 1978

ELIZABETH BISHOP looked at the sheet of paper once more. Of course I may be remembering it all wrong.

When she went back to Brazil, she was received like a convict. Devastated by Lota's death, they acted as if she wasn't devastated. As if she didn't have the right to be. They resisted her taking the things that she and Lota had collected during their fifteen years together, as if she were a sneak thief.

She'd never gone back to the house in Petrópolis. She wouldn't ever go back again. She wanted to sell the house in Ouro Preto. She hadn't been happy there.

Nevertheless, Brazil continued to figure in her life. She compiled an anthology of Brazilian poetry with Emanuel Brasil. They were already beginning a second collection. With Ricardo Sternberg, she gave a presentation in New Bedford on the poetry in Brazilian music. She liked Caetano Veloso; she loved his song "Unidentified." Brazil was, above all, embedded in the poems that she finally was succeeding in finishing, in her verses, praised verses, award-winning verses.

And Lota! Dear Lota. She missed Lota enormously. To this day she couldn't accept what had happened. The devotion, the intelligence, the beauty of Lota ruined by pettiness. Deliberately. Indecently.

Bishop looks out the window. There are already a good number of ships at the dock.

She remembers Lota arriving in New York, prostrated, mortally wounded. Brazil killed Lota, she says to herself.

Scribitur ad narrandum, non ad probandum
One writes to narrate, not to prove.

Titus Livius

# SOURCES

## INTERVIEWS BY THE AUTHOR

Lilli Correia de Araújo
Walkíria Barreto
Edith Behring
Enrico Bianco
Emanuel Brasil
Antônio Callado
Sandra Cavalcanti
Zette Van Erven Lage
Manoel Portinari Leão
Luiza Barreto Leite
Leila da Silveira Lobo
Roberto Burle Marx

Ethel Bauzer Medeiros
Luiz Emygdio de Mello
   Filho
Mary Stearns Morse
Monica Morse
José Alberto Nemer
Linda Nemer
Fernanda Noviz Oliveira
Renata Pallottini
Rosy Bleggi Peixoto
Stella Batista Pereira
Rachel de Queiroz

Maria Augusta Leão da
   Costa Ribeiro
Joana dos Santos
Carlos Scliar
Oscar Maria Simon
Pedro Teixeira Soares
Ricardo da Silveira Lobo
   Sternberg
Julio Cesar Pessolani
   Zavala

## OTHER PRIMARY SOURCES

Correspondence between the author and Ashley Brown, author's archive

Correspondence of Lota de Macedo Soares, private archive

Appointment book of Lota de Macedo Soares, private archive

Manuscripts of Elizabeth Bishop, Archive of Vassar College Libraries, Special Collections

Correspondence of Elizabeth Bishop, Archive of Vassar College Libraries, Special
   Collections

## WORKS BY ELIZABETH BISHOP CONSULTED

Bishop, Elizabeth. *The Complete Poems, 1927–1979*. New York: Farrar, Straus and
   Giroux, 1991.

———. "In the Village." In *The Collected Prose*. New York: Farrar, Straus and Giroux,
   1984. Copyright 1984 by Alice Helen Methfessel. Excerpt reprinted by permission
   of Farrar, Straus and Giroux, LLC.

———. *One Art*. Ed. Robert Giroux. New York: Farrar, Straus and Giroux, 1994.

———. "On the Railroad Named Delight." *New York Times Magazine*, 7 March 1965.

———, ed. *An Anthology of Twentieth Century Brazilian Poetry*. Selected and edited with
   Emanuel Brasil. Middletown, Conn.: Wesleyan University Press, 1972.

## POEMS BY ELIZABETH BISHOP CITED IN THE TEXT

The poems are listed in order of appearance in the text.

"Crusoe in England"

"Santarém"
"Arrival at Santos"
"The Shampoo"
"Brazil, January 1, 1502"
"The Wit"
"Questions of Travel"
"Under the Window: Ouro Preto"
"Going to the Bakery"
"Manuelzinho"
"Electrical Storm"
"Pink Dog"
"Rainy Season; Sub-Tropics"
"Song for the Rainy Season"
"The Burglar of Babylon"
From *The Complete Poems, 1927–1979* (New York: Farrar, Straus and Giroux, 1979, 1983). Copyright 1979, 1983 by Alice Helen Methfessel. Reprinted by permission of Farrar, Straus and Giroux, LLC.

## BRAZILIAN NEWSPAPERS AND MAGAZINES

*A Noite, A Notícia, Correio da Manhã, Diário de Notícias, Gazeta de Notícias, Jornal do Brasil, Jornal do Commercio, Jornal dos Esportes, O Globo, O Jornal, Tribuna da Imprensa, Última Hora; Anhembi, Cadernos Brasileiros, Diretrizes, Módulo, O Cruzeiro Internacional, Revista de Engenharia do Estado de Guanabara*

## SONGS

"Ai, seu Mé," Luis Nunes Sampaio and Freire Júnior
"Vovozinha," popular song
"Dona cegonha," Armando Cavalcanti and Klecius Caldas
"Gosto que me enrosco," Sinhô
"Brigite Bardot," Miguel Gustavo and Jorge Veiga
"The Laziest Gal in Town," Cole Porter
"Rambling on My Mind," Robert Johnson
"Lover Man," Jimmy Sherman and Roger "Ram" Ramirez
"Acontece," Cartola
"Praia do flamengo," Luiz Wanderley and Fausto Guimarães
"Todo mundo enche," Pedro Caetano and Alexandre Dias Filho
"Cinco bailes da história do Rio," Silas de Oliveira, D. Ivone Lara, and Bacalhau
"Juvenal," Wilson Batista and Jorge de Castro
"A linda rosa juvenil," popular song
"Não identificado," Caetano Veloso

## SECONDARY SOURCES

Aeschylus. *Agamemnon. The Oresteian Trilogy.* Trans. W. Bidell Stanford. New York: Viking, 1956.

Alves Abreu, Alzira, and Israel Beloch, eds. *Dicionário histórico biográfico Brasileiro, 1930–83*. Rio de Janeiro: Forense Universitária/FGV/Sineo, 1984.

de Andrade, Mário. *Poesias completas*. São Paulo: Martins, 1980.

——. *Portinari, amico mio: Cartas de Mário de Andrade a Candido Portinari*. Campinas: Mercado de Letras/Editora Autores Associados; Rio de Janeiro: Projeto Portinari, 1995.

Assis, Machado de. *Memórias póstumas de Brás Cubas*. Rio de Janeiro: Jackson, 1946.

Bell, Pearl K. "Dona Elizabetchy: A Memoir of Elizabeth Bishop." *Partisan Review*, 1991.

Brown, Ashley. "Elizabeth Bishop in Brazil." *Southern Review*, 13 October 1977.

——. "Elizabeth Bishop's Brazilian Writers." Paper delivered at a conference, 1994.

——. "An Interview with Elizabeth Bishop." *Shenandoah* 27, no. 2 (1966).

Callado, Antônio. "Poeta deu trégua à angústia em Petrópolis." *Folha de São Paulo*, 11 June 1994.

——. "Um sábio entre bugres." *Correio da Manhã*, 21 August 1958.

Caminha, Pero Vaz de. *Carta a el Rey Dom Manuel*. Modern edition by Rubem Braga. Rio de Janeiro: Record, 1981.

Camões, Luís de. *Redondilhas, canções, sonetos*. Rio de Janeiro: Real Gabinete Português de Leitura, 1980.

Carroll, Lewis. *Alice's Adventures in Wonderland*. New York: Dutton, 1999.

Castro, Fernando de. "Paternalismo e antiamericanismo." *Correio da Manhã*, 28 March 1965.

Costello, Bonnie. *Elizabeth Bishop: Questions of Mastery*. Cambridge: Harvard University Press, 1991.

Cunha, Angela Regina. "A verdade sob o aterro." *O Globo*, 2 July 1974.

David. Psalm 38. In *The New Jerusalem Bible*. Ed. Henry Wansborough. New York: Doubleday, 1985.

Dickinson, Emily. "Presentiment—is that Long Shadow—on the Lawn." In *Complete Poems*. Boston: Little, Brown, 1960.

Dostoevsky, F. M. *White Nights and Other Stories*. Trans. Constance Garnett. New York: Grove Press, 1960.

Drummond de Andrade, Carlos. *Antologia poética*. Rio de Janeiro: Record, 1987.

Eliot, T. S. "The Waste Land." In *Collected Poems, 1909–1962*. New York: Harcourt, Brace and World, 1963.

Fonseca, José Paulo Moreira da. "Anotação poética." In *Antologia da nova poesia brasileira*. Ed. Fernando Ferreira de Loanda. Edições Orfeu, 1970.

Fonseca, Mariano José Pereira da, marquês de Maricá. *Máximas, pensamentos e reflexões*. Ed. Souza de Silveira. Rio de Janeiro: Casa de Rui Barbosa, 1958.

Fountain, Gary, and Peter Brazeau. *Remembering Elizabeth Bishop*. Amherst: University of Massachusetts Press, 1994.

du Gard, Roger Martin. *Jean Barois*. Trans. Stuart Gilbert. New York: Viking, 1949.

Goldensohn, Lorrie. *Elizabeth Bishop: The Biography of a Poetry*. New York: Columbia University Press, 1991.

Herbert, George. "Love" and "Love Unknown." In *The Poems of George Herbert*. London: Oxford University Press, 1961.

Homer. *The Iliad and The Odyssey*. Trans. Robert Fagles. New York: Penguin, 1999.

Jekyll, Gertrude. *On Gardening*. New York: Charles Scribner's Sons, 1964.

Katz, Leonel, and Salvador Monteiro, eds. *Floresta Atlântica*. Rio de Janeiro: Editora Alumbramento, 1991–1992.

Lacerda, Carlos. *Depoimento 1914–1977*. Rio de Janeiro: Nova Fronteira, 1987.

Lessa, Elsie. "Lota de Macedo Soares." *O Globo*, 6 October 1967.

Lispector, Clarice. *Laços de família*. São Paulo: Alves, 1960.

Macedo Soares, Maria Carlota C. de. "A urbanização do aterrado Glória-Flamengo." *Revista de Engenharia do Estado de Guanabara* 29 (January–February 1962).

McCarthy, Mary. *The Group*. New York: Harcourt Brace Jovanovich, 1991.

Medeiros, Ethel Bauzer. *O lazer no planejamento urbano*. Rio de Janeiro: Editora da Fundaçao Getúlio Vargas, 1971.

Millier, Brett C. *Elizabeth Bishop: Life and the Memory of It*. Berkeley: University of California Press, 1993.

Mindlin, Henrique. *Modern Architecture in Brazil*. Rio de Janeiro and Amsterdam: Colibris, 1960.

Moore, Marianne. *The Complete Poems*. New York: Viking Penguin, 1987.

Morley, Helena. *Minha vida de menina* (My life as a girl). Rio de Janeiro: José Olympio, 1988.

Mumford, Lewis. *The City in History*. New York: Farrar, Straus and Giroux, 1979.

O'Connor, Flannery. *The Habit of Being*. Correspondence selected and edited by Sally Fitzgerald. New York: Farrar, Straus and Giroux, 1979.

Oliveira Reis, José de. *A Guanabara e seus governadores*. Rio de Janeiro: Prefeitura da cidade de Rio de Janeiro, 1977.

Pallotini, Renata. "Interurbano." In *Noite afora*. São Paulo: Brasiliense, 1978.

Peixoto, Enaldo Cravo. "O Parque do Flamengo." *Módulo* 37 (1964).

Queiroz, Maria Lucia de. "Elizabeth Bishop: Exilio de la Poesia." *O Cruzeiro Internacional*, 1 March 1963.

Queiroz, Rachel de. "O aterro da glória." *O Cruzeiro*, 18 October 1961.

——. "Carta para Lota de Macedo Soares." *O Cruzeiro*, 16 February 1972.

——. "Lota." *O Jornal*, 8 October 1967.

Shakespeare, William. *Macbeth*. In *The Complete Works*. New York: Harcourt, Brace and World, 1948.

Singer, Dorothea Waley. *Giordano Bruno; His Life and Thought*. Annotated translation of his work, "On the Infinite Universe and Worlds." New York: Greenwood Press, 1968.

Sophocles. *Oedipus Rex*. Trans. Dudley Fitts and Robert Fitzgerald. New York: Harcourt, Brace and World, 1960.

Spires, Elizabeth. "The Art of Poetry XXVII—Interview with Elizabeth Bishop." *Paris Review* 23 (1981).

Starbuck, George. "The Work!—Conversation with Elizabeth Bishop." *Ploughshares* 3, nos. 3 and 4 (1977).

Whitman, Walt. *Leaves of Grass*. Laurel Poetry Series. New York: Dell, 1959.

# ABOUT THE AUTHOR
# AND TRANSLATOR

CARMEN L. OLIVEIRA is a Brazilian novelist. NEIL K. BESNER is a
professor of English at the University of Winnipeg in Canada.